HARVARD EAST ASIAN MONOGRAPHS

88

Studies in the Modernization of
The Republic of Korea: 1945-1975

Urbanization and Urban Problems

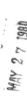

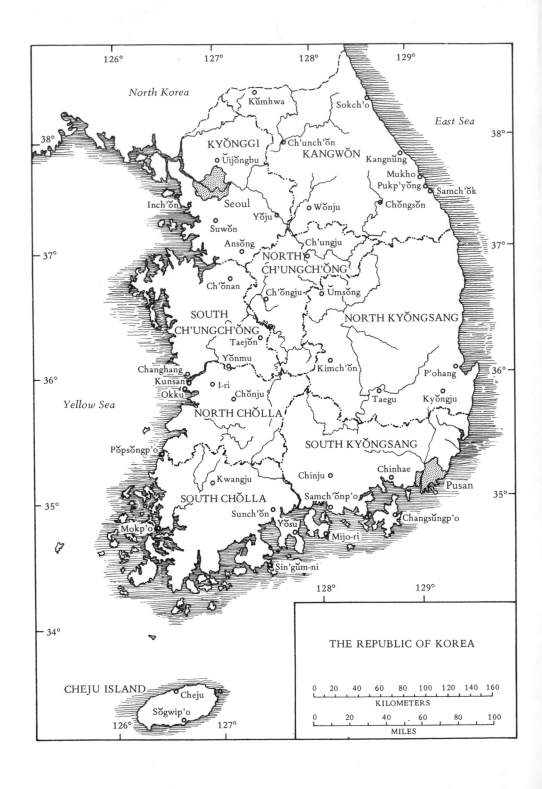

North Korea

126°   127°   128°   129°

○ Kŭmhwa
○ Sokch'o

East Sea

38°   38°

KYŎNGGI   ○ Ch'unch'ŏn
○ Ŭijŏngbu   KANGWŎN   ○ Kangnŭng
                              ○ Mukho
                              Pukp'yŏng ○ ○ Samch'ŏk
Inch'ŏn ○
Seoul   ○ Wŏnju   ○ Chŏngsŏn
○ Yŏju
37°   ○ Suwŏn   37°
     ○ Ansŏng   ○ Ch'ungju
          NORTH
          CH'UNGCH'ŎNG
     ○ Ch'ŏnan
               ○ Ch'ŏngju ○ Ŭmsŏng   NORTH KYŎNGSANG
SOUTH
CH'UNGCH'ŎNG
          ○ Taejŏn
          ○ Yŏnmu
Changhang ○   ○ Kimch'ŏn   ○ P'ohang
36° Kunsan ○   36°
     Okku ○ ○ I-ri   ○ Kyŏngju
               ○ Chŏnju   ○ Taegu
          NORTH CHŎLLA

Yellow Sea
                              SOUTH KYŎNGSANG
Pŏpsŏngp'o ○
                              ○ Chinhae
          ○ Kwangju   ○ Chinju   Pusan
35°   35°
          SOUTH CHŎLLA   Samch'ŏnp'o ○
     ○ Sunch'ŏn   ○ Changsŭngp'o
Mokp'o ○   ○ Yŏsu
                    ○ Mijo-ri
                                   128°   129°
          ○ Sin'gŭm-ni

34°

THE REPUBLIC OF KOREA

CHEJU ISLAND   ○ Cheju
          Sŏgwip'o ○   0 20 40 60 80 100 120 140 160
     126°   127°   KILOMETERS

                    0   20   40   60   80   100
                              MILES

Studies in the Modernization of
The Republic of Korea: 1945–1975

Urbanization and Urban Problems

EDWIN S. MILLS

AND

BYUNG-NAK SONG

PUBLISHED BY
COUNCIL ON EAST ASIAN STUDIES
HARVARD UNIVERSITY

Distributed by
Harvard University Press
Cambridge, Massachusetts and London, England
1979

The Council on East Asian Studies at Harvard University publishes a monograph series
and, through the Fairbank Center for East Asian Research, administers research projects
designed to further scholarly understanding of
China, Japan, Korea, Vietnam, Inner Asia, and adjacent areas.

The Harvard Institute for International Development
is Harvard University's center for interdisciplinary research, teaching, and technical assistance
on the problems of modernization in less developed countries.

The Korea Development Institute
is an economic research center, supported in part by the Korean government
that undertakes studies of the critical development issues and prospects of Korea.

Library of Congress Cataloging in Publication Data

Mills, Edwin S.
Urbanization and urban problems.

(Studies in the modernization of the Republic of
Korea, 1945–1975) (Harvard East Asian monographs ; 88)
Bibliography: p.
Includes index.
1. Cities and towns—Korea—Growth. 2. Urbaniza-
tion—Korea. I. Song, Byung-Nak, joint author.
II. Title. III. Series. IV. Series: Harvard East
Asian monographs ; 88.
HT147.K6M54   301.36'1'09519   79–22494
ISBN 0–674–93133–5

Foreword

This is one of the studies on the economic and social modernization of Korea undertaken jointly by the Harvard Institute for International Development and the Korea Development Institute. The undertaking has twin objectives; to examine the elements underlying the remarkable growth of the Korean economy and the distribution of the fruits of that growth, together with the associated changes in society and government; and to evaluate the importance of foreign economic assistance, particularly American assistance, in promoting these changes. The rapid rate of growth of the Korean economy, matched in the less developed world (apart from the oil exporters) only by similar rates of growth in the neighboring East Asian economies of Taiwan, Hong Kong, and Singapore, has not escaped the notice of economists and other observers. Indeed there has been fairly extensive analysis of the Korean case. This analysis, has been mainly limited to macroeconomic phenomena; to the behavior of monetary, fiscal, and foreign-exchange magnitudes and to the underlying policies affecting these magnitudes. But there are elements other than these that need to be taken into account to explain what has happened. The development of Korean entrepreneurship has been remarkable; Korea has an industrious and disciplined labor force; the contribution of agricultural development both to overall growth and to the distribution of income requires assessment; the level of literacy and the expansion of secondary and higher education have made their mark; and the combination and interdependence of government and private initiative and administration have been remarkably productive. These aspects together with the growth of urban areas, changes in the mortality and fertility of the population and in public health, are the primary objects of study. It is hoped that they will provide the building blocks from which an overall assessment of modernization in Korea can be constructed.

Economic assistance from the United States and, to a lesser extent, from other countries, has made a sizable but as yet unevaluated contribution to Korean development. A desire to have an assessment undertaken of this contribution, with whatever successes or failures have accompanied the U.S. involvement, was one of the motives for these studies, which have been financed in part by the U.S. Agency for International Development and, in part, by the Korea Development Institute. From 1945 to date, U.S. AID has contributed more than $6 billion to the Korean economy. There has also been a substantial fallout from the $7 billion of U.S. military assistance. Most of the economic assistance was contributed during the period before 1965, and most of it was in the form of grants. In later years the amount of economic assistance has declined rapidly and most of it, though concessional, has been in the form of loans. Currently, except for a minor trickle, U.S. economic assistance has ceased. The period of rapid economic growth in Korea has been since 1963, and in Korea, as well as in other countries receiving foreign assistance, it is a commonplace that it is the receiving country that is overwhelmingly responsible for what growth, or absence of growth, takes place. Nevertheless, economic assistance to Korea was exceptionally large, and whatever contribution was in fact made by outsiders needs to be assessed. One of the studies, *The Developmental Role of the Foreign Sector and Aid,* deals with foreign assistance in macroeconomic terms. The contribution of economic assistance to particular sectors is considered in the other studies.

All the studies in this series have involved American and Korean collaboration. For some studies the collaboration has been close; for others less so. All the American participants have spent some time in Korea in the course of their research, and a number of Korean participants have visited the United States. Only a few of the American participants have been able to read and speak Korean and, in consequence, the collaboration of their colleagues in making Korean materials available has been invaluable. This has truly been a joint enterprise.

The printed volumes in this series will include studies on the growth and structural transformation of the Korean economy, the foreign sector and aid, urbanization, rural development, the role of entrepreneurship, population policy and demographic transition, and education. Studies focusing on several other topics—the financial system, the fiscal system, labor economics and industrial relations, health and social development—will eventually be available either in printed or mimeographed form. The project will culminate in a final summary volume on the economic and social development of Korea.

Edward S. Mason

Edward S. Mason
Harvard Institute
for International Development

Mahn Je Kim

Mahn Je Kim
President,
Korea Development Institute

A Note on Romanization

In romanizing Korean, we have used the McCune-Reischauer system and have generally followed the stylistic guidelines set forth by the Library of Congress. In romanizing the names of Koreans in the McCune-Reischauer system, we have put a hyphen between the two personal names, the second of which has not been capitalized. For the names of historical or political figures, well-known place names, and the trade names of companies, we have tried to follow the most widely used romanization. For works written in Korean, the author's name appears in McCune-Reischauer romanization, sometimes followed by the author's preferred romanization if he or she has published in English. For works by Korean authors in English, the author's name is written as it appears in the original publication, sometimes followed by the author's name in McCune-Reischauer romanization, especially if the author has published in Korean also. In ordering the elements of persons' names, we have adopted a Western sequence—family name first in all alphabetized lists, but last elsewhere. This is a sequence used by some, but by no means all, Koreans who write in English. To avoid confusion, however, we have imposed an arbitrary consistency upon varying practices. Two notable exceptions occur in references to President Park Chung Hee, and Chang Myon, for whom the use of the family name first seems to be established by custom and preference. Commonly recurring Korean words such as si (city) have not been italicized. Korean words in the plural are not followed by the letter "s." Finally, complete information on authors' names or companies' trade names was not always available; in these cases we have simply tried to be as accurate as possible.

Geographic Terms (from largest to smallest)

Urban
   si – city
   pu – old term for a city
   ku – borough
   tong – precinct; (see rural tong)
   t'ong – sub-precinct
   pan – neighborhood

Rural
   to – province
   kun – county
   ŭp – town (formerly the county seat)
   myŏn – township
   tong – group of villages
   i (~ri, ~ni) – village
   purak – hamlet

Acknowledgments

Many people have helped the authors of this volume. Other scholars working on the modernization project have provided valuable comments during the research and writing. They and many Korean officials and scholars edified the American author on Korean events. Bertrand Renaud read the entire manuscript and made many wise suggestions. John Sloboda kindly wrote Chapter 5, as part of his research on Korea. Research assistance was provided by Yŏng-il Ch'oe, Sa-hŏn Kim, Sŭng-nae Mun, Ŭi-sŏp Sim, Chong-sun Paek, Tong-hun Chŏn, Un-bang Yŏ, and Kang-yu Yi.

Contents

Contents

Contents

Tables

Abbreviations

BOD	biochemical oxygen demand
BOK	Bank of Korea
CBD	central business district
EPB	Economic Planning Board
EPB/BOS	Economic Planning Board, Bureau of Statistics
GDP	gross domestic product
GNP	gross national product
KHB	Korea Housing Bank
KHC	Korea Housing Corporation
KIFP	Korean Institute for Family Planning
KIST	Korea Institute of Science and Technology
LDC	less developed country
MAF	Ministry of Agriculture and Fisheries (Forestry)
MHA	Ministry of Home Affairs
MOC	Ministry of Construction
NACF	Natural Agricultural Cooperative Federation
SDS	Special Demographic Survey
SMSA	Standard Metropolitan Statistical Area

ONE

Introduction

Economic development is everywhere associated with rapid urbanization, and the basic reasons for the correlation are not hard to find. Economic development entails an increasing ability of a society to produce goods and services with the human, man-made, and natural resources at its disposal. Development may be brought about by technical progress, the spread of technology, capital accumulation, improved education and training of the labor force, improved market organization, and similar changes. In poor countries, most economic activity consists of extraction of food, fuel, and other materials from the earth's surface and sub-surface. Extractive activities such as agriculture and forestry tend to be land-intensive and dispersed; poor countries are therefore mostly rural.

As development proceeds, inputs are transferred from extractive industries to those that process extracted materials into consumption and capital goods or to industries that provide services with the help of processed goods. Processing and service industries are much less land-intensive than extractive industries. It is therefore possible to undertake these activities in close proximity to each other. Furthermore, whereas extraction must take place where the materials to be extracted are found, processing and service industries can be located far from sites of extraction. People are motivated to bring large numbers of processing and service activities together in high-density settlements so they can trade among themselves, with employees, and with customers. Close proximity permits exchanges to be made without expensive long-distance movement of goods and of people in making transactions. Thus, processing sectors tend to be located in large, dense, urban areas. The tendency is even stronger in service sectors. Services are consumed as they are produced, and most require that producer and consumer be physically near each other. Service delivery requires the movement of people rather than of goods, and people are much more expensive to move than goods. Thus, the basic reason that urbanization always accompanies economic development is that resources are transferred to activities in which other inputs can be substituted for land and in which proximity permits producers and consumers to economize on transportation and communication.

By way of elaboration, urbanization serves three basic functions in developing and developed countries. First, urbanization permits a wide range of specialized processing and service activities to be carried on at a scale at which scale economies can be realized. An important problem in developing countries is that markets are too small to permit production at efficient scales. This is obvious and widely appreciated in manufacturing, but it is true also in service industries. Although the absolute scale needed to attain efficient production is not large in service production, firms tend to be highly specialized. A substantial market is required to be able to support enough firms to ensure competition in many service sectors. Evidence for this is the much greater variety of services found in large urban areas than elsewhere in developing countries. Especially in countries where incomes are low, large urban areas are necessary to provide a large enough market to support a wide range of activities.

Second, and closely related, transportation over long distances is expensive, especially in less developed countries (LDCs),[1] where transportation systems are poorly developed. Urban areas enable consumers and businesses to find a wide range of products and services close at hand, thus avoiding expensive shipments over long distances. Transportation systems are much better developed in urban areas than elsewhere, especially in LDCs, because facilities can be used intensively, the costs spread over many users. The road system is a good example. Road costs per user are very high in rural areas, because roads are used at low intensity. In urban areas, roads are used intensively, and costs per user are much lower. The contrast is much greater for public transit systems. Public transportation is so costly unless used at high intensity that many LDC rural areas have almost none.

Third, many cities serve the physical and service requirements of international trade in LDCs. Most developing countries have large international sectors and many have only a few good natural harbors. Furthermore, it is expensive to duplicate elaborate port facilities in many places. Thus, international trade tends to be concentrated in one or two ports in many LDCs. It is frequently advantageous to locate processing activities close to ports from which processed goods will be exported. It is then advantageous for related enterprises, employees, and activities providing goods and services to employees also to locate near ports. The same considerations induce users of imports, processors of imports, and related activities to locate near ports. Consequently, it is often advantageous to have large urban areas at ports.

The abstract statements in previous paragraphs hide one of the most important components of economic development. It has frequently been observed that LDCs have recently urbanized more rapidly than presently developed countries—even more rapidly than presently developed countries urbanized at comparable stages of development. In the United States and Western Europe, the proportion of the population living in urban areas grew about one percent per year during the third quarter of the twentieth century. Kingsley Davis[2] reports that the proportion grew about 1.5 percent per year during the decade of most rapid growth in the nineteenth century. In most LDCs, the proportion has grown between 2 and 3 percent per year during the quarter century 1950–1975; in Korea, at an astounding 4.1 percent per year.

These figures represent a massive shift of human resources in many LDCs, and nowhere has the shift been greater than in Korea. Indeed, over the course of human history, migrations of larger magnitudes have resulted only from the terrible exigencies of war or from political oppression. But recent rapid urbanization in LDCs represents primarily an economic response to opportunities to improve the quality of life. Incomes are higher and employment opportunities more plentiful in urban than in rural areas in almost all LDCs. This results in part from the push away from agriculture because of farm mechanization and high rural birth rates. It results even more from the pull of the cities because of expanding employment and rising incomes, and because of the attractions of city life. Thus, people move to cities in developing countries to lift themselves from the destitute poverty common in the countryside. Not only are incomes higher in the cities, but a much greater variety of goods and services is available; and public and quasi-public services, such as education and health care, are of much higher quality. All these phenomena attest to the high levels of human productivity that cities facilitate.

Urbanization as rapid as that recently observed in Korea and other developing countries inevitably raises serious problems for migrants, for long-term urban residents, and for those remaining in rural areas. The tendency in the 1970s has been to emphasize these problems rather than the benefits of urbanization. Urban migrants lack the education, training, and experience of long-term urban residents. Educational opportunities are poorer in rural than urban areas in most countries, and migrants are poorly equipped to cope with the complexity of urban life. Migrants find it difficult to compete for jobs and housing with other urban residents. Migrants experience high unemployment rates and long periods in the informal sectors of the urban economy. Their incomes are often very low during the transitional phase. The result is poor housing, poor clothing, poor nutrition, and often poor health. Of course, none of these problems is absent in rural areas, and most are more serious there than in cities. But more attention is focused on them in urban areas, where they are more concentrated and visible, the sufferers are better organized, and the media are based.

This volume focuses on both the positive and normative aspects of Korean urbanization and presents two economists' views of Korean urbanization. It naturally emphasizes economic aspects of urbanization. Although the economic may be the most important aspects in a developing country, there are many others that deserve study—political, sociological, and cultural, for example—that are almost completely ignored here.

The book presumes no prior knowledge of Korea. In addition, most of it can be read by those lacking a deep knowledge of economics. Readers unversed in modern microeconomics may have to take a few things on faith. Although Chapters 3, 4, 6, 7, and 8 contain some technical analysis, large parts of those chapters and the other chapters introduce almost nothing unfamiliar to those who have completed an introductory economics course.

We hope this book will be valuable to several groups of people. Non-Korean economists can gain insight into urbanization and urban problems in one of the world's fastest growing economies. To assist them, we have included extensive statistical appendixes. Laymen should be able to learn something about the dramatic changes that urbanization has caused in the economic life of Koreans. Finally, Koreans may be interested in a view of their country from the vantage point of urban economics, still an essentially Western specialty.

TWO

A Survey of Urbanization in Korea

We begin with a brief description of the urban concepts used in Korean data sources. Basic data on Korea come from the National Population Census, taken at five-year intervals in years ending in zero and five. People are counted as urban if they live in a municipality of at least 50,000 people. The Korean definition of urban is more restrictive than the U.S. definition, under which people are counted as urban if they live in a place of at least 2,500 people. To qualify as a city (si), a Korean municipality must have at least 50,000 residents, and being a city entails a basically different pattern of local government finance. Fifty thousand residents in the central city is also the requirement for a Standard Metropolitan Statistical Area (SMSA) or an Urbanized Area in the United States. A city is a local government jurisdiction in Korea, whereas the U.S. SMSA or Urbanized Area includes not only the legal central city, but also surrounding urbanized counties or suburbs. Korean data sources do not define a metropolitan area concept but, with the significant exception of Seoul, Korean cities include all the residents in the generic urban area.

GROWTH AND URBANIZATION
OF THE POPULATION

Table 1 shows Korea's total population and the urban percentage for census years from 1915–1975, with comparable data from Japan and the United States. Urbanization is a very recent phenomenon in Korea. Until after 1930, Korea was at least 95 percent rural by the restrictive criterion used. That Korea was extremely rural is confirmed by the fact that the population was 90 percent agricultural in 1930. Around 1930, the Japanese Colonial Government began to place somewhat greater emphasis on manufacturing production, with a consequent acceleration of urbanization. Japan has been more urbanized than Korea as far back as the data go. By 1950, Korea had not reached the urban percentage that Japan had attained a quarter century earlier.

The pace of Korean urbanization during much of the middle half of the twentieth century may have been as rapid as any ever observed during a substantial historical period in a country larger than a city-state.[1] The urban percentage of the population has grown an average of nearly one percentage point per year during the half century. During the quarter century following the end of World War II, the urban percentage of the population tripled. The largest increases recorded in the table are those during the most recent decade, 1965–1975. The 1970–1975 increase of 7.8 points is off only slightly from the 9.2 point increase during the 1965–1970 interval.

Most developed countries are 65 to 80 percent urban. After they reach roughly Korea's 1975 level of urbanization, the pace of urbanization tends to decelerate. After the urban percentage

TABLE 1 Total and Urban Populations of Korea,
Japan, and the United States
1915–1975
(1,000s)

Year	Korea		Japan		United States	
	Population	Urban %	Population	Urban %	Population	Urban %
1915	16,278	3.1				
1920	17,289	3.3	55,391	18.1	106.0	51.2
1925	19,020	3.5	59,179	21.7		
1930	20,438	4.5	63,872	24.1	122.8	56.2
1935	22,208	7.4	68,662	32.9		
1940	23,547	11.6	72,540	37.9	131.7	56.5
1945	19,369	14.5	71,998	27.8		
1950	20,167	18.4	83,200	37.5	150.7	59.6
1955	21,502	24.4	89,276	56.3		
1960	24,954	28.3	93,419	63.5	178.5	63.1
1965	28,327	33.9	98,275	68.1		
1970	31,435	43.1	103,720	72.2	203.2	73.5
1975	34,709	50.9				

Sources: The Korean data from 1915 to 1940 include North Korea and are obtained from *Chōsen Sōtokufu tōkei nenpō, 1915, 1920, 1925, 1930, 1935, 1940.* The data from 1945 to 1975 are tor South Korea and are obtained from EPB, *Korea Statistical Yearbook 1965, 1970* and *Report on Population and Housing Census, 1975.* U.S. data are obtained from U.S. Government, *Statistical Abstract of the U.S.,* 1974. Japanese Data are from Edwin S. Mills and Katsutoshi Ohta, "Urbanization and Urban Problems," in Hugh Patrick and H. Rosovsky, eds., *Asia's New Giant—How the Japanese Economy Works* (The Brookings Institution, 1976).

reaches 70 or 75, the remaining rural population urbanizes only slowly in nearly all countries. Thus, although we expect Korean urbanization to maintain a rapid pace, it is unlikely that the extremely rapid urbanization of the 1965–1975 period will continue for as long as another decade.

The data in Table 1 imply that the urban population grew at an average annual rate of 6.1 percent between 1945 and 1975. Natural increase has been less in urban than rural areas, because urban birth rates have been much lower than rural. More than two-thirds of post-war urban growth has resulted from rural-urban migration.[2] It has been estimated that about half the population of Korea's largest cities was born elsewhere.

Table 2 shows some comparisons between Korea and developing and developed countries in 1950 and 1975. In 1950, Korea was only slightly more urbanized than the average developing

TABLE 2   Urban Population Percentage in Developing and
Developed Countries, 1950 and 1975

Area	Year	
	1950	1975
All Developing Countries	16.5	28.3
All Developed Countries	51.6	66.9
World Average	28.2	38.9
Korea	18.4	50.9

Sources: Korean data for 1950 refer to 1949 and are obtained from Pyŏng-nak Song, "Han'guk sudokwŏn ŭi konggan kyŏngje punsŏk," Korea Development Institute, Research Report No. 75–16 (December 1975), p. 72. Data for other countries are obtained from The World Bank, "The Task Ahead for the Cities of the Developing Countries," Staff Working Paper No. 209 (July 1975), p. 3.

country. Although developing countries have urbanized rapidly during the ensuing quarter century, Korea has urbanized much more rapidly. In 1975, Korea was about as urbanized as the average developed country shortly after World War II. Although Korea's urban percentage is now much closer to that of developed countries than it was in 1950, the gap is still substantial. This confirms our suggestion that the pace of urbanization will continue to be brisk in Korea during coming years, but will slacken somewhat, as in developed countries.

In Korea, the percentage of the population that was urban has been similar to the percentage of the labor force that was non-agricultural[2] throughout the period of rapid urbanization. In 1925, 10.7 percent of the labor force was non-agricultural, and 3.5 percent of the population was urban. In 1975, the corresponding figures were 54.1 and 50.9 percent. These figures do not provide a precise comparison because labor-force participation rates differ between urban and rural areas. But they indicate that the rural non-farm population has been only a few percent of the total for half a century. In the United States, by contrast, about one-fourth the population is rural, but only about 5 percent of the labor force is in agriculture. Thus, a much larger percentage of non-agricultural production takes place in rural areas in the United States than in Korea. In Korea, non-agricultural activities are strongly concentrated in urban areas.

URBAN STRUCTURE

Urban structure refers to the kinds, locations, and densities of activities in urban areas. Housing is the dominant urban activity in terms of land use, asset values, and social concern. But the major employment activities are also important in the analysis of urban structure.

Although each city has many unique characteristics, cities throughout the world have many characteristics in common. In almost all countries, service and manufacturing sectors are more urbanized than other sectors; in many, services are even more urbanized than manufacturing. Within cities, employment is more concentrated toward the center than is housing, with services the predominant land use in central business districts. In all cities, housing is the dominant land use, occupying about half the land in many. In many Asian cities, land use is often mixed, with retailing, processing, and dwellings sharing the same structure. Since employment is more centralized than housing, inward commuting to work is more common than outward commuting. But in most cities, origin-destination patterns for work and other trips are complex and diverse. In market economies, land prices are highest near city centers and fall off rapidly even a short distance from the center. Much of the very high land value in central business districts results from the large number of related activities within walking distance. Further from city centers, land values vary greatly from one parcel to another because of variations in access and neighborhood conditions, but show little systematic relationship to distance from the city center. Land is used most intensively for housing and employment near city centers, and densities of both uses fall rapidly a short distance from the center. Beyond a few kilometers from the center, housing and employment densities vary little with distance from the center, but vary a great deal from one neighborhood to another. Most land is used for employment very near city centers, but the percentage varies little with distance beyond a few kilometers from the center. Population and employment densities are greater in large cities than in small cities. Average urban population density varies from one country to another, but apparently not as much as do rural densities.

Korea is an extremely crowded country. Its population density of more than 350 people per square kilometer is greater than any country in the world with at least four million people, except for Bangladesh and Taiwan. Population per square kilometer is 287 in Japan, 172 in India, 83 in China, and 22 in the United States. Like Japan, Korea is a mountainous country where only about a fifth of the land is flat enough for agriculture or urban uses. Belgium and the Netherlands, on the other hand, with comparable population densities, are flat, and most land there is suitable for agriculture and cities.

Since Korea's overall population density is 16 times that of the United States, it is not surprising that almost any collection of non-agricultural activities and its associated households is classified as urban in Korea. Urban areas are everywhere defined explicitly or implicitly by density and any such collection is likely to reach a density that would be called urban in a country as crowded as Korea. Korea's cities are characterized by high population densities. The average population density of Korea's 35 cities is 3,700 people per square kilometer,[4] whereas the average density of the approximately 250 urbanized areas in the United States is about 1,300. Nevertheless, it is remarkable that Korea's urban population density is only 2.8 times that in the

United States whereas its overall density is 16 times that in the United States. This illustrates a pattern that is typical: among countries, rural densities differ much more than urban densities. It would be much more accurate to refer to Asia's teeming countryside than to its teeming cities! The existing literature offers no suggestions as to why rural densities should vary so much more than urban densities among countries.

Among the world's largest cities population densities are, in fact, remarkably similar. Table 3 compares Seoul with the world's two largest metropolitan areas, Tokyo and New York. Seoul is a much smaller metropolitan area than the other two, with little more than half the population of New York and one-third that of Tokyo. Land beyond 40 kilometers from the center of Seoul is not in the Seoul metropolitan area and much of it within 20 kilometers of the center is rural. New York and Tokyo have similar population densities, about 10,000 people per square kilometer within 20 kilometers of the center, whereas Seoul's density is less than half as great at the same distance. The difference between Seoul and New York and Tokyo is even greater at distances between 20 and 40 kilometers from the center, since much of the land that far from Seoul is rural. The lesson of these data is clear: although Seoul is a large and rapidly growing metropolitan area, it is not populous or dense in comparison with New York and Tokyo.

Table 4 presents more detailed data for the central business districts of the three cities. Population densities are typically small in central business districts because most land is devoted to employment instead of housing. It is remarkable that the New York and Seoul central business districts have high and similar population densities, both much higher than Tokyo's. In Tokyo, most land within 3 or 4 kilometers of the center is devoted to employment, and few people live there. But large numbers of people live in the Seoul and New York central business districts. In Seoul, many people live in the buildings where they work. Although that arrangement is rare in Manhattan, large numbers of people are able to continue to live in the central business

TABLE 3 Population Density Patterns in Seoul, Tokyo, and New York

	Distance[a] from Center			
	0–20	*20–40*	*40–70*	*Total*
Seoul (1970)				
Population[a]	6,053	1,571	1,270	8,894
Population Share	68.1	17.7	14.3	100.0
Area[a]	1,422	3,501	6,648	11,571
Density[a]	4,256	449	191 (average)	769
Tokyo (1970)				
Population[a]	11,964	7,733	5,048	24,745
Population Share	47.8	31.6	20.6	100.0
Area[a]	1,067	3,293	9,193	13,552
Density[a]	10,960	2,348	549 (average)	1,806
New York (1963)				
Population[a]	8,188	5,176	2,698[b]	16,062
Population Share	51.0	32.2	16.8[b]	100.0
Area[a]	791	3,725	8,042[b]	12,558
Density[a]	10,351	1,390	335[b] (average)	1,279

Sources: Data for Korea are from Pyŏng-nak Song, "Han'guk sudokwŏn ŭi konggan kyŏngje punsŏk," p. 110, and for other countries are from Mills and Ohta, "Urbanization and Urban Problems."

Notes: [a]Population in thousands, distances in kilometers, areas in square kilometers, and density in people per square kilometer.
[b]40–80 kilometers.

district because employment is concentrated in very tall buildings. Thus, although more people work in the Manhattan than in the Seoul or Tokyo central business districts, there is enough land remaining in Manhattan for large numbers of people to live there. It seems likely that more modern office buildings will be built in the Seoul central business district in coming years, and that the employment density will therefore grow there and

TABLE 4 Population of Central Business Districts
of Seoul, Tokyo, and New York

(1,000s)

	Seoul 2 ku (boroughs)	Tokyo 2 wards	Manhattan sub-area	Seoul 3 ku (boroughs)	Tokyo 3 wards	Manhattan sub-area
Population	322	178	518	684	402	1,539
Population density	18,927	8,250	21,400	23,949	9,790	26,540
Area[a]	17	22	24	29	41	58

Sources: Data for Seoul are from Pyŏng-nak Song, "Han'guk sudokwŏn ŭi konggan kyŏngje punsŏk," and for Tokyo and New York from Mills and Ohta. Seoul data are for 1973, Tokyo for 1970, and Manhattan for 1963. Manhattan sub-area is part of Manhattan south of Central Park.

Note: [a]square kilometers.

14

population density will shrink. If so, the Seoul central business district will become more like Tokyo's and less like New York's.

Korea's other large cities are less dense than Seoul. Pusan, the second largest, has an average population density about half that of Seoul. Taegu, the third largest, has a density about two-thirds that of Seoul. Other large cities, such as Inch'ŏn and Taejŏn, have densities about half that of Seoul.

Decreasing urban population densities are characteristic of industrialized countries throughout the world. Urban population densities have declined in the United States since the beginning of the twentieth century. The same trend has been observed in Europe, Australia, and Japan, at least during the period since World War II. Careful analysis indicates that rising incomes and improved transportation are the important causes of decreasing densities. Rising real incomes lead to increased housing demand, and housing is cheaper in more distant suburbs where land values are low. Improved transportation increases the accessibility of suburban housing sites to central employment locations, thus enabling workers to commute long distances from dispersed dwellings. There has been almost no study of urban dispersal within cities in developing countries. We report such a study for Korea in Chapter 6.

As for the structure of employment in cities, in Korea, as elsewhere, urbanization has been strongly correlated with the movement of workers from agriculture to other sectors. The growth of manufacturing employment is cited most frequently as the driving force behind urbanization. During the period of most rapid urbanization in Korea, from 1953 to 1974, the percentage of the labor force engaged in manufacturing grew from less than 3 to more than 17. But it is important not to overemphasize the importance of manufacturing as a cause of urbanization. Among countries of the world for which data are available, the percentage of the labor force in manufacturing explains only about half the variance of the population percentage that is urban. In the United States the percentage of the labor force in manufacturing reached a peak of about 25 in the 1920s, although urbanization proceeded briskly during the subsequent half century.

Several industries are more urbanized than manufacturing. In 1970, 45.5 percent of total employment in Korea was in cities and towns with more than 20,000 population; 79.7 percent of manufacturing employment was in the same set of cities and large towns. But the percentage of construction employment was 92.2; of retailing and wholesaling, 89.1; and of banking and real estate, 92.8. As in the United States and elsewhere, services are the most highly urbanized industry, and the growth of the service sector has been an important cause of urbanization.

Cities tend to specialize in certain industries, but they become less specialized as they grow and as incomes rise. Table 5 shows the employment pattern in Korea's four largest cities. Pusan is a center of heavy industry and has the largest concentration of workers in Manufacturing. Seoul has the smallest concentration of workers in Manufacturing. Seoul's largest employment concentration is in Other Services, which include government and education, the activities that differentiate Seoul from other large Korean cities. Although the four cities contain much of Korea's manufacturing employment, manufacturing accounts for only 27.5 percent of their total employment. The service sectors, including Retailing and Wholesaling, Transportation and Communication, and Other Services, are much larger.

As in most countries, only limited data are available on locations of economic activities within Korean urban areas. Comprehensive data are available mainly for the Seoul area. Table 6 presents data for the Seoul, Tokyo, and New York regions on a geographical basis comparable to that in Table 3. As suggested above, Seoul's central employment density is even smaller than its population density relative to Tokyo and New York. A larger share of Seoul's employment is within 20 kilometers of the center than in Tokyo and New York, mainly because Seoul is a smaller metropolitan area than the other two. In fact, much of the employment beyond 20 kilometers from the center of

TABLE 5 Employment by Industry in Large Korean Cities, 1971

	Total	Agriculture & Fishery	Mining	Manu-facturing	Construction	Electricity & Water	Retailing & Wholesaling	Transportation & Communication	Other Services
Seoul	1,575,648 (100.0)	25,012 (1.6)	3,508 (0.2)	331,537 (21.0)	155,857 (9.9)	23,334 (1.5)	407,482 (25.9)	101,567 (6.4)	527,351 (33.5)
Pusan	503,640 (100.0)	21,920 (4.4)	1,200 (0.2)	163,240 (32.4)	30,760 (6.1)	2,160 (0.4)	111,000 (22.0)	30,080 (6.0)	143,280 (28.5)
Taegu	321,200 (100.0)	10,300 (3.2)	400 (0.1)	96,800 (30.2)	29,600 (9.2)	700 (0.2)	104,000 (32.4)	16,700 (5.2)	62,700 (19.5)
Kwangju	153,500 (100.0)	6,200 (4.0)	–	40,400 (26.3)	10,000 (6.5)	400 (0.3)	54,900 (35.8)	10,700 (7.0)	30,900 (20.1)

Sources: Data for each city are from statistical yearbook of each city. See Sŏul [Seoul] T'ŭkpyŏlsi, Sŏul [Seoul] t'onggye yŏnbo, 1971; Pusan, *Pusan-si t'onggye yŏnbo,* 1971; Taegu, *Taegu-si t'onggye yŏnbo,* 1971; Kwangju, *Kwangju-si t'onggye yŏnbo,* 1971.

TABLE 6 Employment Density Patterns in Seoul, Tokyo, and New York

| | Distance[a] from Center | | | |
	0–20	20–40	40–70	Total
Seoul (1970)				
Employment[a]	1,407	379	355	2,141
Employment Share	65.7	17.7	16.6	100.0
Density[a]	1,003	129	64 (average)	216
Tokyo (1970)				
Employment[a]	7,028	2,840	2,254	12,122
Employment Share	58.0	23.4	18.6	100.0
Density[a]	6,587	862	234 (average)	895
New York (1963)				
Employment[a]	4,188	1,977	799[b]	6,964
Employment Share	60.1	28.4	11.5[b]	100.0
Density[a]	5,295	531	99[b] (average)	555

Sources: Same as Table 3.

Notes: [a]Employment in thousands, distance in kilometers, area in square kilometers, and density in employees per square kilometer.
[b]40–80 kilometers.

Seoul should not be thought of as being in the Seoul metropolitan area. These distant places beyond the green belts contain some industrial areas that are only loosely related to the Seoul metropolitan area.

Table 7 presents trends restricted to manufacturing employment in the Seoul area. Seoul city represents a smaller area than the 20-kilometer radius data in Table 6, since Seoul city has an average radius of about 14 kilometers. Although the comparison is not exact, Tables 6 and 7 suggest that manufacturing employment is more concentrated than total employment near the center of the Seoul metropolitan area. In 1970, 89 percent of manufacturing employment was in Seoul city, whereas only

TABLE 7 Trends in Manufacturing Employment Location
in Seoul Metropolitan Area, 1960–1973
(1,000s)

	1960		1966		1970		1973	
	No.	%	No.	%	No.	%	No.	%
Seoul Metro. Area	80.3	100	197.6	100	319.6	100	431.4	100
Seoul City	64.1	80	180.2	91	284.9	89	383.5	89
Periphery	16.2	20	17.4	9	34.7	11	47.9	11
Entire Country	275.2	–	566.7	–	861.0	–	1,157.8	–

Source: Byung-Nak Song, "The Distribution and Movement of Jobs and Industry—
Seoul Metropolitan Region," Korea Development Institute, Working Paper
74-11 (November 1974), p. 12.

65.7 percent of total employment was within the larger, 20-
kilometer radius. The imprecision comes from the fact that the
total area, which determines the denominators in the two tables,
may not be the same. If manufacturing employment is more
concentrated than total employment near the center of Seoul,
it differs from the United States pattern.

Table 7 reflects the spectacular increase in Korean manufacturing employment, the 1970 figure being more than 3 times the
1960 figure for the entire country. The growth in the Seoul
metropolitan area has been even more spectacular, Seoul having
increased its share of Korea's manufacturing employment from
29.2 percent in 1960 to 37.1 percent in 1970. In Chapter 4, we
shall present data that indicate a trend away from location of
manufacturing in the Seoul area, perhaps starting in the late
1960s, but certainly by the 1970s. This trend is suggested by the
fact that Seoul's share of manufacturing employment remained
virtually unchanged from 1970 to 1973. The most surprising
data in Table 7 are those indicating an increasing share of Seoul
city in the metropolitan area's manufacturing employment from
80 to 89 percent during the 1960s. In the United States and
Japan, there is strong evidence of an increasing dispersion of
manufacturing toward the peripheries of metropolitan areas. But

the boundaries of Seoul city have been enlarged as the city grew during the 1960s and 1970s, and it is therefore not easy to interpret the evidence of increasing centralization in Table 7. It is consistent with the possibility that most new manufacturing located itself on the outskirts as the metropolitan area grew. This difficulty in interpreting data based on legal city boundaries is the primary reason for studying urban structure by density functions, as we do in Chapter 6, instead of relying on data based on legal boundaries.

URBAN AND RURAL INCOME
AND CONSUMPTION PATTERNS

Incomes are higher in urban than rural areas in most countries. Where urban-rural income differences are substantial, people migrate to cities in search of higher living standards. There is no reason to expect that migration should equalize income levels between urban and rural areas. There are non-pecuniary advantages to certain occupations which cause workers to prefer them even at lower incomes. Farming may be such an occupation for people raised in rural areas. In addition, price levels are higher in urban than rural areas. Manufactured goods are somewhat cheaper in cities because they must be shipped further when sold in rural areas and because there is less competition among rural than urban retailers. But services are more expensive in urban than rural areas because they must be produced where they are consumed, and urban workers must be paid more than rural workers to compensate for higher land values in urban areas. Finally, some people believe that urban workers must be paid higher wages to compensate for congestion in cities. This argument is incorrect because what is relevant is the transportation cost from origin to destination, and such distances are mostly much shorter in urban than rural areas because densities are so much greater. In any case, against the possibility of greater urban congestion and perhaps pollution must be set the greater variety of goods and services available in urban than in rural areas, the greater anonymity, and reduced social pressure. Thus, several factors might explain modest urban-rural income disparities in one direction or the other. Migration, however, always results from substantial income disparities.

Precise measurement of the effect of income differences on migration is complicated by the fact that the average urban income is not available to most migrants. Most migrants are less well educated, less experienced in urban occupations, and less familiar with urban life than most long-term urban residents. Consequently many urban migrants spend their first years in low-paying jobs, often selling goods or performing personal services in what is referred to as the informal sector. In fact, it appears that the patterns of entry in the informal sector and gradual movement to the formal sector are less common in Korea than in many developing countries.

Measurement of the income advantages to urban migrants is complex and the subject has inspired research and controversy in recent years. In Korea, the data indicate that there have been large disparities between urban and rural incomes during the period of rapid urbanization. The basic data come from urban- and farm-household expenditure surveys compiled each year from small samples of households. As shown above, there are substantial numbers of rural non-farm residents, but there are no income data for that group. The data are believed to be more reliable for the 1970s than for the 1960s and are subject to sampling fluctuations. It is believed that the data understate urban incomes because the sample under-represents high-income recipients.

Table 8 displays income and consumption patterns from expenditure surveys for Seoul, all urban, and all farm residents for selected years from 1963 to 1974. The table shows that urban income per capita exceeded farm income by only 23 percent in 1965, but the urban figure is almost certainly understated. The data show that urban income per capita was more than twice that on farms during the late 1960s, and that the

TABLE 8 Urban and Farm Income and Consumption Patterns, 1963–1974
(in current wŏn)

	1963	1965	1966	1968	1970	1972	1974
Farm (all households)							
Average income							
per household	80,654	105,685	112,458	145,798	225,155	338,529	498,074
per capita	12,622	16,802	18,080	24,219	38,033	59,287	87,999
Saving ratios	3.94	4.91	2.29	1.85	7.72	8.53	12.57
Food (%)	60.3	53.1	50.2	47.4	45.9	48.2	48.4
Housing (%)	3.5	3.8	4.1	4.9	4.2	5.7	7.5
Fuel & light (%)	9.2	7.8	8.3	8.1	7.9	6.7	7.2
Clothing (%)	6.5	8.0	8.7	9.0	8.4	7.3	7.1
Miscellaneous (%)	20.6	27.2	28.8	30.6	33.6	32.1	29.8
Urban (all households)							
Average income							
per household	–	115,200	170,520	325,680	387,240	509,280	656,160
per capita	–	20,719	30,669	58,787	70,664	94,838	125,701
Saving ratios	–	-1.88	4.57	14.55	7.19	9.14	8.38
Food (%)	54.2	56.8	48.5	42.4	40.5	40.7	43.3
Housing (%)	15.0	13.8	17.9	17.2	18.4	19.5	18.5
Fuel & light (%)	6.1	5.8	6.2	5.2	5.5	5.0	5.6
Clothing (%)	5.9	6.4	7.7	10.8	10.1	8.4	8.4
Miscellaneous (%)	18.8	17.2	19.6	24.4	25.6	26.3	24.3

TABLE 8 (continued)

	1963	1965	1966	1968	1970	1972	1974
Seoul (all households)							
Average income							
per household	–	135,480	198,240	353,040	462,000	593,880	673,440
per capita	–	24,108	34,656	64,776	86,196	112,056	129,264
Saving ratios	–	-3.01	4.18	11.05	6.10	7.17	7.13
Food (%)	50.3	53.7	45.4	41.6	38.4	39.4	43.2
Housing (%)	17.1	15.0	19.0	17.8	18.9	20.8	19.5
Fuel & light (%)	6.3	5.4	5.8	4.9	4.7	4.5	5.6
Clothing (%)	5.5	6.1	7.5	10.4	10.0	8.4	7.4
Miscellaneous (%)	20.8	19.8	22.3	25.3	27.9	27.9	24.3

Sources: EPB, Annual Report on the Family Income and Expenditure Survey, 1963–1974, MAF, Report on the Results of Farm Household Economy Survey, 1963 through 1974, 1975.

gap narrowed to 43 percent in 1974. Although the magnitudes are subject to error, it is likely that the urban-farm gap was large and then narrowed, in part because of the massive migration from farms to urban areas.

In most years, per capita income in Seoul was about 15 or 20 percent greater than the average for urban areas. The table shows that the gap narrowed to 3 percent in 1974. Once again, the precise magnitudes may be in error, but a gradual narrowing of the gap between incomes in Seoul and other urban areas is likely.

The expenditure data in Table 8 reveal that food is the largest component of expenditure by all groups in all years, about 40 to 50 percent of total expenditure. For all three groups, food expenditure as a percentage of total expenditure falls steadily as incomes rise. This follows a rule observed everywhere, that food is the highest budget priority in poor households, but that the income elasticity of demand for food is well under 1 even at low incomes and falls steadily as income rises. If rapid economic growth continues, food will soon take less than 40 percent of expenditure in Korean cities. Since the late 1960s, food has taken a smaller share of urban than farm expenditure and a smaller share in Seoul than in all urban expenditures. The reason is that income is highest in Seoul and higher in urban than farm households. The low-income elasticity of food demand dominates the data even though food prices are higher in urban than in rural areas.

The share of housing in total expenditure is much greater in urban than in farm households, and slightly greater in Seoul than in all urban areas. The reason is that the relative price of housing is much higher in urban than rural areas, and the demand for housing is price inelastic. Urban housing is more expensive than rural mainly because of much higher urban land values. In most countries, housing expenditure falls slightly as a fraction of total expenditure as income rises. In urban Korea, the trend has been in the opposite direction. Urban housing expenditure rose from a low of 12.9 percent of total expenditure in 1964 (not shown) to a high of 19.5 percent in 1972.

CONCLUSIONS

Korea has urbanized at an extraordinarily rapid pace during most of the years since World War II. By 1975, half the population was urban. Although continued rapid national development will certainly be accompanied by continued rapid urbanization, it is unlikely that the country will long continue to urbanize at the frenetic pace of the 1960s and early 1970s. In almost all countries, the movement of people from rural to urban areas has slowed once the urban percentage of the population has reached Korea's level of the mid-1970s.

Much of Korea's industry is located in its large cities, and industrialization has been an important cause of urban growth. But in Korea, as elsewhere, service industries are more urbanized than manufacturing. Production and distribution of services are important urban functions in developing and developed countries.

All countries that urbanize rapidly have urban problems, and it is inevitable that the extraordinarily rapid pace of urbanization in Korea would be accompanied by serious problems. There are problems of personal dislocation and adjustment as rural migrants adjust to urban life. It is difficult for housing construction to keep pace with rapid urbanization, and urban housing becomes expensive and scarce. Likewise, public infrastructure becomes overstrained as demands placed on it by urban migrants grow. Water supply, waste disposal, transportation facilities, schools, and many other public facilities are stressed. These are serious problems; some will be discussed in detail in later chapters. But it is worthwhile to pause here to take note of urban problems that Korea has not faced or has substantially solved.

Very rapid economic growth makes almost every problem less serious. In many developing countries, rapid urbanization has been accompanied by high unemployment rates among migrants and by long periods of transition into organized employment sectors in cities. Korea's rapid economic growth has enabled cities to absorb migrants into the urban labor force rapidly. Korea has thus been spared much of the urban discontent, discouragement, and violence that have plagued some developing countries. Although urban housing remains inadequate for many Koreans, homelessness and extremely inadequate housing had been reduced to a small scale by the mid-1970s. Finally, transportation investments have kept pace with Korean urbanization. Otherwise, chaos would have resulted in the largest cities.

Urban problems are always a matter of degree. In all countries, large urban migrations take place because the alternative of remaining in the rural sector is worse. Korea's urbanization has certainly been successful in the sense that the vast majority of migrants have been able to raise their incomes and living standards, improve their education and skills, and open up better opportunities for their children.

THREE

Causes and Comparisons of Urban Growth

In the last chapter, it was shown that the period 1945–1975 was marked by extraordinarily rapid urbanization in Korea, probably matching any comparable experience elsewhere throughout history. This chapter is interpretative, and answers the question why urbanization is so rapid in a rapidly developing country. Many people in Korea and elsewhere believe that rapid urbanization is detrimental to urban migrants and to others. The notion that many developing countries are overurbanized is pervasive. Here we shall show that the concept of overurbanization is vague and that there is no mechanical rule by which to determine the appropriate amount of urbanization in any country in any historical period. Reasons for international differences in urbanization are discussed and some comparative international statistics are presented.

Individuals come to urban areas from the countryside for

many reasons. Many young people come for educational purposes. Dependent children come because their parents have migrated. Elderly people may come because their grown children live in the cities. Adults may come to join their friends or relatives. But the fundamental and pervasive reasons for urbanization are economic. By and large, most people come to urban areas because income and employment prospects for them and their children are better than in the countryside. Very often, the basic economic reasons are indirect. Young people who come to cities to attend colleges and universities do so mostly to prepare themselves for urban jobs. Dependent children who accompany parents are indirectly responding to economic opportunities that have motivated the parents to migrate. It was shown in the previous chapter that incomes in urban areas have been persistently above those in rural areas during the years of rapid urbanization in Korea. The data are not as plentiful or reliable as one might wish, but they make clear the powerful economic motivation for rural-urban migration.

In the 1950s and early 1960s, there was a widespread belief among development specialists that there was or should be a mechanical link between the industrialization of a country and its urbanization. Many studies were published in which the percentage of a country's population that was urban was correlated with the percentage of the labor force employed in manufacturing. Countries whose urban percentage was high relative to industrialization were sometimes claimed to be overurbanized; the term "parasitic cities" was sometimes used to characterize such overurbanization.

It is now realized that the relationship between urbanization and economic development is complex and that no mechanical linkage between urbanization and industrialization should be expected. Recent research, especially by Kelley, Williamson, and Cheetham[1], has provided a sophisticated conceptual framework to analyze urbanization in developing countries. This chapter provides an interpretation of the approach that can be useful in understanding recent Korean developments.

AN INTERPRETATIVE ANALYSIS
OF KOREAN URBANIZATION

Economic development consists in part of increases in the output of goods and services that can be produced with a country's available inputs of labor and other productive resources. Much research, mostly based on techniques developed by Denison[2] and others, has been undertaken in recent years to identify and measure the sources of productivity growth. One important source is capital accumulation. All countries with rapid growth of real gross national product (GNP) have high saving rates. Korea is a good example, with a gross saving rate in excess of 20 percent since the late 1960s. A second and a most important source of productivity growth is the introduction of new technology—in the long run, new products and new techniques of producing old products are the most important sources of productivity growth. In a developing country such as Korea, new technology can be imported and adapted to Korean conditions or it can originate domestically. There are examples of both processes in most developing countries. A third major source of productivity growth is improvements in the education, skills, and experience of the labor force. Other sources of productivity growth are improved resource allocation resulting from better transportation and communication, increased competitiveness in the economy, increased stability because of better government planning, and so forth.

Whatever the relative importance of the various sources of productivity growth, the result is growth in real income per capita. In Korea, growth has been especially rapid, and real income per capita has grown at an average annual rate of more than 8 percent since the mid-1960s. Productivity growth is not uniform among sectors of the economy, but in Korea and other quickly developing countries it has been rapid in agriculture and manufacturing. Less is known about productivity growth in the service sector, in which output is difficult to measure, but the presumption is that productivity growth is slower there than in most other sectors.

As real incomes rise, consumer demands shift dramatically. At very low income levels, people spend more than half their incomes on food. As the last chapter noted, Koreans spent 50–60 percent of their incomes on food in the early 1960s. The income elasticity of demand for food is less than 1 even at low incomes, and declines as incomes rise. Thus, expenditure on food in Korea fell from 60.3 percent of total consumer expenditure in 1958 to 45.4 percent in 1973. In very high income countries in Western Europe and North America, food takes less than 20 percent of total expenditure.

Whereas expenditure on food increases less than proportionately with income, expenditure on manufactured products and on services increases more than proportionately. Expenditure on clothing and related products has risen from 10.2 percent of total expenditure in 1958 to 13.6 percent in 1973. Expenditure on furniture and household equipment has risen from 1.5 percent to 3.4 percent of total expenditure during the same period. In the service category, health and other personal care expenditures rose from 4.0 to 5.3 percent of the total. These statistics reflect the fact that income elasticities of demand for manufactured goods and services are somewhat greater than 1 in Korea. At higher income levels than those reflected in Table 9, growth in service expenditures becomes even more rapid relative to growth in manufactured goods expenditures.

There is nothing mysterious about these statistics; food is necessary to sustain life, and at low income levels people devote most of their resources to it. At somewhat higher income levels, larger parts of income are devoted to clothing, household equipment, and other things that are important to comfort and health. At still higher income levels, larger parts of income are devoted to a variety of services that make life pleasant and rewarding.

The result of these shifts in demand is that a decreasing percentage of the labor force and of other inputs is needed to satisfy the demand for food as incomes rise. Increasing percentages of productive resources are needed to satisfy demands for

TABLE 9 Share of Private Consumption Expenditure
(in 1970 billion wŏn)

	1958		1963		1968		1973	
	Amount	*%*	*Amount*	*%*	*Amount*	*%*	*Amount*	*%*
Private Consumption Expenditure	882.43	100.0	1,055.51	100.0	1,545.55	100.0	2,415.82	100.0
Food	531.80	60.3	568.56	53.9	796.05	51.5	1,097.56	45.4
Beverages	31.29	3.5	36.27	3.4	59.95	3.9	129.32	5.4
Tobacco	11.55	1.3	16.66	1.6	43.87	2.8	91.03	3.8
Clothing and other personal effects	90.19	10.2	117.91	11.2	157.29	10.2	328.69	13.6
Rent and water charges	48.76	5.5	53.66	5.1	64.77	4.2	88.19	3.7
Fuel and light	33.63	3.8	59.28	5.6	71.45	4.6	106.34	4.4
Furniture, furnishing, and household equipment	13.01	1.5	20.61	2.0	41.60	2.7	83.37	3.4
Household operation	10.47	1.2	12.96	1.2	17.05	1.1	25.81	1.1
Personal care and health expenses	35.07	4.0	60.02	5.7	78.65	5.1	127.19	5.3
Transportation and communication	20.89	2.4	41.35	3.9	85.05	5.5	143.26	5.9
Recreation and entertainment	40.30	4.6	43.63	4.1	82.42	5.3	124.12	5.1
Miscellaneous services	27.00	3.0	24.60	2.3	47.40	3.1	70.94	2.9
Statistical discrepancy	−11.53	−1.3	–	–	–	–	–	–

Source: BOK, *Economic Statistics Yearbook, 1976.*

manufactured goods and services. As the demand for labor, capital, and other inputs rises in manufacturing and service sectors and falls in agriculture, the first two sectors bid more for inputs than the third. Thus, wage rates and returns to capital become higher in manufacturing and service industries than in agriculture. As a result, workers move from low-wage farming jobs to high-wage manufacturing and service jobs; and savings are channeled into capital formation in manufacturing and away from farming.

The shift of demand from food to manufactured products and services continues for many decades as incomes rise. This leads to persistently higher wages and other input returns in manufacturing and service sectors, and a continuing movement of labor and other resources from farming to the other sectors. This pattern has persisted for half a century or a century in many countries. The movement of labor out of agriculture has been extremely rapid in Korea since the early 1960s, more rapid than at comparable stages of development in presently developed countries. Employment in agriculture (including forestry and fisheries) fell from 63.1 percent of total employment in 1963 to 48.2 percent in 1974. During that period, manufacturing employment rose from 8.0 to 17.4 percent. But agricultural employment is less than 20 percent of the total in developed countries. In Japan, with a rice-based agricultural economy similar to Korea's, agricultural employment is less than 15 percent of the total. It should therefore be expected that the movement of workers out of Korean agriculture will continue for many years to come.

What has been established so far is that economic development in Korea and elsewhere is accompanied by massive shifts of human and other resources from agriculture to the manufacturing and service sectors. These are, of course, movements between industries; the link to urbanization stems from the fact that manufacturing and service industries are predominantly located in urban areas, whereas agriculture is almost entirely located in rural areas. Thus, the movement between industries tends to produce rural-to-urban migration.

Manufacturing and, to a lesser extent, service industries are subject to substantial scale economies. Productivity is greatest if substantial amounts of labor and other inputs can be employed in one location. Workers, of course, find it advantageous to live close to places of employment, and employers find it advantageous to locate where an adequate labor force is readily available. Likewise, retail suppliers of goods and services to manufacturing employees and their families find it advantageous to locate near potential customers. The desire to avoid high transportation costs motivates a wide range of economic activities that have market interrelationships to locate in close proximity to each other. This motivation is present in some degree for agricultural as well as manufacturing and service sectors, but technology makes proximity less feasible in agriculture. In farming, output and labor input per unit of land are relatively small, and there are stringent limits to the substitution of other inputs for land. In manufacturing and services, proximity is made possible by the fact that relatively little land is required per worker or per unit of output, and large amounts of employment and output can therefore locate on small plots of land. In addition, in both manufacturing and service industries, other inputs can be substituted for land in places where land is expensive. The most visible manifestation of this substitution is tall buildings used for office activities, retailing, processing, and housing where land is expensive. Capital in the form of structures has been substituted for land. In addition, density and proximity are increased by leaving only little land uncovered or unused where it is expensive. These technological facts mean that much larger ratios of output and labor to land are possible and profitable in manufacturing and service sectors than in agriculture.

Thus, technology makes high densities of output and employment possible in manufacturing and service sectors. And the desire to avoid expensive transportation of goods and people provides the motivation to use the high densities made possible by technology. Producers of commodities that are inputs in further processing activities find it profitable to locate near potential customers. Service producers find it advantageous to locate near their business and household customers. Workers find it advantageous to live near their places of work. Retailers find it advantageous to locate near their customers. And so an endless variety of complex locational relationships is built up in an urban area. Although the variety and complexity of relationships are much greater in a large city than in a small hamlet, the principle is the same. Technology permits agglomerations of manufacturing and service activities, and the desire to avoid expensive transportation in moving goods and people among related activities motivates the agglomeration.

The foregoing are the basic technological and economic reasons for the agglomeration of large numbers of people and economic activities in urban areas as countries develop and shift resources from agriculture to predominantly urban sectors. Land values are both the economic reflection and the motivation of the process. Land prices are of course set by supply and demand, as are other prices. Korean data on land values will be surveyed in Chapter 7. In Korea and in all countries in which markets are permitted to set land values, urban land prices exceed agricultural land prices by one or two orders of magnitude. The basic reason, as shown above, is that output per unit of land is much greater in urban than in agricultural activities. Thus, urban land users are able to outbid agricultural land users in places where it is advantageous for manufacturing and service activities to congregate. In such places, the value to manufacturing, service, and housing activities of proximity to other such activities is so great that they bid large sums for land that is near many such activities. This creates intense competition for urban land, and land prices are bid up so that landowners receive the value of land's productivity in its most productive use. This is a socially beneficial mechanism, in that competition ensures that each plot of land is allocated to its most productive use. Urban land allocation is, of course, a complex and slow process, and urban land uses are continually shifting as market participants attempt to find the most productive use for each plot of land.

Although the process is in a continuous state of flux, distinct and persistent patterns of land use are found in urban areas. They will be studied in detail in Chapter 6. Land close to the centers of large urban areas has the greatest proximity value, and prices of such land are very high indeed. It is allocated to uses in which proximity is most valuable and which can to the greatest extent substitute structural capital and other inputs for land. Land on the outskirts of urban areas or in small urban areas has less proximity value, but nevertheless has much greater value than agricultural land. It is used for housing, activities that service nearby residents, and manufacturing. Manufacturing tends, increasingly in most countries, to concentrate in the outskirts of urban areas, partly because proximity is less important in manufacturing than in some service activities. It is important for manufacturing activities to be near their employees, which favors fringe locations where worker residences are concentrated. But fringe locations are of little disadvantage even to manufacturers who buy from and sell to other firms scattered throughout the urban area. Urban areas have highly developed road systems, and goods shipment is relatively inexpensive throughout. Finally, there are more stringent limits to substitution of structural capital for land in manufacturing than in service activities. Many services can be produced in high office buildings as easily as in low structures, but most manufacturing becomes inefficient if materials must be moved among many floors. Thus, manufacturing activities are less able than service activities to economize on land, and therefore they locate on the outskirts of urban areas where land is relatively inexpensive. Even within activities, such as housing and retailing, lower densities and capital-land ratios are employed on the outskirts of urban areas where land is relatively cheap than near the centers. The closer they are to the centers of urban areas, the higher the structures in which shops and houses are located, and the less uncovered land around them.

INTERNATIONAL COMPARISONS

The preceding analysis shows why urbanization is correlated with economic development. It also makes clear that there is no mechanical link between urbanization and development. The percentage of the population that is urban depends on many conditions at each stage of economic development. First, the extent of the demand shift from agricultural products to manufacturing products and services. People in some countries may wish to devote more or less of their incomes to food than in other countries. There may be cultural or traditional features to consumption patterns that affect the allocation of consumer expenditures. Second, the relative productivity levels in the various sectors. Agricultural productivity may vary from country to country, depending on the amount and fertility of arable land, on the kinds of crops grown, and on the speed with which new technology is introduced. Productivity in manufacturing and services also varies from country to country and for similar reasons. Third, the percentage of manufacturing and service output that is located in rural areas, which varies from one country to another for reasons that are not well understood. One factor is certainly the accessibility of rural residents to urban areas. If rural areas are isolated from cities, rural residents cannot easily travel there to obtain goods and services. Finally, the percentage of the population that is urban depends in part on international conditions and on national policies. A country that has a comparative advantage in food production and exports substantial amounts of agricultural products is likely to have a relatively large rural population. Conversely, a country that imports much of its food is likely to be highly urbanized. The effect of comparative advantage on urbanization is affected by national policies. Some governments encourage agricultural production by subsidies, import controls, and export promotion. Some countries also discourage urban growth. Or countries may encourage urbanization by policies that promote industrialization.

Thus, one would expect the correlation between urbanization and economic development to be strong but by no means perfect. We now present an elaborate comparison between urbanization and other development indexes in Korea and other countries.

The comparisons presented in this section are based on calculations and data presented by Chenery and Syrquin.[3] In 1975, they published the most extensive comparison of international development patterns ever undertaken. Their procedure is complex, and their book is recommended for a full description. Building on the work of Kuznets, they started with 26 variables that are systematically related to economic development, here listed in Table 10, and numbered according to the 10 major groups into which they fall. Each of the 26 variables was used as dependent variable in a regression of the form

$$X = \alpha + \beta_1 \ln Y + \beta_2 (\ln Y)^2 + \gamma_1 \ln N + \gamma_2 (\ln N)^2 + \Sigma_i T_i + \epsilon F \tag{3-1}$$

where X equals dependent variable, Y equals GNP per capita, N equals population, F equals imports minus exports of goods and nonfactor services as a share of GDP_1 and T_i equals time period. The hypothesis underlying (3-1) is that the 26 correlates of economic development are nonlinear functions of per capita income and population, and linear functions of the trade balance and of the time variables. Chenery and Syrquin estimated (3-1) for each of the 26 dependent variables, using both cross-sectional and time-series data. The unit observation is a particular country and a particular year. Data were collected from about 100 countries during the period 1950 to 1970. Of course, some data are much more plentiful than others, so sample sizes vary among the regressions.

In Table 10, we compare Korean data with calculations from

TABLE 10 Actual and Normal Economic Structures with Level of Development in Korea, 1953–1974

		1953	1957	1960	1965	1970	1974
Per Capita GNP (in 1964 $)		103.0	108.9	110.5	129.7	193.6	260.9
Population (in millions)		20.2	22.7	24.7	28.3	31.3	33.5
Accumulation Process							
1. Investment							
a. Saving	A	0.083	0.048	0.016	0.079	0.172	0.186
	N	0.088	0.075	0.090	0.120	0.119	0.112
b. Investment	A	0.162	0.154	0.110	0.153	0.273	0.311
	N	0.163	0.180	0.182	0.193	0.220	0.237
c. Capital Inflow	A	0.078	0.106	0.093	0.074	0.101	0.124
	N	0.008	0.020	0.022	0.018	0.015	0.013
2. Government Revenue							
a. Government Revenue	A	0.058	0.089	0.130	0.119	0.193	0.175
	N	0.120	0.122	0.121	0.132	0.148	0.162
b. Tax Revenue	A	0.049	0.075	0.103	0.087	0.153	0.149
	N	0.128	0.132	0.126	0.136	0.149	0.160
3. Education							
a. Education Expenditure	A	0.011	0.034	0.080	0.020	0.030	0.029
	N	0.019	0.023	0.028	0.033	0.034	0.035
b. School Enrollment Ratio	A	0.472	0.568	0.542	0.581	0.714	0.815
	N						

TABLE 10 (continued)

Resource Allocation Processes

		1953	1957	1960	1965	1970	1974
4. Structure of Domestic Demand							
a. Private Consumption	A	0.837	0.843	0.848	0.838	0.731	0.692
	N	0.790	0.762	0.783	0.755	0.735	0.724
b. Government Consumption	A	0.079	0.109	0.145	0.095	0.109	0.108
	N	0.134	0.130	0.125	0.126	0.139	0.151
c. Food Consumption	A	0.482	0.524	0.467	0.500	0.394	0.378
	N	0.435	0.433	0.416	0.382	0.349	0.328
5. Structure of Production							
a. Primary Share	A	0.504	0.487	0.422	0.430	0.324	0.283
	N	0.458	0.435	0.437	0.404	0.316	0.256
b. Industry Share	A	0.099	0.131	0.156	0.210	0.255	0.300
	N	0.189	0.201	0.198	0.212	0.267	0.305
c. Utilities Share	A	0.020	0.047	0.053	0.051	0.072	0.070
	N	0.057	0.061	0.063	0.066	0.073	0.078
d. Services Share	A	0.376	0.335	0.369	0.310	0.349	0.348
	N	0.347	0.369	0.370	0.382	0.419	0.443
6. Structure of Trade							
a. Exports	A	0.020	0.015	0.034	0.086	0.148	0.303
	N	0.160	0.143	0.140	0.151	0.158	0.163
b. Primary Exports	A			0.011	0.022	0.017	0.026
	N	0.113	0.109	0.106	0.102	0.097	0.092
c. Manufactured Exports	A			0.003	0.036	0.089	0.240
	N	0.029	0.030	0.029	0.032	0.043	0.052

TABLE 10 (continued)

		1953	1957	1960	1965	1970	1974
6. Structure of Trade (continued)							
d. Services Exports	A	0.005	0.009	0.020	0.028	0.042	0.036
	N	0.018	0.018	0.018	0.019	0.023	0.026
e. Imports	A	0.098	0.121	0.127	0.160	0.249	0.427
	N	0.163	0.159	0.157	0.165	0.168	0.171
Demographic and Distributional Processes							
7. Labor Allocation							
a. Primary Share	A	0.637	0.622	0.624	0.596	0.516	0.486
	N				0.608	0.542	0.488
b. Industry Share	A	0.115	0.125	0.125	0.140	0.187	0.222
	N				0.123	0.161	0.212
c. Services Share	A	0.263	0.268	0.266	0.281	0.323	0.301
	N				0.269	0.291	0.313
8. Urbanization	A	0.231	0.241	0.283	0.334	0.423	0.498
	N		0.243	0.257	0.296	0.381	0.441
9. Demographic Transition							
a. Birth Rate	A	0.410	0.430	0.430	0.370	0.300	0.240
	N	0.422	0.408	0.409	0.396	0.350	0.315
b. Death Rate	A	0.143	0.130	0.130	0.100	0.090	0.070
	N	0.182	0.173	0.173	0.163	0.132	0.113
10. Income Distribution							
a. Highest 20%	N	0.545	0.548	0.548	0.054	0.561	0.561
b. Lowest 40%	N	0.129	0.128	0.127	0.124	0.117	0.113

Note: Normal economic structure computed on the basis of statistical methods in Chenery and Syrquin.

the Chenery-Syrquin regressions for selected years between 1953 and 1974. For each year and each dependent variable, we present two numbers. *A* is the actual value of the dependent variable that year in Korea. *N* is the value of the variable calculated from the Chenery-Syrquin regression for that year and for values the independent variables took in Korea that year. Thus, the *N*, or normal, observations are predictions for Korea for the year and variable in question from the Chenery-Syrquin regressions. For example, consider Equation 1a in 1974. *A* is 0.186 and *N* is 0.112. Korean savings in 1974 was 18.6 percent of GDP, whereas the Chenery-Syrquin regression predicts the 1974 Korean savings rate to be 11.2 percent. All dependent variables are ratios to GDP or to the national variable in question. For example, saving, 1a, is the ratio of total saving to GDP. The labor allocation variables, 7a–7c, are shares of total labor in the three sectors.

Many interesting comparisons can be made with the data in Table 10. We shall concentrate on those related to urbanization. In 1957, the first year in which the urbanization ratio can be calculated for Korea, row 8 of the table shows that Korea was almost exactly as urbanized as predicted by the Chenery-Syrquin model. After that, Korean urbanization proceeded more rapidly than predicted, and by 1974 Korea was 5 percentage points more urbanized than predicted. This difference is not large, but it is large enough to justify searching elsewhere in the table for explanations.

The answer does not appear to lie in Korea's industrial structure. Lines 7a–7c compare actual and predicted labor-force shares in the primary, industrial, and service sectors. In 1974, Korea's actual labor-force shares were almost exactly as predicted by the Chenery-Syrquin equations. In 1965 and 1970, the actual primary and industry shares were somewhat less than the normal shares, and the service share was larger than the normal. However, the sum of the two urban shares, industry and services, is almost exactly as predicted by the regression equation. A similar story is told by production shares, lines 5a–5d. The primary share is somewhat greater than predicted in almost all years since 1953. The output shares of the three predominantly urban sectors are consistently less than predicted. Thus, the reason for Korea's greater-than-predicted urbanization does not appear to be that the predominantly urban production sectors are larger than predicted.

This conclusion is reinforced by the food consumption data, line 4c. Food has been a larger share of total consumption than predicted throughout the period covered by the table. Thus, the inclusion on the consumption side is the same as on the production side; an unusually small agricultural sector is not the reason for Korea's high level of urbanization.

The answer to the question of why Korea is somewhat more urbanized than predicted appears to be in the international sector. Line 6a shows that Korean exports were much greater than predicted in 1974, and have grown relative to their predicted share throughout the period covered by the table. Imports have also been larger than predicted since the late 1960s. Furthermore, manufactured exports have been much larger than predicted since 1965. Thus, the reason that Korea is more urbanized than predicted appears to be that Korea's international sector, and especially its manufactured exports, are much larger than predicted by the Chenery-Syrquin model. Since all international trade ports are in urban areas, it appears that Korea's manufacturing industry is more concentrated in urban areas, mainly in urban areas with access to ports, than is true in typical developing countries. Although this conclusion is the only explanation suggested by the data in Table 10, it is conjectural and needs to be tested against more precise data. It is, nevertheless, a plausible explanation.

CONCLUSIONS

As this chapter has shown, urbanization results mainly from dramatic shifts in demand from products produced in rural areas to products and services mostly produced in urban areas as real incomes rise. Elaborate international comparisons demonstrate that Korea has been somewhat more urbanized than most countries at its stage of development since the late 1950s. Only in recent years has the difference been significant, and even then it has been modest. This difference appears to reflect the much greater importance of international trade in the Korean economy than in comparable developing countries.

FOUR

Primacy and City Size Distribution

National censuses in many countries have long designated cities in which people live. Data on city populations are among the most plentiful in the social sciences, and in many countries such data go back one, two, or more centuries. Economists, geographers, city planners, and other scholars have been fascinated by city size data, and scholars in many disciplines have studied their distribution.

The most common technique of analysis has been simple curve fitting in which the parameters of a frequency distribution are estimated from data on city populations. Every country or large region has its characteristic distribution, but distributions from many countries and many historical periods bear a strong family resemblance. Invariably, the distribution is highly skewed to the right, since in all countries and all historical periods there are many very small towns and cities and a small number of relatively large cities. Among the distributions that typically fit the data best are the log-normal and the Pareto. Both distributions have been found to describe accurately much socio-economic data that produce skewed distributions, including incomes, firm sizes, and family sizes.

It was formerly believed by many scholars that city sizes inevitably followed the rank-size distribution. This distribution assumes that the population of the Nth largest city is inversely proportional to N. It can be written

$$N = P_1 / P_N \qquad (4\text{-}1)$$

where P_N is the population of the Nth largest city. Putting $N = 1$ shows that P_1 is the population of the largest city. According to this distribution, the second largest city is half the population of the largest, the third largest is one-third the population of the largest, and so on. It is now widely appreciated that the rank-size distribution is no more than an approximation and that other distributions fit much of the data somewhat better than the rank-size distribution. One such distribution is the Pareto, which can be written

$$N = P_1 / P_N^a \qquad (4\text{-}2)$$

where a is a parameter to be estimated from the data. The rank-size distribution is a special case of the Pareto in which $a = 1$. The Pareto provides a convenient classification of city size distributions. If $a > 1$, city sizes fall off faster than proportionately with N, and if $a < 1$, they fall off more slowly than proportionately. The larger a is, the more primate the country is said to be, meaning that the largest city is large relative to the second, third, and subsequent cities in the size distribution. Although a varies somewhat from country to country and from time to time, there is a remarkable tendency for estimates of a to be close to 1.

A less sophisticated measure of primacy has been proposed by

Davis.[1] Davis's measure is the ratio of the population of the largest city to the sum of those of the second, third, and fourth largest cities. The Davis index can be designated D and equals

$$D = P_1 / (P_2 + P_3 + P_4) \qquad\qquad (4\text{-}3)$$

The advantage of this measure is that it does not require the estimation of a specific distribution and does not depend for its value on which distribution is the correct one. Its disadvantage is that it is calculated from an arbitrary subset of the four largest city populations. If the rank-size distribution is correct, Davis's index takes the value $12/13 \approx 0.92$.

The size distribution of cities varies somewhat from country to country, but is remarkably persistent within countries. The form and parameters of the distribution change only slowly from decade to decade. Not surprisingly, therefore, measures of primacy tend also to be persistent over many decades. Large countries tend to have lower primacy measures than small countries, and primacy tends to decrease as a country develops and average income rises. Primacy also depends on government actions. Israel, for example, has vigorously curtailed growth in Tel Aviv and Jerusalem, largely for military and ideological reasons. Many other countries have tried to nudge growth away from capital cities by modest subsidies to firms and workers if they locate elsewhere, with no measurable effect. England and France are examples.

Primacy is a remarkably controversial phenomenon. Public officials, scholars, and others believe that the largest cities are too big in many countries. Excessive primacy is blamed on the colonial legacy, on foreign businessmen, on poor migrants from rural areas, and on government policies in many countries. Controversy over primacy is mostly unrelated to the facts about the size and growth of the largest cities. It stems from the fact that the social costs of large and rapidly growing cities are obvious. Everyone can see the congestion, pollution, expensive housing, and high taxes that frequently result. But the benefits of primacy are subtle and complex. Especially in developing countries, large cities permit economic activities to take place at large and efficient scale because of the large local market, readily available labor supply, and easily accessible inputs. The result is the high real incomes that characterize the largest cities in many developing countries. In addition, large cities make available a range and variety of consumer goods and services that people find advantageous. Finally, the largest city in many countries is not only a manufacturing center, but also the national capital, largest port, and financial, cultural, and educational center. It is expensive to duplicate many of the necessary facilities for these activities in several places, and many need to interact with each other. Such interaction is expensive if the activities are dispersed in several centers and internal transportation is poor.

KOREAN CITY SIZE DISTRIBUTION

Table 11 shows the percentage of urban residents living in cities in various size categories for selected years from 1949 to 1975. The data display an unusually rapid shift of population to large cities during the years of rapid urbanization. During the 26-year period, there was a large decrease in the percentage of urban residents living in cities with fewer than 20,000 residents, and a corresponding increase in the percentage living in cities with more than 100,000 residents. Shifts in the relative importance of cities of intermediate size have been small. So large has been the shift from small to large cities that the number of people living in cities of under 20,000 residents was almost the same in 1975 as in 1949, whereas the number living in cities of over 100,000 residents was five times as large in 1975 as in 1949.

No one can be surprised at a rapid shift of population toward large cities in a country that has urbanized as rapidly as Korea. Table 12 shows the population and rank of Korea's 40 largest cities for selected years from 1960 to 1975. Here we begin to

TABLE 11 Percent Distribution of Urban
Residents by City Size, 1949–1975

City Size	1949	1955	1960	1966	1973	1975
Less than 20,000	72.5	66.1	59.0	51.1	46.1	41.1
20,000 – 50,000	9.2	8.6	12.4	14.7	6.9	8.0
50,000 – 100,000	3.6	5.7	5.7	4.3	4.5	3.6
Over 100,000	14.7	19.6	22.8	30.0	42.6	47.3

Sources: MHA, *Municipal Yearbook of Korea 1972, 1974.* EPB, *Report on Population and Housing Census, 1975.*

see the stability of rank order that is typical of large cities in many countries. There has been no change in rank among Korea's 6 largest cities not only during the 15 years covered by the table but also during the 26 years from 1949 to 1975. By 1975, each of the 6 largest cities in 1949 had reached between 4 and 5 times its 1949 population. The stability of ranks is remarkable in view of the dramatic increases in city sizes.

In 1960, Davis's primacy index, given by D in (4-3), had an average of about 1.42 and a range from 0.51 to 4.64 in the 46 countries of the world which has at least 4 urban areas with at least 100,000 people in each. It is easy to calculate D for Korea for census years. In 1949, D was 1.36. It fell to 0.87 in 1955, rose steadily to 1.53 in 1970, and fell slightly to 1.51 in 1975. The 1975 value of D for Korea is slightly above the 1960 worldwide average of 1.42, but well below its value for such countries as Argentina, France, Hungary, and Mexico. Japan's primacy index was 1.62 in 1960. Thus, despite the concentration of people in Seoul, Korea is not a highly primate country by worldwide standards.

We have also fitted the Pareto distribution to data on city sizes for census years from 1949 to 1975. If we take natural logs of both sides of (4-2), the result is

$$\ln N = \ln P_1 - a\ln P_N \qquad (4\text{-}4)$$

TABLE 12 Urban Population and Ranks

(1,000s)

Rank	1960 City (Si)	1960 Population	1966 City (Si)	1966 Population	1970 City (Si)	1970 Population	1975 City (Si)	1975 Population
1	Seoul	2,445	Seoul	3,805	Seoul	5,536	Seoul	6,889
2	Pusan	1,163	Pusan	1,430	Pusan	1,881	Pusan	2,454
3	Taegu	676	Taegu	847	Taegu	1,083	Taegu	1,311
4	Inch'ŏn	402	Inch'ŏn	529	Inch'ŏn	646	Inch'ŏn	800
5	Kwangju	315	Kwangju	404	Kwangju	503	Kwangju	607
6	Taejŏn	299	Taejŏn	316	Taejŏn	415	Taejŏn	507
7	Chŏnju	189	Chŏnju	221	Chŏnju	263	Masan	372
8	Masan	158	Mokp'o	162	Masan	191	Chŏnju	311
9	Mokp'o	130	Masan	155	Makp'o	178	Sŏngnam	272
10	Ch'ŏngju	92	Suwŏn	128	Suwŏn	171	Ulsan	253
11	Suwŏn	91	Ch'ŏngju	124	Ulsan	159	Suwŏn	224
12	Kunsan	90	Ulsan	113	Ch'ŏngju	144	Mokp'o	193
13	Yŏsu	87	Chinju	107	Ch'unch'ŏn	123	Ch'ŏngju	193
14	Chinju	87	Wŏnju	104	Chinju	122	Kunsan	154
15	Ch'unch'ŏn	83	Kunsan	103	Yŏsu	114	Ch'unch'ŏn	141
16	Wŏnju	77	Yŏsu	102	Kunsan	112	Cheju	135
17	Kyŏngju	76	Ch'unch'ŏn	100	Wŏnju	112	Anyang	135

TABLE 12 (continued)

Rank	1960 City (Si)	Population	1966 City (Si)	Population	1970 City (Si)	Population	1975 City (Si)	Population
18	Sunch'ŏn	69	Cheju	88	Cheju	106	P'ohang	134
19	Ch'ungju	69	Changsŏng	87	Changsŏng	103	Yŏsu	131
20	Cheju	68	Kyŏngju	86	Uijŏngbu	95	Wŏnju	120
21	Chinhae	67	Chinhae	81	Kyŏngju	92	I-ri	117
22	Changsŏng	67	Ch'ungju	80	Chinhae	92	Puch'ŏn	109
23	I-ri	66	Sunch'ŏn	79	Anyang	92	Sunch'ŏn	108
24	P'ohang	60	I-ri	79	Sunch'ŏn	91	Kyŏngju	108
25	Kangnŭng	59	Uijŏngbu	75	Ch'ungju	88	Uijŏngbu	108
26	Andong	53	Ch'ŏnan	71	I-ri	87	Ch'ungju	105
27	Uijŏngbu	51	P'ohang	66	P'ohang	79	Chinhae	104
28	Kimch'ŏn	51	Kangnŭng	65	Ch'ŏnan	78	Ch'ŏnan	97
29	Samch'ŏnp'o	50	Andong	64	Andong	76	Andong	95
30	Sosa	48	Sokch'o	63	Kangnŭng	74	Kangnŭng	85
31	Ch'ungmu	48	Tongduch'ŏn	59	Sokch'o	73	Chech'ŏn	74
32	Sangju	47	Kimch'ŏn	56	Chech'ŏn	62	Sokch'o	72
33	Sokch'o	46	Anyang	54	Kimch'ŏn	62	Yŏngju	71
34	Ch'ŏnan	44	Samch'ŏnp'o	53	Tongduch'ŏn	60	Kimch'ŏn	67
35	Mukho	41	Ch'ungmu	51	Yŏngju	59	Ch'ungmu	67

TABLE 12 (continued)

Rank	1960 City (Si)	Population	1966 City (Si)	Population	1970 City (Si)	Population	1975 City (Si)	Population
36	Chech'ŏn	39	Mukho	50	Sosa	57	Hwangju	61
37	Songt'an	35	Chech'ŏn	50	Mukho	56	Tongduch'ŏn	60
38	Yŏngju	32	Sangju	48	Ch'ungmu	55	Samch'ŏnp'o	60
39	Anyang	31	Yŏngju	46	Samch'ŏnp'o	55	Sindo	59
40	Ulsan	30	Songt'an	44	Sangju	53	Songt'an	57

Sources: MHA, *Municipal Yearbook of Korea 1974,* EPB, *Report on Population and Housing Census 1975.*

For each census year, (4-4) was estimated from a sample consisting of all cities of at least 20,000 population. The results are in Table 13, which shows the remarkable stability in the distribution of city sizes and the tendency for *a* to be close to 1. Most values of *a* are insignificantly different from 1 and no trend in the estimates of *a* is apparent.

TABLE 13 Estimates of Pareto Distribution

Year	Number of sample	lnP_1	a	R^2
1949	35	6.084 (137.7)	0.854 (80.5)	0.995
1955	79	7.147 (95.7)	1.011 (51.5)	0.972
1960	90	7.179 (108.9)	0.978 (56.9)	0.974
1965	113	7.713 (115.2)	1.043 (60.7)	0.971
1970	110	7.357 (137.2)	0.930 (69.8)	0.978
1975	142	7.621 (197.7)	0.939 (97.5)	0.986

Note: Sample includes all cities over 20,000 population. Numbers in parentheses are *t* statistics.

The conclusion is that Korea is only slightly more primate than the average country and shows no tendency to become still more primate. The size distribution of cities has shown remarkable stability during the last quarter century. Almost all Korean cities have grown rapidly, but there is no tendency for Seoul, or any other city, to become increasingly dominant.

To say that the city size distribution has remained unchanged is not to say that the ranks of particular cities have remained unchanged. Though the ranks of the 6 largest cities have not changed since 1949, the same is not true of smaller cities.

GROWTH OF THE
SOUTHEASTERN COASTAL REGION

Much attention in this and other studies has been focused on growth in the Seoul area. But since the late 1960s, the southeastern coastal region has unquestionably emerged as the country's major growth area. In many ways it is natural that this area should develop as Korea industrializes. It is that part of the country closest to sources of raw materials, most of which are imported, and to Japan and other foreign buyers of exports. It has good natural harbors and a mild climate. Unlike Seoul and its port of Inch'ŏn, undeveloped land was available in the late 1960s on the southeastern coast on which to locate large manufacturing facilities. Finally, it is a good location from a military viewpoint, in that it is the most distant part of the country from North Korea, and the only part not overrun during the Korean War. Since the late 1960s, much of Korea's new heavy industry has located in this region. Prominent industries are refining and petrochemicals, other chemical industries, steel, and shipbuilding. The main cities in the region are Pusan, Masan, Yŏsu, Chinhae, Ulsan, and P'ohang. The area in question is bounded by Yŏsu in the southwest and by P'ohang in the northeast.

The growth and shifts of population in the region have been staggering. Most dramatic has been Ulsan. In 1960 it was, as Table 12 shows, Korea's 40th city with a population of 30,000. By 1975, it was 10th, with a population of 253,000, representing a compound annual population growth of 14.2 percent per year. P'ohang rose from the 27th city to 18th in the five years from 1970 to 1975. Some cities in the region are just beginning to industrialize and will undoubtedly grow rapidly during the late 1970s.

During the 1970s, the growth of several cities in the region outstripped Seoul's. Between 1970 and 1975, Seoul's population grew 4.4 percent per year, whereas Pusan grew 5.3 percent, P'ohang 10.6 percent, Masan 13.3 percent, and Ulsan 9.3 percent.

There can be no doubt that manufacturing has been the driving force behind recent growth in the region. Between 1966 and 1973, manufacturing value added increased 34.8 percent per year in current prices in Seoul. In Pusan, the annual growth was only 32.5 percent. But in P'ohang it was 83.9 percent, in Masan 67.4 percent, and in Ulsan 70.5 percent.

PROSPECTS FOR THE CITY SIZE DISTRIBUTION

It is common that countries become somewhat less primate as they develop. Korea is now at the stage at which heavy industry is developing rapidly. On the assumption that such industrial growth will continue at a rapid pace, it seems quite certain that it will quickly lead to a further dispersion of urban growth to the southeast coastal region. This will almost certainly result in slower urban growth in the Seoul-Inch'ŏn area, and should lead to some reduction in primacy during coming decades. We do not, however, believe that Seoul will be replaced as the country's leading city in the foreseeable future.

Of course, recent and likely future growth in the southeast region is not independent of government policy. The natural advantages of the southeast for heavy industry are so great that pressure for growth there would have been inevitable. But the growth could not have taken place without government construction of ports and other infrastructure. In addition, the government has encouraged heavy industry to locate in the southeast region and presumably will continue to do so. It seems impossible and senseless to try to separate the effects of government encouragement from the private inducements to industrialize the southeast coastal region.

FIVE

Migration

Other chapters in this study have considered the emergence of
the urban system of South Korea. In this chapter, the focus
shifts from urbanization as the emergence of a system of settlements to a consideration of urbanization as the increasing
involvement in an exposure of a population to an "urban" way
of life and population movements as an important force during
this process.

Particularly when the colonial period is considered, a distinction must be made between the "urbanization" of the
Korean population and the growth of cities in Korea, since a
substantial fraction of the urban population of the larger cities
was Japanese, while Korean exposure to urban life was
frequently in Osaka, Kobe, or other cities of Japan and Manchuria. It is also important to distinguish between the urbanization of the Korean population that occurred through natural

increase in annexation of peri-urban areas (passive urbanization) and that occurring through migration (active urbanization). There is, in addition, a significant discrepancy between the population in settlements administratively defined as urban and the population that could be defined as following an urban life-style under a reasonable definition.

TRADITIONAL URBANIZATION
AND POPULATION MOVEMENTS

The history of urbanization in Korea is quite short. Censuses conducted in the eighteenth and nineteenth centuries give Seoul an enumerated population of around 190,000, while the second largest traditional urban settlement, P'yŏngyang, prob-ably had no more than 50,000 permanent residents.[2] Probably only 3–5 percent of the population could have been considered urban during the latter half of the Yi dynasty—far below the 10–15 percent commonly estimated for Tokugawa Japan and very near the minimum level of urbanization required for a traditional bureaucratic society to function. As late as 1910, only Seoul and P'yŏngyang had recorded populations of over 50,000.

Population movements were not unknown in the late tradi-tional Korea, however. The Yi dynasty (1392–1910) had seen an apparent acceleration of the movement of the Korean people into the sparsely populated (and aboriginal) northern and north-western districts. This was spurred early in the dynasty by Japanese pirate incursions in southern areas and at the end of the sixteenth century by the widespread devastation suffered during Hideyoshi's invasion.

By the mid-nineteenth century, it seems that the population in both the north and the south was pushing against the social and technological limits of traditional Korean culture, and only with the advent of an "epochal change" would these limits be altered to allow for additional growth. As a consequence of such population pressure into southern Manchuria, the late Yi dynasty saw a significant movement from the northern provinces. In 1890, 5,100 Korean households were reported to be living on the northern bank of the Yalu River, while 60,000 households were reported in the Chientao district north of the Tumen River.[3] Korean emigrants posed difficulties for Sino-Korean relations, and out-migration had long been proscribed by the Yi government. After 1910, however, when the Tumen River was finally fixed as the boundary between China and Korea, the Chientao district was opened to Korean immigrants on the understanding that they would be subject to Chinese law, and by 1910 the number of Koreans in Manchuria had reached 200,000.[4] In the extreme northeast, some 64,000 Koreans were registered in the Russian maritime provinces in 1914.[5]

Other than the Korean settlements in Manchuria and a lesser number in the neighboring Russian maritime provinces, as of 1910 Korean emigrant communities were limited to a few thousand plantation laborers and their families in Hawaii (total perhaps 7,000), less than 1,000 in Mexico,[6] a small community in Japan (790 registered in 1909),[7] and an unknown but presumably small number in China outside of Manchuria.

MIGRATION AND URBANIZATION
DURING THE COLONIAL PERIOD

Although modern urban growth in Korea and the origins of the modern urban hierarchy can be traced to the opening of treaty ports in the 1870s and 1880s and the construction of the Seoul-Pusan railroad and other trunk lines during the first quarter of this century, urbanization of the Korean population became a noteworthy aspect of social change only after 1925. Trends in the urbanization of the Korean population during the colonial period are summarized in Table 14. Indicated are the number

TABLE 14 Urbanization During the Colonial Period
(1,000s)

	1910		1926		1935		1941	
	Person	*%*	*Person*	*%*	*Person*	*%*	*Person*	*%*
Total population	12,934	100.0	19,103	100.0	21,891	100.0	24,703	100.0
Urban areas								
Over 100,000	341	2.6	527	2.8	863	3.9	2,428	9.8
Over 50,000	596	4.6	658	3.4	1,325	6.1	3,163	12.8
Over 20,000	752	5.8	1,378[a]	7.2	1,908	8.7	4,672	18.9

Source: Chōsen *Sōtokufu tōkei nenpō, 1910, 1926, 1935, 1941.*

Note: [a]Including myŏn (townships), which have population over 20,000.

and proportion of Koreans in Korea living in settlements with total populations of over 100,000, over 50,000, and over 20,000.

A substantial fraction of the increase of the Korean urban population in Korea was attributable to periodic redrawing of urban (then called pu rather than si) boundaries and the elevation of new places to urban status.[8] For much of the period, the net number of Korean rural-urban migrants within Korea was substantially less than net emigration from the peninsula.

By 1925, there were already 454,000 Koreans enumerated in Japan and Manchuria, and Tai Hwan Kwon argues that the actual number of Koreans in northeast Asia outside of Korea proper was probably around 776,000 at this time: 589,000 in Manchuria, 184,000 in Japan, and the remaining few thousand in China or elsewhere. Tai Hwan Kwon has made detailed estimates of the volume of total net emigration from Korea between 1925 and 1940, as well as for net emigration to Japan. These are summarized in Table 15.

As Table 15 indicates, the net loss in population through emigration or migration was concentrated principally in southern Korea. Well over half the net loss in population in the four southernmost provinces was attributable to net migration to Japan, at least through 1935. Migration to Japan from the remaining southern provinces was much more modest, and movement from the northern part of the country to Japan appears to have been very limited.[9] Although the north gained population from the south, it lost even more through emigration to Manchuria, especially after 1935.

Until the very last years of the colonial period, emigration to Japan or Manchuria was well in excess of net rural-urban migration within the peninsula. Table 16 attempts a rough estimation of the components of urban population growth between 1925 and 1944. Implied emigration under the same assumptions is also indicated and, although these suggest more emigration than that estimated by Tai Hwan Kwon, the two results are

TABLE 15 Inter-Regional Migration and Emigration of
the Korean Population, 1925–1945

(1,000s)

	1925–1930			1930–1935		
	Both Sexes	*Males*	*Females*	*Both Sexes*	*Males*	*Females*
Total Country						
Net Migration (age 5 & over)	−223.8	−154.3	−69.5	−361.8	−225.0	−136.8
(Including Infants)	(−262.4)	(−173.9)	(−88.5)	(−431.0)	(−260.2)	(−170.8)
Net Migration Rate (%)	−1.3	−1.8	−0.8	−2.0	−2.4	−1.5
Migration to Japan	−202.4	−136.4	−66.0	−223.5	−145.5	−78.0
(Including Infants)	(−239.4)	(−155.2)	(−84.2)	(−266.7)	(−167.5)	(−99.2)
Regions						
South Korea						
Net Out-Migration (age 5 & over)	−239.0	−165.1	−73.9	−279.5	−173.5	−106.0
(Including Infants)	−281.2	(−186.5)	(−94.7)	(−338.5)	(−203.5)	(−135.0)
Net Out-Migration Rate (%)	−2.0	−2.8	−1.3	−2.2	−2.8	−1.8
Emigration to Japan	−195.0	−131.4	−63.6	−215.4	−140.2	−75.2
(Including Infants)	(−230.8)	(−149.6)	(−81.2)	(−257.0)	(−161.4)	(−95.6)
North Korea						
Net Out-Migration (age 5 & over)	−15.3	−10.8	−4.5	−82.3	−51.6	−30.7
(Including Infants)	(−18.7)	(−12.6)	(−6.1)	(−92.7)	(−56.8)	(−35.9)
Net Out-Migration Rate (%)	−0.2	−0.3	−0.2	−1.2	−1.6	−1.0
Emigration to Japan	−7.4	−5.0	−2.4	−8.1	−5.3	−2.8
(Including Infants)	(−8.6)	(−5.6)	(−3.0)	(−9.7)	(−6.1)	(−3.6)

	1935–1940			1940–1945		
	Both Sexes	Males	Females	Both Sexes	Males	Females
Total Country						
Net Migration (age 5 & over)	−810.5	−475.5	−335.0	−596.4	−409.2	−187.2
(Including Infants)	(−978.1)	(−560.5)	(−417.6)	(−626.6)	(−424.5)	(−202.1)
Net Migration Rate (%)	−4.3	−5.1	−3.5	−2.8	−3.8	−1.8
Migration to Japan	−336.1	−177.2	−158.9	−443.2	−305.2	−138.0
(Including Infants)	−418.7	(−219.2)	(−199.5)	(−515.0)*	(−341.6)	(−173.4)
Regions						
South Korea						
Net Out-Migration (age 5 & over)	−801.1	−502.1	−298.9	−513.1	−353.3	−159.8
(Including Infants)	(−954.2)	(−579.7)	(−374.5)	(−543.6)	(−368.7)	(−174.9)
Net Out-Migration Rate (%)	−6.0	−7.4	−4.6	−3.7	−5.1	−2.2
Emigration to Japan	−323.9	−170.8	−153.1	−427.1	−294.1	−133.0
(Including Infants)	(−403.5)	(−211.2)	(−192.3)	(−496.3)	(−329.2)	(−167.1)
North Korea						
Net Out-Migration (age 5 & over)	−9.6	+26.6	−36.2	−83.3	−55.9	−27.4
(Including Infants)	(−23.8)	(+19.4)	(−43.2)	(−83.0)	(−55.8)	(−27.2)
Net Out-Migration Rate (%)	−0.1	+0.7	−1.0	−1.1	−1.5	−0.8
Emigration to Japan	−12.2	−6.4	−5.8	−16.1	−11.1	−5.0
(Including Infants)	(−15.2)	(−8.0)	(−7.2)	(−18.7)	(−12.4)	(−6.3)

Source: Tai Hwan Kwon, Appendix V, Tables A.V, 1-1 - A.V. 1-3.

Notes: The bracketed estimates of net migration include all estimated births to migrant women during the period. Kwon counts only one-half of these as migrants.

Rates have been recalculated to reflect out-migration only among those age 5 years and over at the end of the period. The denominator is the survivors of the initial population.

Kwon only gives estimated total emigration to Japan during 1940–1945 for nation as a whole. Sex, age, and regional breakdown estimated from 1935–1940 pattern.

sufficiently comparable to support the contention that internal rural-urban migration during the period was less important than natural growth or the extension of city boundaries in the increase of the domestic Korean urban population as a whole, although some cities were exceptions to this pattern.

The total ethnic Korean population living outside Korea proper increased by 41 percent between 1925 and 1930, by 50 percent during the next five years and then by 72 percent between 1935 and 1940, and again by 50 percent between 1940 and 1944, based on Kwon's estimates. By 1940 this meant that 10.7 percent of ethnic Koreans in northeast Asia were living outside Korea proper. With full wartime mobilization by Japan after 1940, this proportion increased to approximately 14 percent by 1944. For the most mobile cohorts, males 20-29, it may have exceeded 17 percent. The net movements indicated in the above tables were the outgrowth of an unprecedented amount of gross mobility among the Korean population. In any given inter-censal period, for example, it is not unreasonable to assume that perhaps twice the number of net migrants were exposed to at least a year of residence in Japan, with many more journeying to Japan for shorter periods to work or study. The role of Japanese colonial policies in stimulating this movement was decisive. Strict public health measures enacted by the Japanese at the very beginning of the colonial period to prevent the spread of endemic diseases sharply aggravated pressure on agricultural land in a society having all the structural pre-requisites for a population explosion—universal and early marriage of women, a high value placed on large families and lineages, strong son preference, and an extended family system in which young adult males were not expected to be economically independent before marriage and family formation. Moreover, between 1926 and 1934, the Japanese authorities pursued a Rice Increase Plan to expand production in Korea for export to Japan. The program provided very favorable interest rates to Japanese wanting to invest in paddy land in Korea, and served to quicken the pace at which independent peasant farmers were

TABLE 16 Korean Population in Northeast Asia Outside Korea Proper
(1,000s)

Year	Registered or Enumerated (1)			Estimated (2)			
	Total	Japan	Manchuria	Total	Japan	Manchuria	China & Other
1925	654	121	533	776.1	184.2	589.4	2.5
1930	1026	419	607	1094.2	419.0[a]	672.7	2.6
1935	1292	625	667	1643.8	720.8	915.8	7.2
1940	2715	1265	1450	2821.0	1241.2[a]	1450.4[a]	129.4
1944		1859			1860.0		
		(1867)					

Sources: (1) Yunshik Chang.
(2) Tai Hwan Kwon, p. 390 (Table A.II.1). Kwon's figures are adjusted for estimated under enumeration.

Note: [a]Census figures.

turned into tenant cultivators. With a large reserve army of potential agricultural tenants available and the Japanese gendarmes ready to be mobilized at any sign of union-type activities among Korean farmers, landlords, both Japanese and Korean, were able to evict tenants and otherwise impose terms that weakened the insular solidarity of the traditional village and shook loose large numbers of young adults from the rural social order.

In the mid-1930s Japanese colonial policy shifted from encouragement of agricultural development in Korea to encouragement of industrialization in northern Korea as well as Manchuria. Colonial authorities encouraged movement to the north (and to Manchuria) with transportation subsidies, while at the same time tighter restrictions were imposed on the movement of Koreans to Japan. These intensified during the 1930s when the emigration of Koreans sharply increased. Because it was an avowed policy of the Japanese government to integrate Koreans into the Japanese Empire, even if as second-class subjects, outright prohibition of movement to Japan was not politically feasible and the number of Koreans in Japan nearly tripled between 1930 and 1940. By the early 1930s, the number of Koreans in Osaka alone, the largest single Korean community, exceeded the Korean population in any Korean city other than Seoul or P'yŏngyang. Rural poverty in Korea, aggravated by increasing tenancy among Korean peasants and a relative decline in the price of rice, is commonly cited as the principal reason for this exodus.[10] Other factors may have also played a role, however. Wages received by Korean laborers in the domestic urban sector appear to have declined during the period, while real wages received by Koreans in Japan seem to have risen. Although the urban sector of Korea experienced unprecedented growth in the late 1930s, much of the growth was due to the expansion of the government sector and the commercial or service sector. Industrial expansion was limited to the expansion of heavy manufacturing and mining in the north and a modest amount of light manufacturing in the south, much of which drew largely on female labor. Thus, although the demand for industrial labor increased, the amount and skill level required was such that it could be met out of the pool of displaced ruralities of the rapidly growing urban-born population. A large proportion of the expansion of administrative, office-level white-collar or skilled-laboring jobs went to Japanese, of course. The cost of going to Japan, although not great, served to separate the two labor markets, although there was even considerable seasonal migration of Korean laborers to Japan.[11] Although cross-ties between the urban economies and urban labor markets were extensive, the travel-cost barrier, together with the smaller size and less dynamic expansion of the urban sector in Korea, may explain the apparent discrepancy in the real wages received by Koreans in Japan and in urban Korea.

Short-term employment was not the sole reason for going to Japan, however. Within the economic and political content of the time, some saw it as a step to upward social and economic mobility. Others were drawn to Japanese institutions of higher learning, discouraged by the very few places allotted to Koreans at Keijō (Seoul) National University. Expansion of primary school education in Korea, although belated and promoted as one aim of Japan's imperialist policies, may nonetheless have stimulated the exodus from the rural sector. By 1930, one-sixth of Korean men age 20–30 had attended primary school, while 30 percent of the boys 6–12 years old were currently enrolled. A final factor, one which, although probably of limited importance as a direct stimulus to emigration to Japan but which nonetheless would have had a significant impact on the perceived advantage of permanent emigration, was the greater political freedom enjoyed by Koreans in Japan where police surveillance of political or union activities was somewhat less oppressive. In Manchuria, although Koreans were closely watched for Bolshevik and nationalist tendencies,[12] they enjoyed higher social status than the native Manchurians and were seen by the Japanese authorities as a major vehicle through which Japanese control of the area could be secured.

Finally, as Japan mobilized for war after 1939, the restrictions on Korean emigration to Japan were moderated to offset a shortage of domestic workers. In 1942, the Draft System by Recommendation was inaugurated and strengthened provisions for mobilization of Korean laborers to Japan which had been in effect since 1939. During the period 1939–1944, 692,000 Korean workers were mobilized to Japan,[13] while in 1944 the Personnel Draft Law in Korea was extended beyond military recruitment in order to draft labor for work in factories and mines in the north, frequently to replace more experienced workers being drafted to Japan.[14]

Migration to Japan continued until the sea lanes were interdicted in mid-1945, although the volume of net migration declined as the war neared its end. The Liberation of Korea and the dismantling of the Japanese Empire brought with it the massive repatriation of overseas Koreans, as shown in Table 18. Tai Hwan Kwon estimates that at the time of Liberation there were approximately 1.9–2.0 million Koreans living in Japan.[15] By 1950 this had been reduced by three-fourths. During the same period, perhaps 30–40 percent of the emigrants in Manchuria returned. Since south Korea had been the origin of a majority of emigrants during the colonial period, it was natural that this should be the destination of the vast majority of returnees, even in the absence of the political division of the country. In addition, there was substantial movement of returnees and refugees from the Soviet Zone of occupation between 1945 and 1949. The actual volume of net migration between the zones remains a matter of some dispute. Irene B. Taeuber and George W. Barclay argued in 1950 that there was probably a strong upward bias in both the registration figures and the 1949 census figures on repatriation and refugees from the north.[16]

Tai Hwan Kwon's figures,[17] on the other hand, are consistent with the decline in the overseas Korean population indicated by the 1950 Japanese census and the 1953 Chinese population survey. Kwon's estimates also show a very consistent ratio to the number of enumerated repatriatees from each overseas area.

TABLE 17 Proportion of Residents and Repatriates from Japan

	Proportion of Residents in Japan (1938) (South Korea only) (1)	Proportion of Enumerated Repatriates from Japan (1949) (2)	Sex Ratio of Repatriates (Female=100)
Seoul	1.9%	3.1%	207
Kyŏnggi province	1.1%	3.7%	431
Kangwŏn province	1.1%	1.5%	735
N. Ch'ungch'ŏng province	2.9%	3.4%	336
S. Ch'ungch'ŏng province	3.7%	6.5%	347
N. Chŏlla province	6.3%	6.4%	265
S. Chŏlla province (incl. Chejn Island)	21.4%	12.6%	175
N. Kyŏngsang province	23.9%	22.5%	147
S. Kyŏngsang province	38.9%	37.4%	124
Number		936.0	168

Sources: (1) Based on a 1938 study of the *honseki* of Koreans living in Japan. Only 27,061 or 3.4% of the 799,878 registered Koreans in Japan at the time of the study were from North Korean provinces. Sang-hyŏn Kim, p. 44.
(2) *Preliminary Report of the 1949 Census of Korea.* Calculated from data reported Office of Public Information, in Ehn-Hyun Choe, p. 33.

TABLE 18 Alternative Estimates of Repatriates and Refugees to South Korea, 1945–1949
(1,000s)

Origin	Registration Ministry of Home Affairs (1)	Figures Ministry of Social Affairs (2)	1949 Census (3)	Estimates	
				Chol Kim (4)	Tai Hwan Kwon (5)
Japan	1,118	1,407	936	1,300	1,397
Manchuria & other	423	619	270	430	416
North Korea	649	456	481	150	740
Total	2,190	2,482	1,687	1,880	2,535

Sources: (1) BOK, *Economic Statistics Yearbook, 1949.*
(2) Han'guk Sanŏp Unhaeng, *Han'guk kyŏngje 10-nyŏnsa,* 1971.
(3) Taehan Min'guk Kongbosil, *Han'guk ŭi 1949-nyŏn in'gu sensŏsŭ sokpo,* 1950.
(4) Chol Kim, *Kankoku no jinkō to keizai* (Tokyo, 1965).
(5) Tai Hwan Kwon, "Population Change," p. 247.

This ratio is 1.50±.05 which is virtually identical to the ratio between estimated and enumerated net internal rural-urban migration during the 1960s.

As Tai Hwan Kwon points out, the fact that there were only 75,000 persons with permanent residences in north Korea living in south Korea in 1940 compared to 300,000 persons with south Korean residences living in the north suggests that south-north movement after 1945 was probably quite limited, with 50,000 persons a probable maximum.[18]

Concurrent with the influx of Korean expatriates and refugees to South Korea, 460,000 Japanese soldiers and civilians living in South Korea at the time of the Liberation were repatriated to Japan, together with another 420,000 Japanese formerly in North Korea.

On the basis of permanent domicile data for 1940, Tai Hwan Kwon argues that no more than one-third of the north-south movement was due to the return of former migrants from South Korea.[19] While this neglects to consider substantial movement from south to north Korea between 1940 and 1945, Kwon's judgement does appear to be supported by other evidence:

1) A much lower estimated sex ratio among migrants from north Korea (110) compared to that for migrants from Japan (164) or Manchuria (142), suggesting a predominance of family migration

2) The concentration of enumerated migrants from north Korea in Seoul (45 percent), Kyŏnggi province (24 percent), and Kangwŏn province (10 percent) adjacent to the 38th parallel

3) A distribution of origins among enumerated north Korean migrants while correlated much more closely to population size and nearness to the 38th parallel than to the absorption of south-north migrants during the colonial period.

The settlement pattern of migrants from Manchuria was substantially different from that of north Korean migrants, showing a much higher ratio of men to women (140:100) and a smaller proportion settling in Seoul (28 percent), with a large number settling in the more southern and rural provinces, the principal origins of out-migrants during the preceding two decades. Like migrants from Japan, those from Manchuria seem to have been dominated by returning emigrants.

Repatriates from Japan, the largest component of the influx, settled principally in the three southern provinces which had been the principal areas sending migrants to Japan, as Table 17 shows. The influx of returning emigrants and refugees contributed greatly to the growth of the urban population during the U. S. Military Government period. The vast majority of the Koreans from Japan had been living in urban or industrial areas, and upon their return a large proportion—at least 40 percent—settled in urban areas,[20] chiefly in their native provinces.

The Korean urban population in 15 administratively defined cities increased at an average annual rate of 11 percent between 1944 and 1949, even after adjustment is made for changes in city boundaries. The proportion of the total population of South Korea in urban areas grew from 13 percent to 17 percent during the period. This growth was broadly distributed: 10 of the cities had growth rates in excess of 10 percent a year and only 2 experienced growth rates under 8 percent a year.

The concentration of returnees and refugees in urban areas in spite of the depressed state of the post-Liberation economy was probably a function of three factors. First, most of the returnees from Japan had been living in urban or industrial areas, as had probably a substantial number of the returnees and refugees from Manchuria and North Korea. The first choice of many of these may have been to settle in areas where whatever skills or experience they had acquired would be put to use. Moreover, a substantial component of the returnees from Japan and Manchuria were long-term emigrants who, like refugees from North Korea, had no native village into which they could easily reintegrate. Finally, refugee relief activities were concentrated in urban areas, the natural entry and distribution points for food and reconstruction materials.

The estimated contribution of migration to urban growth

during this period far exceeds that for any previous period, both in absolute and relative terms. In absolute terms, growth in Seoul and the cities of Kyŏnggi province accounted for 49.7 percent of the total gain to urban areas, while the urban section of South Kyŏngsang province accounted for 19.7 percent, that of North Kyŏngsang province for 9.1 percent, that of South Chŏlla province for 8.2 percent, and that of North Chŏlla province for 6.1 percent.

Both the urban exposure experienced by the Korean population during the colonial period and the resettlement pattern of repatriated emigrants and refugees after Liberation may have contributed to the substantial inter-urban migration which occurred during the 1960s.

WARTIME POPULATION DISPLACEMENT AND REFUGEE MOVEMENTS

The dramatic loosening of the Korean population from its village base which occurred during the colonial period was painfully accelerated during the Korean War. The wartime statistics on deaths, displaced persons, and refugees from North Korea significantly underestimate the actual mortality and movement during this period, but Tai Hwan Kwon has attempted to estimate wartime deaths and population movements from the 1949 and 1955 censuses.[21] Kwon uses life-table survival ratios based on expected mortality during the period under non-war conditions to estimate the net population loss in each province during 1949–1955, reflecting the combined effects of wartime mortality and population movements. His estimates are summarized in Table 19. Although the highest proportional loss was experienced in Kangwŏn province (–26.9 percent), high absolute losses were also experienced in South Chŏlla province and North Kyŏngsang province—battle zones during the North Korean assault on the Pusan Perimeter. The surprisingly low rate of loss from Seoul and Kyŏnggi province, also devastated during the

TABLE 19 Population Loss and Movement, 1949–1955
(1,000s)

Province	Loss or Gain due to Wartime Mortality or Migration	Rate of Gain or Loss[a]	Net Increase without North Korean Refugees (includes births)	Change due to North Korean Refugees
Seoul	−165.5	−9.4%	−24.3	+58.5
Kyŏnggi	−166.6	−6.8	+51.4	+100.7
Kangwŏn	−275.4	−17.5	−195.5	+121.5
N. Ch'ungch'ŏng	−98.4	−7.4	+74.0	+6.3
S. Ch'ungch'ŏng	−96.7	−4.1	+189.0	+22.7
N. Chŏlla	−178.2	−7.6	+109.8	+17.9
S. Chŏlla	−201.8	−8.3	+149.6	+10.3
N. Kyŏngsang	−263.3	−7.2	+200.4	+19.0
S. Kyŏnsang	+215.8	+6.0	+586.3	+92.9
Cheju Island	−22.6	−7.9	+5.2	+2.3
Total	−1,252.7	−5.8	+1,145.9	+452.1

Note: [a]Rate based on estimated number of survivors from the beginning of period. Calculated from data presented by Tai Hwan Kwon "Population Change," pp. 285, 287.

war, is partially explained by rapid repopulation after 1953 and the influx of North Korean refugees. Only South Kyŏngsang province showed an increase during this period—and the estimated gain of 216,000 from 1949–1955 does not adequately reflect the number of refugees in the province during the height of the conflict.

The 1955 census reports 452,000 wartime refugees from North Korea who survived to the census date (Table 20). Tai Hwan Kwon assumes that wartime refugees were under-enumerated by about the same extent as North-South refugees in the 1949 census, which raises his estimate of the number of wartime refugees to 650,000, a figure very consistent with place-of-birth data in the 1960 census. Kwon's higher estimate of North Korean refugees raises the estimated wartime loss to the South Korean population to over 1.9 million persons. Of these he maintains that as many as 286,000 may have been taken north forceably as civilian captives or prisoners of war.[22] In view of the extreme sex ratio of South-North wartime movement derived either from records or residually from census data, Kwon discounts the possibility of much voluntary movement north during the war.[23]

The sex ratio and age structure of wartime refugees from North Korea appear to have been quite similar to those of pre-war North-South migrants, and family unit movements appear to have predominated. A large proportion of these wartime refugees (40.5 percent) were found in rural areas of the two front-line provinces in 1955, while another 21.6 percent were enumerated in the urban areas of these provinces or in Seoul. Another 21 percent had settled in South Kyŏngsang province,— almost entirely in urban areas, principally Pusan. Tai Hwan Kwon concludes on the basis of refugee residence in 1955 that over half the refugees may have been from Hwanghae province and the northern portions of Kyŏnggi province and Kangwŏn province, which were lost during the war.[24]

Internal wartime movements in South Korea took two forms. One was movement from Seoul and other urban areas of the

TABLE 20 Population Changes 1949–1955 Due to the Korean War
(persons)

	Reported			Estimated (Tai Hwan Kwon)		
	Male	*Female*	*Total*	*Male*	*Female*	*Total*
Killed	293,078 (29,294)	109,815	403,893 (29,294)	837,000	802,000	1,639,000
South-North Movement	143,978 (65,601)	6,155	150,133 (65,601)	264,000	22,000	286,000
Missing or Prisoners of War	358,943 (105,672)	49,941	408,884 (105,672)			
North-South Movement	248,100	204,100	452,200	354,000	292,000	646,000
Total Net Change Due to War	-547,899 (-200,567)	+38,189	-509,710 (-200,567)	-747,000	-532,000	-1,279,000

Sources: Official registration figures taken from BOK, *Economic Statistics Yearbook, 1955* (figures for civilians based on those issued by the ROK Office of Public Information, those for military personnel issued by the Headquarters of the United Nations Forces). Estimates from Tai Hwan Kwon, "Population Change," p. 291.

Note: Figures in parentheses are for ROK military personnel.

war-torn northern provinces to Pusan, Taegu, and other cities of the southeast. This movement occurred principally in December 1950 and January 1951 when the United Nations forces were being pushed back toward the 38th parallel following the entry of Chinese Communist forces into the conflict. A second stream was from rural and urban areas of the war zone to rural areas of nearby provinces, as some urbanites sought refuge with rural relatives, or fled from the war zone. Those who fled to rural areas appear to have returned home soon after the Armistice of 1953, while refugees who had moved to the urban areas of the southeast which experienced war-induced expansion were slower to resettle. Contributing to this was the continuation of full military mobilization until 1957 and restrictions on the movement of civilians to Seoul in the immediate post-war years. The devastated capital did not fully recover its central political and economic functions until the late 1950s.

Associated with or occurring concurrently with wartime and post-war refugee movements, there appears to have been considerable non-refugee rural-urban migration after the war zone became stabilized around the 38th parallel in 1952. Tai Hwan Kwon attempts to estimate net rural-urban migration during 1949–1955 but admits that the assumptions required to do so preclude great confidence in the results. The number probably lies in the range of 650,000–750,000.[25]

The general pattern of net internal rural-urban movement appears to have been: 1) extreme out-migration from the rural sector of Kangwŏn province (21 percent of the population during this period); 2) extensive out-migration from Kyŏnggi province, moderated by a substantial flow into the rural sector of the province from Seoul and the cities within the province (yielding an overall rural out-migration rate of 5.3 percent); 3) rates of net rural out-migration in North and South Ch'ungch'ŏng province of less than 2 percent for the period, due presumably to an influx of refugees from the war zone, some of whom had not returned by 1955; 4) low rates of net rural out-migration in North and South Chŏlla provinces (2–3 percent for the period); and 5) high rates of rural out-migration in North and South Kyŏngsang provinces (4–5 percent). Only in North Ch'ungch'ŏng and North and South Kyŏngsang provinces did the net gain to the urban sector of the province through internal migration exceed the net loss from the rural sector. The urban sector of South Kyŏngsang province (including Pusan) appears to have absorbed over 500,000 net in-migrants, exclusive of North Korean refugees, nearly 4.5 times the number of net out-migrants from the rural sector of the province. The gap between net urban in-migration and net rural out-migration in South Kyŏngsang was equivalent to more than 80 percent of the exodus from provinces having net out-migration during the period.

While rural-urban migration in provinces other than South Kyŏngsang may be explainable in terms of wartime damage to the agricultural infrastructure, the concentration of war relief efforts in the cities, and the urbanward movement of individuals who had lost or become separated from parents or spouses, the substantial urbanward movement in South Kyŏngsang province is less explainable in these terms.

Presumably the rise in the relative price of agricultural goods in the face of war-caused declines in output during the war and post-war years[26] may have been expected to reduce out-migration from rural areas that experienced little war damage. Moreover, land reform following the Korean War, which distributed confiscated Japanese lands and divided most large landholdings, was principally carried out in the immediate post-war period. This too should have lessened off-farm migration, if indeed rural-urban migration during this period was principally off-farm movement. Apparently, however, the pressure of natural growth on limited land resources was sufficiently severe to give rise to substantial rural out-migration even under war-time conditions. With movement to Japan no longer possible, the movement to the cities was perhaps inevitable. On the other hand, the substantial out-migration from urban areas of South Kyŏngsang after 1960 suggests that this movement was war-related and temporary: the movement of families to be near men still on active duty, movement into the war-swollen urban economies of the area behind departing refugees, and so on.

MIGRATION DURING THE POST-WAR PERIOD 1955–1960

The 1955 census provides the benchmark for the study of contemporary demographic processes in the Republic of Korea. Although there is clear evidence of deliberate age misreporting in the 1955 census and some apparent confusion over the age concept employed,[27] it provides a reasonable basis for considering internal migration during the period of post-war recovery. Migration during the period 1955–1960 appears to have been of two types. Part of the movement was returning war refugees. Tai Hwan Kwon estimates that a third of this movement took place after 1955.[28] Such movement was principally out of the urban areas of the southeast. In addition to this movement, however, there appears to have been substantial rural-urban movement of the more classical type. But no direct data on internal migration exist for this period, and it is necessary to rely on residual estimates derived from the 1955 and 1960 censuses.

Tai Hwan Kwon provides estimates of net age-sex specific migration for the rural and urban sectors of each province as well as for each city, using the forward projection census survival ratio method.[29] To obtain these estimates, substantial adjustments had to be made to the 1955 census data owing to numerous changes in provincial and city boundaries between the censuses, and a change in the enumeration of those in military service from de facto assignment to the place of encampment in the 1955 census to assignment of military personnel back to the de jure residence of the household of pre-service membership. A further source of error is the existence of deliberate age misreporting in 1955 by males liable for military conscription and uncertainty about the extent to which ages in the 1960 census were reported according to traditional Korean age reckoning.[30] Total net rural-urban migration during 1955–1960 is estimated at 584,000 persons. This was equivalent to 34.8 percent of the total growth of population in urban areas. Of the urban growth, 54.9 percent was due to natural increase[31] and 10.3 percent to administrative reclassification or changes in urban boundaries.[32] There was apparently a very large excess of female over male migration during this period, with only 79 net male rural-urban migrants per 100 net female migrants. Net out-migration from urban areas appears to have occurred among males in their twenties and over age fifty, although the actual extent of net out-migration among young adult males is likely to be exaggerated by under-enumeration and age misreporting in the 1955 census among males eligible for military service. As Tai Hwan Kwon notes, however, the excess of net female migration served to offset a heavily male dominant rural-urban movement during the war, and may well have been stimulated by the earlier movement.

Many of the cities of the southeast which had served as wartime refugee centers showed substantial out-migration among young adults of both sexes during this period. Although 12 of the 25 cities in 1955 realized net in-migration during 1955–1960, only 5 cities realized net in-migration of both males and females in the cohorts age 15–24 in 1955. These were Seoul, Taegu, Wŏnju, Taejŏn, and Inch'ŏn, all of them away from the major refugee centers. With only 3 exceptions, all other cities lost both sexes in these age groups, with the rate of net out-migration greater among men than women in all but two cases. Prolonged military mobilization had created a concentration of young adult males in many of the southern and port cities. With demobilization and a slowing of the inflow of direct reconstruction aid, the economies of these areas which had been stimulated by the presence of military encampments went into a decline, which accelerated as Seoul and other northern cities recovered their natural functions.

While Pusan experienced an estimated net out-migration of

48,800 (40,900 over age 5), this was quite modest considering the large number of refugees who had settled in the southern port. Kwon estimates that about 300,000 internal refugees resided in Pusan at the time of the 1955 census—one-third of the city's total population. Together with refugees from North Korea and migrants from rural areas of the same province, Pusan gained about 500,000 net in-migrants between 1949 and 1955.[33]

INTERNAL MIGRATION SINCE 1960

With virtually all war refugee return migration completed by 1960, migration patterns assumed a fairly regular pattern in respect to the age-sex structure of gross and net rural-urban migration; a pattern of interregional movement has emerged in which Seoul is the predominant destination of rural out-migrants from all areas except North and South Kyŏngsang provinces and Cheju Island.

Between 1960 and 1966, the urban population increased by 40 percent (31 percent in constant 1966 boundaries), while the rural population increased by 8 percent, the town population by 11 percent, and the population of the nation as a whole by 17 percent. Within the rural sector, the lowest population growth occurred in the rice-dominant areas along the lower Naktong River, the Kŭm River, and in the lowland areas of the southwest. In these areas numerous counties experienced an absolute decline in population. In some mountain districts, however—specifically the Sobaek Range region and the area northeast of a line running from Seoul to P'ohang—population growth exceeded that for the nation as a whole. Rural coastal areas recorded increases of 12–14 percent, which was above the rural average but below that for the nation.

Rates of rural out-migration also varied significantly between provinces, with the highest rates in South Kyŏngsang followed by South Ch'ungch'ŏng province and North Kyŏngsang province. All provinces but Kangwŏn experienced net rural out-migration, and in Kangwŏn net in-migration was solely a function of the repopulation of front-line areas. Of total net rural-urban migration during this period, Seoul absorbed nearly 70 percent. Only in Kyŏnggi province and Cheju Island did net in-migration to the urban sector of the province exceed rural net out-migration, while in all other provinces net urban in-migration was substantially less than half of local rural out-migration. Although net rural-urban migration largely favored the growth of Seoul, the movement was not in all cases principally from the rural sector of a province directly to the capital. Evidence from the 1966 Special Demographic Survey indicates that overall about 43 percent of gross rural out-migrants to urban areas went to non-metropolitan cities generally within the same province. Net rural-city migration, equivalent to 32 percent of net rural out-migration in the 1966 SDS, was almost entirely offset by net city-metropolitan movement. The greater the accessibility to Seoul, however, the greater the proportion of direct rural-metropolitan movement.

Twelve cities[34] actually lost population through net out-migration during this period, including most of the small port cities. Presumably this was due in part to the continuing diminution of the economic role of these lesser transshipment points compared to the colonial period when substantial volumes of rice and other foodstuffs were shipped to Japan and light consumer goods moved the other way.

For the cities losing population through out-migration (or gaining very little through net in-migration) the typical pattern was a modest loss (or slight gain) in the age groups 10–19, a substantial loss in the age group 20–24 among both males and females, a more modest loss (or net gain) among men and women in their late twenties and thirties, and relatively high rates of net out-migration among men age 40 and over. Among women however, net out-migration after age 40 typically moderated among the cohorts over age 55 or actually reversed to net in-migration. Among the 18 cities outside the capital experiencing net in-migration overall, only Kwangju, Wŏnju,

Ulsan, and Cheju city showed net in-migration among men over age 50 and only 8 of these cities had net in-migration among women in these ages.

As discussed in some detail below, however, this net out-migration at later ages should not be simply interpreted as a return to farming activities in the later years of life. While net in-migration of males to farm households can be observed after age 35, by age 55 relatively little mobility is observed among the male farm population.

The pattern of age-specific net rural-urban migration rates shifted significantly in the case of men between 1955–1960 and 1960–1965. In particular, a broad trough can be observed in the male net-migration-rate profile for those in their twenties and early thirties, followed by a strong secondary peak. This can be largely explained in terms of the larger proportion of the eligible male cohorts in military service prior to the 1957 demobilization. This caused a reduction of the period during which "free" migration could take place and a tendency for migration to be delayed. This explanation is consistent with Tai Hwan Kwon's contention that most of the post-1955 migration by war refugees was inter-urban movement rather than rural-urban movement. Furthermore, the pattern of female net migration rates is very similar to those in subsequent periods and shows no evidence of a substantial returning refugee component.

With the farm population continuing to grow absolutely in each province through 1966, migration to the cities, and ultimately to Seoul, served to vent rural population pressure which had previously been released through overseas migration.

SIX

Structure of Cities

Rapid urbanization of populations throughout the world has been one of the most dramatic and important characteristics of the twentieth century. Almost equally dramatic, and even more controversial, has been the decentralization of people and jobs within urban areas.

In the United States, people have been strongly aware that jobs and population have been increasing rapidly in metropolitan suburbs, and shrinking or stagnant in central cities since shortly after World War II. Many Americans believe that suburbanization is mainly a post-war United States phenomenon. But careful research makes it clear that urban areas have been decentralizing all over the industrialized world throughout the twentieth century.[1] Recent research[2] has established that Japanese urban areas have decentralized rapidly during most of the post-war period.

Furthermore, careful studies indicate that the most important causes of urban decentralization are the growth of metropolitan areas, rising real incomes, and improved urban transportation. In small urban areas, the purchases of the entire urban area's population are needed to support its commerical and industrial activities, and they are therefore located centrally. As the population and real income of an urban area grow, it becomes possible to support shopping and employment centers with the customers and labor force of only part of the urban area. Thus, subcenters of stores and work places appear away from the central business district. Thus, fewer people are tied to the city center for jobs and shopping, and they are attracted to suburban residences because of lower land values and correspondingly lower population densities. Real income growth has an additional important effect. As income rises, a family's housing demand rises and it is induced to move further from the center to take advantage of low land values. Improved transportation, whether by public transit or automobile, has the same effect. It increases accessibility to the central business district from distant parts of the urban area, thus permitting people to take advantage of cheap suburban land for housing.

Suburbanization is remarkably controversial in most countries. In the United States it is blamed on racism and crime and high taxes in central cities. There and elsewhere, it is blamed for devouring land needed for agriculture. In most countries, it is blamed for destroying an attractive lifestyle based on high density living. Yet is it not known whether cities are suburbanizing in developing countries and, if so, whether more rapidly or more slowly than in the developed world. Nor is it known what the causes and consequences of suburbanization might be in developing countries.

MEASURES OF SUBURBANIZATION

In the United States, the most common measure of suburbanization is changes in the fraction of the urban population living or working in the legal central city. This measure is feasible only because large parts of most U.S. urban areas are outside central cities. It is, nevertheless, unsatisfactory because central city boundaries are moved from time to time and because the fraction of people and jobs in the central city varies greatly from one urban area to another. The measure is entirely unfeasible in urban areas in most other countries because legal city boundaries enclose all or most of the urban area, and are enlarged so they will continue to do so as the urban area grows.

These considerations have motivated scholars to seek simple equations that accurately describe density patterns of population and, to a lesser extent, jobs, and that can be estimated from available data. The parameters of such equations provide measures of suburbanization. The equation that has been found to describe density patterns best in many countries and at many times is the exponential function

$$D(x) = D_O\, e^{-gx} \qquad\qquad (6\text{-}1)$$

where $D(x)$ is the density, say residents per square kilometer, x kilometers from the center of the urban area, D_O and g are parameters to be estimated from the data, and e is the base of the natural logarithm. D_O is the estimated density at the center of the urban area[3] and g describes the rate at which density falls with distance. Specifically, it is the percentage decrease in density per kilometer of distance from the center. For example, if average density decreased 10 percent per kilometer of distance from the center, g would be 0.10. Thus, the larger g is, the faster density falls with distance from the center. Therefore g provides a natural measure of suburbanization. The smaller g is, the more suburbanized is the urban area. One can compare g both among points in time for a particular city and among cities. It is a measure of suburbanization that is independent of the locations of jurisdictional boundaries. Both D_O and g, however, depend on the units in which density and distance are measured.

Equation 6-1 can easily be estimated from samples of density in an urban area. Many countries publish population data either for small enumeration districts or for small local government jurisdictions in urban areas. If the land areas of the enumeration districts are published or can be estimated, then population density in them can be calculated. Distance to the city center can be calculated from maps. Thus, from Equation 6-1, the natural log of density can be regressed on distance for the sample of density-distance data in the urban area, and D_O and g can be calculated.

In Korea, 12 cities have the requisite data. The statistical yearbook of each of the 12 cities gives data on population and area at the level of tong (precinct), the smallest administrative unit in Korea. The size of a tong varies from city to city. In Seoul the average area and population of the 468 tong in 1975 were 1.4 square kilometers and 14,000 people respectively.

A random sample of 40 tong for Seoul and about 20 tong for the other 11 cities was taken for the estimation of the population density and land price functions. However, owing to data problems arising mainly from changes in the boundary, some tong were eliminated from the sample. As a result the sample size for each city may not be identical. Only limited accuracy can be expected in estimating density functions from our relatively small samples. Readers should also be aware that parameter estimates are sensitive to choice of functional form, as is shown by comparison between the results in Tables 21 and A-6-2. However, in the case of employment density function for Seoul, the sample size was increased to 95.

KOREAN DENSITY FUNCTIONS

Table 21 presents estimates of density functions for 12 Korean cities for years for which requisite data are available. These estimated density functions follow, to a remarkable extent, the pattern found in other countries. First, large cities are more decentralized than small ones. Seoul's and Pusan's gradients are the smallest of those in the table. Although there are exceptions,

TABLE 21 Urban Density Functions for 12 Cities

City	Year	D_O		g		R^2	Population (in 1,000s)
Seoul	1961	64,861	(45.3)	0.350	(10.6)	0.747	2,577
	1965	73,130	(46.6)	0.328	(10.0)	0.728	3,471
	1970	60,476	(49.0)	0.223	(7.3)	0.587	5,536
	1973	56,387	(48.3)	0.185	(6.1)	0.492	6,290
Pusan	1966	44,445	(23.5)	0.263	(4.3)	0.548	1,430
	1970	28,538	(29.5)	0.134	(2.8)	0.350	1,881
	1973	27,834	(30.9)	0.109	(2.4)	0.282	2,072
Taegu	1966	92,042	(30.6)	0.777	(0.1)	0.786	847
	1970	91,858	(31.2)	0.739	(8.5)	0.776	1,083
	1972	82,043	(20.3)	0.666	(7.3)	0.717	1,164
Kwangju	1966	34,614	(28.0)	0.651	(7.9)	0.767	404
	1970	40,498	(30.0)	0.658	(8.5)	0.793	503
	1973	39,735	(31.9)	0.643	(8.8)	0.802	552
Inch'ŏn	1966	55,050	(27.9)	0.453	(6.5)	0.679	529
	1970	56,613	(29.3)	0.410	(6.1)	0.653	646
	1973	55,271	(29.3)	0.378	(5.7)	0.617	714
Taejŏn	1966	46,583	(51.7)	0.838	(10.7)	0.858	316
	1970	46,864	(49.1)	0.703	(8.5)	0.784	415
	1973	44,267	(52.4)	0.622	(8.1)	0.765	463
Ch'ŏngju	1966	28,396	(40.9)	1.087	(10.4)	0.851	124
	1970	30,394	(40.0)	1.082	(10.1)	0.842	144
	1973	30,853	(39.9)	0.994	(9.2)	0.817	167
Andong	1966	15,093	(37.9)	1.042	(9.1)	0.814	64
	1970	18,509	(39.0)	1.076	(9.6)	0.830	76
	1973	19,910	(41.2)	1.078	(9.9)	0.839	87
Suwŏn	1966	24,294	(30.4)	1.031	(7.6)	0.783	128
	1970	28,283	(32.0)	0.975	(7.5)	0.776	171
	1973	28,796	(30.3)	0.946	(7.5)	0.779	192

TABLE 21 (continued)

City	Year	D_O		g		R^2	Population (in 1,000s)
Ch'ŏnan	1966	11,159	(30.2)	0.839	(7.7)	0.719	71
	1970	14,285	(31.7)	0.937	(8.3)	0.748	78
	1973	13,849	(31.1)	0.937	(8.0)	0.737	85
Kangnŭng	1966	53,615	(23.0)	0.588	(5.3)	0.621	65
	1970	61,734	(23.5)	0.616	(5.5)	0.644	74
	1973	68,431	(24.4)	0.617	(5.7)	0.656	82
Samch'ŏnp'o	1960	5,292	(18.3)	0.461	(4.1)	0.549	50
	1966	5,764	(18.3)	0.461	(4.1)	0.545	54
	1970	6,358	(18.3)	0.487	(4.2)	0.565	55
	1973	7,112	(18.4)	0.500	(4.3)	0.575	57

Note: Numbers in parentheses are t statistics.

the smaller cities have, on the whole, steeper density functions than larger cities. Second, the density functions become flatter as time passes, with only a few exceptions. Thus, Korean cities display the pattern of decentralization that has been found to characterize cities throughout the developed world. Third, the larger cities have higher central densities than the smaller cities, as measured by the estimated D_O values. By and large, densities are greater near the centers of large cities than of small cities.

The previous paragraph indicates that large cities have both smaller density gradients and larger central densities than small cities. These two facts together imply that, the larger the city, the greater its average density. This is hardly a startling conclusion, but it is important that density functions be consistent with what the data tell us directly about average urban densities. It is reassuring that the Korean density functions are consistent with data on average density by city size.

Table 22 provides an instructive comparison between average density gradients for the Korean cities in Table 21 and average gradients for similar samples or urban areas in Japan and the

United States. The samples of urban areas are by no means random. In Japan and the United States, sample urban areas were chosen to avoid those constrained by mountains and other geographical barriers and to avoid urban areas that had grown together. In Korea, the sample consists of all the largest cities in the country, and indeed all the cities for which data are available.

The data in Table 22 show a remarkable pattern, comparing urban areas in countries at three very different stages of development. All three countries show the same tendency of urban

TABLE 22 Average Density Gradients for Samples of Urban Areas in Korea, Japan, and the United States

Korea		Japan		United States	
Year	Average Gradient	Year	Average Gradient	Year	Average Gradient
1966	0.701[a]	1965	0.457	1960	0.199
1970	0.670	1970	0.391	1970	0.123
1973	0.639				

Source: The average gradients for Korea are computed from Table 21. Figures for Japan and the United States are from Mills and Ohta.

Note: [a]Includes 1965 estimate for Seoul.

decentralization. In all three countries the average density gradient flattens rapidly as time passes. Measured by absolute annual decline in the gradient, Japanese cities decentralized most rapidly during the period covered by Table 22—0.0132 points per year. The Korean average declined 0.0089 points per year, and the United States average declined 0.0076 points per year. An annual decrease of 0.0133 points per year in density gradients represents rapid suburbanization indeed by the standards of observations that have been made in the developed world.

The other main characteristic of the data in Table 22 is that decentralization has proceeded less far in Korean cities than in

Japanese and U.S. cities, and less far in Japanese than U.S. cities. That is, the average Korean density function is steeper than the average in Japan, and much steeper than the average in the United States. There are probably three reasons for this. Most important, the higher the income level of a country, the more decentralized its urban areas are likely to be. High incomes stimulate housing demand and people move to the urban fringes to find inexpensive land. Second, the lower the relative price of land, the more decentralized the city should be. If land is cheap, much is consumed by low density housing. The relative price of land is strongly correlated with population density, and the rankings of the three countries in Table 22 by population density are the same as those by average gradients. Third, large urban areas are more decentralized than small urban areas, and the United States urban areas included in Table 22 are larger than the Japanese, which in turn are larger than the Korean.

The findings in Tables 21 and 22 can be illustrated and made more specific by considering density functions for three urban areas of about the same population, one each in Korea, Japan, and the United States. Table 23 presents the 1970 density functions for Suwŏn in Korea, Mito in Japan, and Binghamton, N.Y., in the United States. The three urban areas had almost identical populations in 1970, about 170,000. The three density functions are typical of the averages in Table 22. The Korean city has the highest central density and the steepest gradient, followed by the Japanese city, then the United States urban area.

The dramatic differences in urban structure implied by these density functions are shown in Table 24. Suwŏn has a radius about one-third greater than that of Mito, whereas Binghamton's is 4 times as great as Mito's. Suwŏn's total area, as calculated from the density function, is somewhat less than twice that of Mito, whereas Binghamton's is 16 times as great as Mito's. Correspondingly, Suwŏn's population density is somewhat greater than half Mito's, whereas Binghamton's is only 6 percent of Mito's. Although these are small urban areas, the comparisons

TABLE 23 Illustrative Density Functions
            1970

Urban Area	D_O	g	Total Population
Suwŏn	28,283	0.975	171,000
Mito	13,630	0.382	174,000
Binghamton	953	0.136	167,000

Source: For density functions for Suwŏn see Table 21; for Mito and Binghamton, see Mills and Ohta.

are typical. Conditions in the United States make its urban areas voracious users of land. But the comparison between Suwŏn and Mito is more instructive for the purposes of this paper. As measured by the density gradient, Suwŏn is much more centralized than Mito. But, because Suwŏn has a much higher central density than Mito, Suwŏn's average density is much smaller than Mito's. This illustrates the important fact that an urban area can be decentralized although it has a high average population density. For a city of a given population, average density depends on the intercept of the density function as well as on the gradient.

The data presented in this section suggest strongly that, as incomes rise and urbanization continues in Korea, not only will cities grow but they also will continue to decentralize. Average

TABLE 24 Illustrative Urban Structures
            1970

Urban Area	Radius of Urban Area	Area of Urban Area	Average Density of Urban Area
Suwŏn	4	50	3,404
Mito	3	28	6,157
Binghamton	12	452	369

Source: Computed from Table 22.

urban densities may increase for some time if cities grow rapidly, but density functions will continue to flatten. When the percentage growth rate of urban areas slows, as it must eventually, average urban densities will begin to fall as they have in Japan, the United States, and elsewhere.

These findings suggest strongly that it would be desirable to study more specifically the determinants of urban decentralization. Such a study is reported below.

DETERMINANTS OF SUBURBANIZATION IN KOREA

The data presented and analyzed above have made it clear that, in a general way, urban areas become more decentralized the larger they become and the higher the incomes of their residents. There is great variation among city sizes within a country, and that part of the hypothesis is therefore easy to test with data from Korean cities. Incomes among cities within a country vary much less than city sizes, and there are much fewer data, but it is nevertheless possible to do some testing and estimation. The relative scarcity of land is the third factor suggested above as a major determinant of urban decentralization. But land scarcity pervades a country, and this part of the hypothesis must be tested by comparisons either among countries or over long periods of time. Lack of data prevents comparisons among density functions estimated over long historical periods, and cultural and other characteristics may be important determinants of international differences in urban structure. For example, cities where detached houses predominate are likely to be more decentralized than cities where people are willing to live in multi-family dwellings. But attitudes toward multi-family dwellings differ from one society to another, and such differences may affect international comparisons of density functions.

The foregoing discussion suggests that differences in city

sizes and residents' incomes should be the main determinants of urban decentralization within a country. This conjecture has been verified statistically by studies in Japan and the United States. These studies have shown that density gradients can be related quite accurately to the logarithms of urban population and average incomes in the urban area. Specifically, the relationship can be expressed as

$$g_i^* = a_0^* + a_1^* \, lnP_i + a_2^* \, lnY_i \qquad (6\text{-}2)$$

where g_i^* is the density gradient of the ith city when it has adjusted to the values of the independent variables, lnP_i is the natural log of population of the urban area, and lnY_i is the natural log of per capita income. The a_i^* are parameters to be estimated from the data. For example, a_1^* represents the effect of a given percentage change in population on the density gradient.

The hypothesis embodied in (6-2) is that the density gradient flattens as the urban population grows and as per capita income increases. But this is a complex process, involving construction, demolition and alteration of buildings, and conversion of land from rural to urban uses. All these changes require notoriously long times, and many people have speculated that the lag between a change in a determinant of urban structure and the resulting change in urban structure is among the longest in an economic system. Inevitably, this implies that the urban structure is always moving toward a new equilibrium form, but not getting there before the equilibrium has shifted. Thus, the data on urban structure provide observations on the actual density gradient g, but not on its equilibrium value g^* in (6-2). It is then necessary to hypothesize a relationship between g and g^*, that is, a mechanism by which g adjusts gradually to its equilibrium value g^*. A simple such mechanism, which has been found useful in analyzing adjustments in urban structure in other countries and in analyzing many other kinds of economic adjustments, is the distributed lag adjustment equation. It assumes that g adjusts each year by an amount that eliminates a certain fraction of the difference between g and g^*,

$$g_i = g_{i-1} + \lambda(g_i^* - g_{i-1}) = \lambda g_i^* + (1-\lambda)g_{i-1} \qquad (6\text{-}3)$$

In (6-3), g_i^* is the equilibrium density gradient, g_i is the actual density gradient, and g_{i-1} is the density gradient at some earlier time. λ is the fraction of the difference between g_i^* and g_{i-1} by which g_i adjusts between observations. If λ were one, g_i would adjust each period to the new equilibrium. If λ were zero, there would be no adjustment and the density gradient would not respond to the variables in (6-2). Realistic cases are between the extremes. λ can be estimated from the data and provides a measure of the speed with which urban structure adjusts in disequilibrium. There is some evidence that urban structure adjusts more slowly in some countries than in others, depending on legal and institutional resistance to such changes.

If (6-2) is used to eliminate g_i^* from the right side of (6-3), the resulting equation is

$$g_i = a_0 + a_1 \ln P_i + a_2 \ln Y_i + (1-\lambda)g_{i-1} \qquad (6\text{-}4)$$

Equation 6-4 is suitable for estimation from the data in that it does not contain the unobservable variable g_i^*. It shows that the density gradient g_i is related to total population and to per capita income of the ith urban area and to the lagged value of g_i. Each a_j in (6-4) is related to the corresponding a_j^* coefficient in the equilibrium equation (6-2) by $a_j = \lambda a_j^*$. Thus, λ and each a_j can be estimated from (6-4), and estimates of the a_j^* can be calculated from estimates of a_j and λ. In this way it is possible to estimate both the magnitude of the dependence of the density gradient on the population and income of the urban area and the speed with which the gradient adjusts when it is out of equilibrium.

The sample observations of the dependent variable in (6-4) are the 12 1973 estimates of g_i in Table 21. The sample lagged values of g_i are the 12 1970 estimates of g_i in the table. Sample P_i observations are the 1973 populations of the 12 cities in Table 21. Sample Y_i values are 1974 per capita incomes of the 12 cities. For convenience of reference, all sample data used in estimation of (6-4) are brought together in Table 25.

The estimate of (6-4) from the data in Table 25 is

$$g_i = 0.1075 - 0.0223\, lnP_i + 0.0097\, lnY_i + 0.9194g_{i\text{-}1}$$

$$\quad (0.3272)\ (-1.7178)\quad\ (0.1157)\qquad (20.3482)$$

$$R^2 = 0.994 \qquad\qquad\qquad\qquad\qquad\qquad\qquad (6\text{-}5)$$

The coefficient of lnP_i has the anticipated sign and is significantly different from zero at about the 5 percent significance level. The estimated value of -0.0223 means that a 10 percent increase in a city's population is associated with a decrease of 0.00223 in the city's density gradient three years later. The coefficient of lnY_i has the opposite sign from that anticipated and found in similar studies in other countries. It implies that the density function becomes steeper as income increases. Theoretical models indicate that a positive effect of Y_i on g_i is possible, but only in the presence of unlikely combinations of housing demand and travel cost parameters. One component of such a combination is a low income elasticity of demand for housing. In Chapter 8 we shall present evidence that the Korean income elasticity of housing demand may indeed be very low. But the evidence is weak. Furthermore, the evidence from (6-5) that $a_2 > 0$ is also weak since the t-value of the estimated a_2 is only about 0.1. The safest conclusion is that g_i hardly responds to changes in Y_i.

The estimate of 0.9194 for the coefficient of $g_{i\text{-}1}$ implies an estimate of λ equal to $0.0806 = 1 - 0.9194$. Thus, g_i adjusts by about 8 percent of any disequilibrium between successive observations. Since the observations are at 3-year intervals, the implication is that g_i adjusts by about 2.7 percent of any disequilibrium per year. This confirms the belief that cities decentralize only slowly in response to changes in the underlying

TABLE 25 Data for Density Gradient Regressions

Urban Area	Density Gradient 1973	Density Gradient 1970	Population 1973 (1,000s)	Per Capita Income 1974 (1,000s)
Seoul	0.186	0.223	6,290	152.5
Pusan	0.109	0.134	2,072	135.0
Taegu	0.666	0.739	1,200	130.0
Inch'ŏn	0.378	0.410	714	120.0
Kwangju	0.643	0.658	552	115.0
Taejŏn	0.622	0.703	463	113.0
Suwŏn	0.946	0.975	192	120.0
Ch'ŏngju	0.994	1.082	167	136.8
Andong	1.078	1.076	87	124.9
Samch'ŏnp'o	0.500	0.487	57	77.0
Kangnŭng	0.617	0.616	82	117.6
Ch'ŏnan	0.937	0.937	85	99.6

Sources: Density gradients are from Table 21.
Data on income are from EPB, *Special Labor Force Survey Report,* 1974.
Population data are from EPB, *Report on Population and Housing Census,*
1975. Per capita income is in thousands wŏn (exchange rate: W/$ = 404.6
in 1974).

determinants of the equilibrium pattern. It also implies that studies of decentralization that ignore the pervasiveness of disequilibrium are likely to be grossly inaccurate.

Remembering that $a_j^* = a_j/\lambda$, we can estimate the equilibrium coefficient in (6-2) from the coefficients in (6-5). The estimated coefficients in (6-2) are

$$g_i^* = 1.334 - 0.277 \, lnP_i + 0.120 \, lnY_i \qquad (6-6)$$

Equation 6-6 shows the long-run relationship between density gradients and population and income in cities. It makes clear why large cities have flatter density functions than small cities, despite the fact that large cities have higher average incomes. The coefficient of lnP_i is more than twice that of lnY_i, so that a given percentage increase in P_i and Y_i will result in a reduction in the density gradient in the long run. But large cities have 10 to 100 times as many people as small cities, whereas high-income cities are unlikely to have more than twice the per capita income of low-income cities. Thus, lnP_i rises much more rapidly with city size than does lnY_i. Therefore, the effect of population dominates the effect of income on density gradients, if large and small cities are compared. Much the same conclusion emerges from the study by Mills and Ohta of Japan, where income varies less among cities than in Korea.

Calculations based on (6-6) indicate that Korean cities are far from equilibrium. Using the data in Table 25, (6-6) implies that the equilibrium density gradient for Suwŏn, for example, is about 0.452 at its 1973 population and 1974 income level. This implies that Suwŏn's equilibrium density gradient is only about half its actual 1973 density gradient. Similar calculations imply that some of the largest cities have negative equilibrium density gradients. That conclusion is not to be taken seriously, since the equilibrium density gradient is presumably not really a linear function of lnP_i and lnY_i at extreme values of these variables. But the basic point is that both population and income have grown rapidly in Korean cities, and the cities are therefore much more centralized than they would be if they were in equilibrium. The conclusion is inescapable that, even if there were no further growth of city populations and incomes, Korean cities would continue to decentralize rapidly during many years to come. Of course, population and income will continue to grow in cities, and the result will undoubtedly be to reinforce the tendancy to decentralize. The reinforcement will be greater the more rapidly city population grows and less the more rapidly income grows, according to (6-6). Undoubtedly, income growth will be large and population growth will be small in the largest cities, and the reverse in small cities. Thus equilibrium density gradients will fall most in small cities. But all will continue to experience rapid decentralization.

Urban decentralization inevitably breeds conflict and controversy. Farm land must be developed for urban uses, and small towns near expanding metropolitan areas must be absorbed into the metropolitan areas. Although it is important to plan and prepare for expansion at urban fringes, it is not desirable to prevent urban decentralization. Korean cities are extremely dense and congested. As incomes rise, people reduce the disadvantages of congestion by seeking to live at lower densities. This is an important component of increases in well-being that higher incomes make possible. Very high land values, the subject of Chapter 7, act as a severe check on excessive suburbanization in Korea. They force people to economize on land in residential uses.

SEVEN

Land Values

Land values are a cause of confusion, anxiety, and controversy in countries that are urbanizing and developing rapidly.
People do not understand what it is that determines land values,
why they rise so rapidly, and what government policy should be.
People are anxious because land costs are a large proportion of
the costs of housing and of production facilities. People fear
that land values will become so high that they will be unable to
afford decent housing or housing of traditional kinds. Land
values are extremely controversial because land is a non-
produced resource. If a person buys a house, he understands
that the builder has devoted valuable labor and produced
materials for its construction. But no resources have been
devoted to production of the land; it is a natural resource.
Therefore, people resent paying high prices for something no
one sacrificed resources to produce. Land is an ideological issue
in all countries. Many people believe that land prices should be

controlled by government or that land should be removed from private ownership and market allocation.

Land is an input in the production of all goods and services. If it is cheap relative to structures and other inputs, a great deal of it is used per unit of output. If it is expensive, other inputs are used instead. In manufacturing, low factories can be built on large plots with much open space or high factories can be built on small plots with little open space. For residences, high land values induce builders and residents to prefer high-rise apartments on small plots, whereas low land values lead to single-family detached dwellings on large lots.

The function of land prices is to allocate land to valuable uses. The most casual traveler in Japan and Korea observes that people economize on land in ways that are almost unheard of in the United States, because land is a very scarce and valuable resource and its price is correspondingly high. Where land markets are permitted by governments to work, land prices are determined by supply and demand, just like the prices of other commodities. The important difference between land and other commodities is that land, being non-produced, is available in fixed or inelastic supply, regardless of its price. Leveling topography and filling swamps and estuaries are relatively minor exceptions. Landowners, like other asset owners, invest in land to obtain the highest return they can on their asset. They therefore sell or rent their land to the potential user who offers the most for it. The largest amount that it is worthwhile to pay for the use of a plot of land for a year is the value of the marginal product of the land during the year when it is devoted to its most valuable use. This is the annual rent of the land. The most it is worthwhile to pay to buy the land is the present value at time of purchase of anticipated future rents from the land discounted at an appropriate interest rate. Although misuse may impair land's productivity in agriculture, urban uses do not impair land's productivity. Urban land lasts forever. If R_t is the rent anticipated on a plot in year t, and i is the interest rate, then the price of the plot in year zero, P_0, is

$$P_0 = \sum_{t=0}^{\infty} \frac{R_t}{(1+i)^t} \qquad\qquad (7\text{-}1)$$

If the anticipated rent, R_t, is a constant R, this formula reduces to $P_0 = R/i$. For example, if the annual rent of a plot were 100 and the interest rate were 10 percent, then the plot's price would be 1,000.

The main reason for this excursion into land value theory is that it helps explain a fact in some developing countries that would otherwise be puzzling. It is sometimes observed that land values are very high relative to land rents at the time. In rapidly developing countries, productivity of land and other inputs increase rapidly. Anticipated future increases in land's productivity become capitalized in the land's price, and the price becomes large relative to current rent. Land close to urban centers is the most valuable of all, usually one or two orders of magnitude more valuable than agricultural land. As urbanization proceeds and cities grow, high land values spread further from urban centers. Thus, high and rising land values are always associated with rapid urbanization.

The extraordinarily high productivity of urban land arises from its proximity to related economic activities. Central business district land is extremely valuable because it is within walking distance of an enormous range of densely packed and related activities. The closest surrounding residential land is valuable because it provides access to central employment and shopping at low transportation cost. More distant residential land falls off in value as access deteriorates. Many studies have shown that land values are extremely high at city centers, fall off very rapidly with short distances from the center, and show little variation with distance beyond a few kilometers from the centers of even large metropolitan areas.

Land is an extremely valuable resource in a crowded and rapidly developing and urbanizing country like Korea. It is therefore important that it be used efficiently. Market clearing prices are valuable in ensuring that land is devoted to its most valuable use. Governments are frequently tempted to introduce price controls on land, because users complain about high prices and speculators. Land price controls can obscure the scarcity of land, but they cannot change it. Land price controls inevitably create excess demand for land. At artificially low prices, there are more demands to use land than there is land available; then government is inevitably placed in the position of having to allocate land among competing interests, substituting a political for a market allocation procedure. In addition, when land is artificially cheap, those who are permitted to use it inevitably want to use it at lower intensity than market prices would dictate; government is forced to decide in detail not only who can use land but also how it is to be used. Although most economists oppose land price controls, most believe governments should regulate land uses to some degree. Virtually all governments regulate land uses by government ownership, taxation of land, zoning, and other land use controls. How much control governments should exercise over land uses is controversial in most countries.

NATIONAL TRENDS IN LAND VALUES

In part because high land values have made the subject a matter of national concern, the Korean government collects excellent data on land values. The Korea Appraisal Board has conducted Land Price Surveys in urban areas, including ŭp (towns), since the 1960s. The Korea National Agricultural Cooperative Federation has published data on land values for the entire country including rural areas since 1971.

Using these published data, we have estimated the market value of land in Korea, as shown in Table 26. We excluded streams, lakes, rivers, and public uses such as roads, railroads, and parks. For residential, arable, and forest land, we drew a 20-percent random sample from the published data in each region. We then "blew up" the sample to obtain total land

TABLE 26 Korean Land Values, 1975

	Total Area (million p'yŏng)	Price per p'yŏng (wŏn)	Total Land Value (million wŏn)	Value (million dollars)
Entire Country	26,817	626	16,777,654	34,593
Residential	507	14,665	7,437,240	15,334
Arable	6,671	1,245	8,304,954	17,124
Forest	19,638	53	1,035,460	2,135
Urban Areas	1,060	7,181	7,609,776	15,690
Residential	142	45,423	6,453,299	13,305
Arable	332	3,306	1,097,956	2,264
Forest	586	100	58,551	121
Semi-Urban Areas	1,917	872	1,671,953	3,447
Residential	87	7,069	614,539	1,267
Arable	617	1,576	972,493	2,005
Forest	1,213	70	84,921	175
Rural Areas	23,840	314	7,495,925	15,456
Residential	278	1,328	369,432	762
Arable	5,722	1,090	6,234,505	12,855
Forest	17,840	50	891,988	1,839

Sources: Computed from land value data in Han'guk Kamjŏngwŏn, T'oji siga chosa, 1975.
Korea National Agricultural Cooperative Federation, National Land Values Survey, 1974 and MHA Naemubu, Chijŏk t'onggye, 1973.

values by multiplying sample average land values by total land area in each category. The unit of area in the table is the p'yŏng, of which there are about 1,224 per acre. According to the government classification, about 4 percent of Korea's land is urban, and another 7 percent is semi-urban, consisting of the partly urbanized small towns; 67.2 percent of Korea's land is forested; only 22.5 percent, not all in rural areas, is arable.

Our estimate is that the market value of Korea's land was

16,778 billion wŏn in 1975, or 34.6 billion dollars (W484=$1). By comparison, Korea's 1975 GNP was 9,080 billion wŏn.[1] Thus, we estimate that total land values in Korea are about 1.85 times annual GNP. A comparable U.S. estimate concludes that the market value of U.S. land was about 0.7 times U.S. GNP in 1966. A 1973 Japanese estimate is that land in Japan was worth about 3.3 times annual GNP. All these estimates are subject to substantial margins of error, because most land is not sold in a given year and its value must be estimated, and because it is difficult to separate the value of developed land from the value of structures on it.

Regardless of inaccuracies, these data make clear that land values vary greatly in relation to GNP among countries. In Japan, land values in relation to GNP are twice the Korean value, which in turn is more than twice the U.S. value. Undoubtedly, the main explanation for these differences is the relative scarcity of land. Japan and Korea are very dense countries, whereas the United States is among the most land-rich of industrialized countries. But this cannot be the entire explanation. In the United States, it is reasonable to assume that land rents are capitalized into land values at an interest rate of about 10 percent. That assumption and the fact that land values are about 70 percent of GNP imply that a constant land rent would be about 7 percent of GNP according to Equation 7-1. That is very close to the conclusion of the best estimate of land rents in the United States. Ten percent is a low interest rate to assume for capitalizing land rents in Japan and Korea. Even that low rate would imply that land rents are 17 percent of GNP in Korea and 33 percent of GNP in Japan. It is not possible to check this against the GNP accounts because land rents are not reported separately from other GNP components. But the Japanese figure of 33 percent of GNP exceeds the percentage of all property income in GNP, and much of property income is clearly from produced capital. The Korean figure is less than the percentage of all property income in Korean GNP, but it seems very unlikely that land rents are as much as 17 percent of

Korean GNP. Undoubtedly, the resolution of this paradox is that the forecast of rapid future growth of land rents has been capitalized into land values in Japan and Korea. As explained above, this can cause land values to be high relative to land rents. Thus, the expectation of continued rapid economic growth is an important explanation of the high ratio of land values to GNP in Korea and Japan.

In Korea, as elsewhere, urban land prices are much greater than rural land prices. The data in Table 26 imply that the average p'yŏng of urban land is worth 23 times as much as the average rural p'yŏng. In fact, the 4 percent of the land that is urban is worth more than the 89 percent of land that is rural. The reason for this is of course that, in urban activities, structures and other inputs can be substituted for land much more easily than in agriculture and other rural activities.

Table 26 shows that the average price of urban residential land was 45,423 wŏn per p'yŏng, or 100,000 dollars per acre. This category includes all developed urban land. This is certainly somewhat higher than the average price of urban residential land in the United States, but probably about one-fifth of the comparable Japanese figure.[2] A traditional urban single-family Korean home might be on a plot of about 365 p'yŏng, or 0.3 acres. The value of such a plot was about 2.6 million wŏn or 5,425 dollars in 1975. This compares with average family income of about 660,000 wŏn or 1,364 dollars in urban Korea. The figures imply that the residential plot is worth about four years' family income.

It is not possible to construct aggregate land value figures for earlier years. But data are available for Korea's 12 largest cities. An index for the 12 cities and separate indexes for the 3 largest cities are presented in Table 27 for the period 1963–1974.[3] The wholesale price index and an index of GNP are presented for comparison. Land values have risen rapidly indeed in the 12 cities during the 11-year period covered by the table. In 1974, the 12-city index was nearly 26 times its 1963 level.

TABLE 27 Land Price Indexes

	Average for 12 Major Cities	Seoul	Pusan	Taegu	Wholesale Price Index	GNP
1963	100	100	100	100	100	100
1965	203	225	191	188	148	165
1970	1,233	1,445	1,208	1,458	215	530
1972	2,056	1,966	1,649	2,070	267	790
1974	2,582	2,610	2,321	2,668	406	1,381

Source: Computed from land price data in Han'guk Kamjŏngwŏn, *12 chuyo tosi chiga chisu*, June 1975. The twelve cities are: Seoul, Pusan, Taegu, Kwangju, Taejŏn, Inch'ŏn, Ch'unch'ŏn, Chŏnju, Suwŏn Ch'ungju, Masan, Cheju.

This represents a compound average annual growth of 29 percent. Part of this extraordinary gain is, of course, the result of inflation. In 1974, the wholesale price index was about 4 times its 1963 level, representing an average compound inflation rate of 13 percent. But these data imply that the average real rate of return to land holding was 14 percent in urban Korea during the 11-year period. This return is in addition to the return in the form of annual rents that would be paid for the use of the land. The implication is that holding urban land must have been one of the most profitable investments in Korea during the recent period of very rapid growth.

A final remarkable fact about the data in Table 27 is that land values in the 3 largest cities have risen at about the same rate as those for the 12-city average during the 11-year period. Land values in the largest cities are, of course, much higher than in smaller cities. But since, as shown in Chapter 2, the largest cities have grown faster than other cities, it might be expected that their land values would grow faster as well. But that seems not to have happened. In fact, since 1970, land values have risen more slowly in the three largest cities than in the group of 12 cities.

Less reliable land value indexes go back to 1956 for the same

12 cities. These data suggest that urban land value increases of between 25 and 30 percent per year were common between 1956 and 1963.

The data in Table 27 make it almost inevitable that the share of land rent in GNP has risen during the 11-year period. During the period, GNP in current prices has increased at a compound annual rate of about 24 percent. Since land values increased at a compound annual rate 5 percentage points faster than GNP, it means that the ratio of land values to GNP doubles in 14 years. Undoubtedly, the share of land rents in GNP will not double in 14 years, since current rents have undoubtedly been capitalized into land values at lower rates in recent years than in earlier years, as expectations about future growth in land rents have been revised upward. But the share of land rents in GNP must be increasing somewhat as the ratio of land values to GNP increases.

Furthermore, the Japanese experience suggests that Korean land values may continue to increase faster than GNP in coming years. Land values are higher relative to GNP in Japan than in Korea, as has been pointed out. Presumably, the reason is that rapid economic growth has been of longer duration in Japan than in Korea, and anticipated future increases in rents have been more fully capitalized into land values. If so, continuation of rapid economic growth in Korea will almost inevitably mean that land values will continue to rise faster than GNP.

Very rapidly rising land values always create social problems. Many people believe that speculators are the cause of high land values and demand controls on land prices. Economists mostly believe that speculation can keep prices above equilibrium for only short periods of time and that, in fact, speculation is likely to make land prices more, rather than less, stable. But popular beliefs persist despite economists' arguments.

Perhaps of more importance, many people believe that rapidly rising land values make income distribution more unequal. Stories of large fortunes made from land sales appear in the media, and some people believe that a large part of social wealth is being placed in the hands of a few wealthy landowners. In fact, the opposite conclusion is more likely. Land is much less unequally distributed than any other important asset in most societies. In Korea, 69 percent of housing was owner-occupied in 1970, and most farmland is in the hands of owner-operators. It is almost inevitable that land is more widely held than corporate assets, the other major category of wealth. If so, rapid increases in land values have the effect of decreasing the concentration of wealth ownership.

STRUCTURE OF URBAN LAND VALUES

Fortunately, Korean land value data are published for sub-areas within a few large urban areas. These data make it possible to study the pattern of land values within urban areas in the same way that population density within urban areas was studied in Chapter 6. In that chapter, it was shown that population density falls off systematically with distance from the centers of urban areas. Urban land use theory indicates that land values should be closely realted to population density within urban areas.

Urban land owners, like other asset owners, sell or rent their asset to the user who pays the most for it. The value of a plot of urban land depends mainly on its accessibility to urban activities on nearby land and on technology that determines its productivity. The former determinant of urban land values has long been recognized and analyzed. If a given plot is close to shopping and employment centers, it provides access to these activities at lower transportation costs than more distant plots. Potential residents are willing to pay more for this plot than for others by an amount that represents the saving it permits in transportation costs. The most important focus for shopping and employment is the central business district in urban areas. Therefore transportation cost savings resulting from improved access fall off with distance from the central business district. If transportation cost is proportional to distance traveled, access accounts for a linear decline in land values with distance from the central business district.[4]

In fact, land values fall off less rapidly than linearly with distance, following the pattern of first rapid and then gradual decline with distance characteristic of urban population density patterns. This characteristic non-linearity results from the pecularities of production technology, and has been recognized and analyzed by scholars only in recent years. Production technology for housing, commerce, and manufacturing is such that other inputs, especially capital, can be substituted for land, but at the cost of some loss of productivity of inputs employed in relatively large quantities. A single-family detached dwelling employs a large input of land, but a relatively small input of capital. A high-rise apartment dwelling economizes on land, but requires much more capital. The same is true, in varying degrees, of office and industrial activities. The implication is that, as land becomes more expensive because of better access as one moves toward the city center, capital is substituted for land through the use of tall buildings with only small amounts of surrounding uncovered land. Substitution of capital for land raises the productivity of land and therefore raises its value. Thus, as one moves toward the center, land values rise faster than linearly; the linear increase resulting from improved access and the additional increase resulting from input substitution.

It is input substitution that accounts for rising employment and population densities as one approaches the central business district (CBD). Employment and resident population are roughly proportionate to floor space, and floor space per unit of land rises as capital is substituted for land. These basic ideas can be embodied in a number of specific mathematical models of demand for housing and production technology. Several such models imply that population density and land values are related in the following specific way:

$$D(x) = BV(x)^{1-\beta} \qquad (7\text{-}2)$$

In this formula, $D(x)$ is, as in Chapter 6, population density x kilometers from the CBD, $V(x)$ is land value per unit x kilometers from the CBD, and β is a constant. β is zero if the price elasticity of housing demand is unity. Then, density and land value are proportional. If, as seems likely from evidence to be presented in Chapter 8, housing demand is somewhat inelastic, β is positive. It was concluded in Chapter 6 that population density falls off approximately exponentially with distance from the urban center. Then land values should also fall off exponentially, but with a smaller exponent than density.[5]

The prediction from this theoretical discussion is that land values should be approximately exponential in distance from the central business district if population density is exponential, and the exponent of the land value equation should be about the same as, or somewhat smaller than, that of the population density equation. From a scholarly point of view, comparison between land value and density patterns is worthwhile because very few countries have sufficiently plentiful land value data to make the comparison. Thus, the theoretical notions put forth above are virtually untested. From a practical point of view, estimation of urban land value functions is important because it helps ascertain whether markets are allocating land to the most valuable use. If the data confirm the theoretical relationship between land values and population density, they suggest, but do not prove, that markets are allocating land efficiently. A final practical use of land value functions is that they provide an economical and accurate method of estimating the trend of total land values in an urban area.

Our procedure in estimating land value functions has paralleled that for estimating population density functions. Start by assuming land values fall exponentially with distance from the center of the urban area,

$$V(x) = V_0 e^{gx}. \qquad (7\text{-}3)$$

Here, V_0 is land value per square kilometer at the center, and g

is the percentage decrease in land value per square kilometer per kilometer of increased distance from the center. For our sample, we chose the 3 largest cities—Seoul, Pusan and Taegu—and a smaller city—Suwŏn—with a 1975 population of 224,000. In each city, land values were recorded in a small random sample of tong (precincts). Sample sizes varied from 21 to 47 tong in a given city and year, depending on the amount of data available. Data for industrial land values could not be used because sample sizes were too small. In other respects, the procedure for estimating the land value functions was identical to that employed in Chapter 6 to estimate density functions.

Table 28 shows some land value functions for 4 Korean cities estimated for recent years for which data are available. Separate estimates are shown for residential and commercial land. Population density gradients are shown from Table 21 for ease of comparison. The estimates in Table 28 provide a rare and remarkable comparison between density and land value functions.

As should be expected, commercial land values are higher than residential land values. Each commercial V_0 is larger than the corresponding residential V_0, in most cases by a factor of 2 or more. This indicates that commercial land near the city center is much more valuable than residential land equally near the city center. In most, but by no means all cases, commercial land values fall off more rapidly than residential land values with distance from the center. Despite this, commercial land values remain higher throughout the urban area. For example, the 1975 Seoul land value functions indicate that residential land values would exceed commercial land values only at distances in excess of 56 kilometers from the center. That is far beyond the radius of the urban area. The relationship between commercial and residential land values is similar for other years and other urban areas. An intriguing question is whether the findings that commerical land values exceed residential land values indicate resource misallocation. If land can be converted freely from one use to the other, owners convert land to commercial use as long as its value in that use exceeds its value in residential use. One is tempted to say that land use controls restrict land use for commercial purposes and thus keep its price higher than similarly located land used for residences. However, that inference may be erroneous. Not all land x miles from the center provides equal access. Land on main arteries provides better access than land on side streets. The former is more likely to be used for commercial purposes than the latter. This fact can account for the finding that commercial land values exceed residential land values at each distance from the center. No government intervention and no resource misallocation are implied.

A second finding is that land value gradients show the same tendency to decline through time that was found for density gradients. For example, the residential land value gradient for Seoul declines from 0.201 in 1970 to 0.126 in 1975. As with the density gradients, there are exceptions to the general rule. Urban land use theory, embodied in (7-2), tells us that the ratio between the density and land value gradients should not change rapidly through time. If so, then as the urban area decentralizes and the density gradient falls, the land value gradient should also fall. In this respect, the estimates in Table 28 are consistent with land value theory.

The most striking finding in Table 28 is the remarkable agreement between the relationship between the land value and density gradients and that indicated by urban land use theory. The theory implies that land value gradients should be about the same as or somewhat less than the corresponding density gradients. This is true in every case in which the land value and density gradients are available for the same year in the table. For example, the 1973 Pusan density gradient is 0.109, whereas the residential and commercial land value gradients are 0.094 and 0.089. The consistency of this relationship is remarkable indeed. Even when density and land value gradients are not available for the same year, interpolation between neighboring years indicates strongly that the relationship holds. This finding

TABLE 28 Land Value Functions for Selected Korean Cities

	SEOUL							PUSAN						
	V_0		g			R_2		V_0		g			R_2	
	Res.	Comm.	Res.	Comm.	Pop.	Res.	Comm.	Res.	Comm.	Res.	Comm.	Pop.	Res.	Comm.
1965					0.328									
1966												0.263		
1968														
1970	183,000 (44.6)	417,000 (40.2)	0.201 (10.2)	0.188 (7.5)	0.223	0.724	0.582	83,000 (34.3)	222,000 (22.5)	0.112 (6.4)	0.111 (3.4)	0.134	0.661	0.355
1972														
1973	176,000 (48.0)	469,000 (43.7)	0.163 (9.2)	0.187 (7.9)	0.186	0.671	0.611	101,000 (38.3)	314,000 (25.5)	0.094 (5.8)	0.089 (2.9)	0.109	0.612	0.288
1975	242,000 (74.8)	627,000 (46.3)	0.126 (10.2)	0.143 (6.1)		0.723	0.483	191,000 (43.9)	547,000 (30.0)	0.091 (5.6)	0.072 (2.5)		0.600	0.232

TABLE 28 (continued)

TAEGU

Year	V_0 Res.	V_0 Comm.	g Res.	g Comm.	g Pop.	R_2 Res.	R_2 Comm.
1965							
1966							
1968							
1970	101,000 (48.2)	369,000 (41.0)	0.508 (11.1)	0.574 (8.3)	0.739	0.867	0.785
1972					0.666		
1973	100,000 (58.5)	483,000 (31.4)	0.348 (19.2)	0.526 (5.6)		0.818	0.621
1975	139,000 (65.0)	784,000 (36.7)	0.316 (8.7)	0.520 (6.0)			

SUWŎN

Year	V_0 Res.	V_0 Comm.	g Res.	g Comm.	g Pop.	R_2 Res.	R_2 Comm.
1965			0.733 (10.7)			0.718	
1966					1.031		
1968	13,000 (17.0)		0.833 (13.9)			0.812	
1970					0.975		
1972							
1973	51,000 (33.9)	210,000 (38.2)	0.675 (14.6)	0.819 (10.8)	0.946	0.827	0.795
1975	69,000 (41.5)	261,000 (38.9)	0.581 (14.4)	0.766 (9.9)		0.821	0.765

suggests that land uses are in competitive equilibrium in Korean cities. Not only are owners allocating land to its most valuable use, but also the markets appear to be competitive and to be approximately in equilibrium. This finding does not prove that urban land use is efficient in Korea; that depends mainly on whether external effects such as pollution and noise cause competitive equilibrium to deviate from an optimum allocation of land. But the finding does suggest that land markets are competitive and are doing their job of allocating land to its most valuable use.

Table 28 also makes clear that, as in the United States and elsewhere, land values have risen less rapidly in the central parts than elsewhere in Korean cities. It was pointed out above that total urban land values increased 29 percent per year in large Korean cities during the period 1963–1974. Annual growth rates of V_0 values in Table 28 are much lower. In Seoul, for example, both the residential and commercial V_0 estimates grew between 5 and 6 percent per year during the period 1970–1975. Growth rates of V_0 estimates are higher for the other cities in the table, but none is as high as 29 percent. Thus, land values near the centers of Korean cities have risen less than land values on the outskirts, and land values near the center of Seoul appear to have risen less than land values near the centers of smaller cities. Although this finding may appear paradoxical in a country where urbanization is rapid and big cities are growing faster than small cities, it is a familiar story in the United States and elsewhere. But there is no real paradox in the finding in Korea or anywhere else. We have found that cities decentralize as they grow and as transportation improves. That inevitably means that suburban densities and land values rise relative to those near urban centers. The relatively slow rise in central urban land values is merely a reflection of the inexorable pattern of urban decentralization.

TAXATION AND CONTROL OF URBAN LAND

Almost all countries tax and regulate the use of land. Taxation of land and structures is the main source of local government revenue in the United States and to a lesser extent, other Anglo-Saxon countries. In the United States, annual urban real estate taxes are typically 2 to 4 percent of the market value of land and structures, or an average of about 25 percent of land rent. Land taxation is an efficient source of government revenue in that land is a non-produced input and taxation therefore does not reduce its supply or affect its gross value or rent. Some economists believe that land taxes should be as high as annual land rents, but this is certainly unwise. Resources must be devoted to finding the most valuable use of land, and no one would commit those resources if all the resulting rent were taxed away. But land taxes can presumably be a substantial fraction of annual rent without loss of efficiency. Taxation of structures is always distorting to some degree, although there is much controversy about the magnitude of the resource misallocation it causes. Equity aspects of land taxation are even more controversial. Land being more widely held than other assets, its taxation is less progressive than other wealth taxes. But whether land taxes are regressive is unknown. The answer may not be the same in every country.

The most basic economic rationale for land use controls is very simple: certain land uses affect the welfare of users of surrounding land; for example, industrial users generate smoke, noise, vibration, and traffic hazards that may affect nearby residents adversely. Zoning and other land use controls are intended to segregate such activities to minimize their effects on others. Although this idea is very simple and has been understood for many decades, land use controls are subject to endless variety in actual practice. Western countries employ a panoply of land use controls, including not only zoning but also housing and building codes, subdivision controls, discriminatory real estate taxation, and architectural controls. Furthermore, the motivation for and effects of land use controls are most commonly not the control of external diseconomies. They are most commonly used to exclude unwanted groups. Sometimes the unwanted group is one that would provide competition for local workers or merchants. Sometimes it is a group that cannot afford the taxes to pay their share of the costs of local government services voted by an affluent majority of residents. Sometimes the unwanted group is a racial, ethnic, or religious group.

Urban land use controls are extensive in area, but their history cannot be described here. Recently, steps have been taken to improve land use controls in Korea. The 1972 National Land Use Management Act gives the Minister of Construction broad power to regulate urban and rural land use. Land can be classified into several exclusive land categories, and nonconforming uses can be legally prevented. The act is being used to promote orderly growth in new and expanding urban areas and to redirect growth away from the largest cities. There appears to be no information available yet on the law's implementation or its effects on urban growth and structure.

In 1967, an anti-speculation tax was enacted. It applied in Seoul, Pusan, and other areas specified by presidential decree. It is now incorporated into the income tax system. It imposes a 50 percent tax on capital gains on land and a 30 percent tax on capital gains on dwellings. In both cases, the tax is calculated on sales price less purchase price less capital improvements less appreciation at the rate of increase of the wholesale price index. Thus, the law basically taxes only real and not money capital gains. Basing the tax on real rather than money capital gains represents a degree of economic sophistication that is rare among governments. One effect of the tax seems to have been to reduce sales of land and developed property. This is a rational response of property owners to the tax only if they expect the tax to be temporary.

EIGHT

Housing

The quality and quantity of housing are viewed as serious social problems in most developing and developed countries. The basic reasons for deep concern are that housing is an important determinant of people's welfare, life-style, and social status, and that, in most countries, it takes a larger fraction of people's income than any commodity group except food. The immediate reason for public concern over housing is controversy surrounding the role of governments in the housing sector. In most countries, governments build, own, and tax housing, and regulate its construction and use in a variety of complex ways. There is continuing controversy about the number, kinds, and efficiency of government programs.

In a rapidly developing and urbanizing country like Korea, concern focuses on housing in urban areas. The influx of people, especially the poor, to cities means that urban housing becomes scarce, expensive, and inadequate compared with social norms. Urban squatter settlements are the symbol of this problem in many developing countries.

Housing is among the most stringently regulated and taxed sectors in many countries, and much housing is built and owned by governments. Direct controls on housing are less stringent in Korea than in many countries, but Korea has tried important experiments in housing programs. Perhaps of more significance, the national government appears to exercise an important indirect influence on the allocation of investment resources between housing and industrial capital formation.

TRENDS IN KOREAN HOUSING

Korean housing data are remarkably rich for years since 1970, but are sparse for earlier years. Thus housing status can be surveyed and compared with other countries in recent years, but trends are difficult to identify.

Table 29 displays data on the adequacy of Korean housing in 1970 and, when available, 1960. There can be no doubt that Korean houses are small on the average. The 6.6 square meters of floor space per person in 1970 compares with 18.6 square meters per person in Japan at the same time. Although the Japanese frequently complain about their small houses, they have nearly three times the space per person that Koreans have. Space per person in the United States is nearly twice that in Japan, or about five times the Korean figure. The housing shortage data tell much the same story. In 1970, 24 percent of Korean households had no separate dwelling. This group consists mostly of married couples living in the parents' dwellings and of families taking in roomers.

As in many rapidly urbanizing countries, housing is scarcer in urban than rural areas. According to Table 29, space per person in cities is less than 75 percent of what it is in rural areas. And the housing shortage data indicate that doubling up of families in dwellings is predominantly an urban phenomenon. Urban housing is less adequate than rural despite higher urban incomes. One reason is that the relative price of housing is higher in urban

TABLE 29 Housing Data

	1960	*1970*
Space: persons per room		
Korea	2.5	2.3
Urban	2.8	2.7
Rural	2.4	2.1
Seoul	2.8	2.7
Space: square meters per person		
Korea	–	6.6
Urban	–	5.5
Rural	–	7.5
Seoul	–	5.9
Facilities: percent of dwellings with piped water		
Korea	–	26.6
Urban	–	57.0
Rural	–	4.0
Seoul	–	64.9
Age: percent of dwellings 10 years old or less		
Korea	30.7	21.0
Urban	45.7	38.9
Rural	24.8	12.6
Seoul	51.8	50.5
Housing shortage: percent of household without separate dwelling		
Korea	17.4	24.2
Urban	–	43.4
Rural	–	9.5
Seoul	–	45.5

Source: EPB, *Report on Population and Housing Census, 1960, 1970.*

than rural areas, owing mainly to much higher urban than rural land values. Probably of more importance, the massive recent rural-urban migration has left a stock of under-utilized rural housing and has placed great stress on the urban construction industry to keep up with the influx of migrants to cities.

There is certainly no room for complacency regarding housing in Korea. It is important, however, to keep the problem in perspective. The urban housing stock was, of course, devastated during the invasion from the north in the early 1950s. Furthermore, in the mid-1970s, Korea's per capita income was one-fifth that in Japan, yet housing space per capita in Korea was more than one-third that in Japan. Housing expenditures usually rise somewhat less than proportionately with income, indicating that the income elasticity of housing demand is somewhat less than one. Not all increased expenditures go to increased space; some go to increased quality. Nevertheless, it does not appear that housing in Korea is less adequate relative to Korean incomes than in Japan and elsewhere.

Persons per room is the only measure of housing quantity that is available for enough countries to make extensive international comparisons. It is an inadequate measure, in that rooms are used quite differently in many Asian countries than in the West. But the United Nations publishes comparable data on both income per capita and on persons per room.[1] Among countries with 1970 per capita incomes within 25 percent of Korea's, Algeria had 2.8 persons per room, Morroco 2.4 and Tunisia 3.2. Among countries with incomes substantially below Korea's, India had 2.8 persons per room and Sri Lanka 2.5. Among countries with incomes well above Korea's, Israel had 1.5 persons per room, Singapore 2.9, Mexico 2.5 and Japan 1.0. The U.S. figure was 0.6. These data do not suggest that Korean house space at 2.3 persons per room is out of line with its income level. It is more important to ask whether Korean housing is improving rapidly as incomes rise than it is to ask about the adequacy of present housing. Unfortunately, data on space per person are not available before 1970. But the persons-per-room data are not encouraging. The decrease from 2.5 to 2.3 persons per room from 1960 to 1970 represents an increase in space per person of 9 percent during the decade. The urban figures represent only 3.6 percent improvement in space per person during the decade. These are only modest improvements compared with other rapidly growing countries. In Japan, space per capita increased more than 35 percent during the same decade.

Data on housing age are equally discouraging. Table 29 shows that the percentage of dwellings no more than 10 years old fell from 31 to 21 during the 1960s. In urban areas the percentage fell from 46 to 39. Although the housing stock is aging in both urban and rural areas, it is aging more rapidly in rural areas.

Housing-start data are somewhat more encouraging. Housing starts increased from 49,000 to 181,000 from 1962 to 1973. The later figure is 3.7 times the earlier one and indicates a rapid growth of dwelling construction. But the 1973 housing-start figure is only about 4 percent of the housing stock. There are no data on depreciation and removal from the stock of housing in Korea. However, if one assumes a 30-year life for the average house, 3.3 percent must be replaced each year to maintain the stock intact. Thus, recent housing-start data probably imply no more than a one percent annual growth of the housing stock, little more than half the population growth rate. Japan, with about 3 times the Korean population, had 10 times as many housing starts as Korea in the early 1970s. But in the early 1960s, when Japanese real incomes were somewhat greater than current Korean incomes, Japanese housing starts were about the same multiple of present Korean housing starts as Japanese population to Korean population.

Total housing investment is a better indication of housing growth than housing-start data, since investment data take account not only of numbers of new houses but also of the size and quality of new houses and of investment in improving the existing housing stock. Table 30 shows data on housing and other investment in relation to GNP from 1960 to 1974. As a share of GNP, housing investment reached a low of 1.6 percent

TABLE 30 Housing Investment

(in current billion wŏn)

	(A) Gross National Product	(B) Total Capital Formation	(C) Housing Invest- ment	C/A × 100	C/B × 100
1960	246	27	5	2.2	19.9
1964	700	102	11	1.6	10.8
1968	1,598	428	49	3.1	11.4
1970	2,589	705	88	3.4	12.5
1971	3,152	805	101	3.2	12.6
1972	3,860	805	105	2.7	13.0
1973	4,902	1,289	158	3.2	12.3
1974	6,747	2,102	299	4.4	14.2

Source: BOK, Economic Statistics Yearbook, 1977.

in 1964 and a high of 4.4 percent in 1974. Although the former figure is small, the latter figure is substantial in comparison with many countries. Housing investment is usually between 4 and 4.5 percent in the United States, whereas it has been about 7 percent in Japan in recent years.

It is clear that Koreans have given highest priority to industrial investment during most of the period since 1960. But by the mid-1970s, priorities were shifting and more attention was being paid to housing needs.

Owner-occupancy is the traditional form of housing tenure in Korea, as in Japan, the United States, and elsewhere. Table 31 displays recent data. The 69 percent owner-occupancy for 1970 is above the comparable figures of 63 percent in the United States and 58 percent in Japan. As in Japan, but in contrast with the United States, the percentage of owner-occupancy fell in Korea during the 1960s. In the United States, ease in obtaining mortgages for owner-occupants and large tax advantages to owner-occupancy keep the rates high. In Korea and Japan, there is no tax advantage to owner-occupancy.

One reason for the drop in owner-occupancy has been urbanization. Owner-occupancy is less common in urban than rural areas because high urban land costs provide incentive to apartment living and apartments lend themselves to owner-occupancy less than single-family detached homes. Thus, as the percentage of the population living in urban areas grows, apartment living becomes more common and owner-occupancy decreases. Owner-occupancy has decreased within urban areas, in part for the same reason. As urban areas grow and land values rise, apartments become more common, with a consequent decline in owner-occupancy.

It is likely that financing problems have been an additional cause of decreased owner-occupancy. Mortgages on owner-occupied homes are almost unheard-of in Korea. As land values have skyrocketed, savings and other sources of finance for owner-occupied homes have become less adequate. It may be that apartment owners and builders of large rental developments

TABLE 31 Housing Tenure

(%)

	1970		1960		1955	
	Owner-Occupied	Rented	Owner-Occupied	Rented	Owner-Occupied	Rented
Whole Country	69.0	24.7	79.1	14.9	79.5	16.6
Urban	48.4	43.5	62.0	34.2	56.1	35.2
Rural	84.3	10.7	86.0	7.1	87.2	10.5
Seoul	48.1	51.9	56.5	39.8	45.5	46.6

Source: EPB, *Report on Population and Housing Census 1970, 1960, 1955.*

have better access than owner-occupiers to credit necessary to finance housing. We shall return to this issue in the section on housing finance.

In Korea, along with the private sector, both national and local governments build housing. Some government housing is built for use by special groups, like government employees and the military, but most is for low-income families. Government-built housing has averaged about 15 percent of total housing construction since the early 1960s, but rose above 20 percent in recent years. In the mid-1970s most government-constructed housing was small apartments built by the Korea Housing Corporation, a national government body, for low-income families.

A MODEL OF URBAN HOUSING SUPPLY AND DEMAND

A supply and demand model for housing can help illuminate how responsive housing demand is to rising incomes and housing prices, and how much and how rapidly housing supply adjusts as demand rises. The model should help anticipate future trends in housing demand as incomes rise and project likely further housing price increases as urbanization proceeds.

It would be desirable to estimate the model separately for each urban area, or at least to use each urban area as a sample observation in estimating the model. But data limitations compel us to estimate an aggregate model for housing in all urban areas. The sample observation from which to estimate the model consists of annual totals or averages for all urban areas in Korea.

The only previous urban housing model estimated from Korean data is that by Song and Struyk.[2] But that attempt failed to produce a useful supply equation. The present study employs a different model and different data. Our basic notion is that housing demand and supply refer to the entire stock of urban housing. Demand is related to households' incomes and to housing prices. Supply is related to housing prices and to construction costs. At any given time, the stock of housing is fixed, and demand determines the price of housing. If the resulting price of housing is high relative to construction costs, the stock expands, gradually bringing the price down. Eventually, the price falls to a level at which the stock remains constant. During much of our sample period, government has constrained the flow of funds into housing, placing priority instead on industrial investment. A goal of our estimation is to discover the extent to which government influence has affected housing markets.

Demand growth is driven by rising incomes and by growth of urban population, both exogenous variables in our model. Thus, in practice, supply is always trying to catch up to a growing demand. It is the failure to take account of the fact that housing supply adjusts only gradually that causes many housing models to produce unintelligible results. Increases in housing supply are by no means the result only of new construction. Supply can also be adjusted by accelerating or decelerating the rate of demolition and by accelerating or decelerating the rate of conversion of structures to and from housing and from and to commercial and industrial uses. All such supply changes take time. Our model allows for gradual adjustment of the housing stock and permits us to estimate the speed of adjustment.

The functional form of our equations is exponential. Much experience of economists has shown that this form fits most supply and demand data as well as any usably simple functional form. In addition, the estimated exponents can be interpreted as demand and supply elasticities. Finally, taking logarithms of all variables yields equations that are linear in the coefficients, thus permitting standard computer programming packages to be used.

Housing demand per urban household is

$$h_D = A p^{\alpha_1} y^{\alpha_2} \tag{8-1}$$

Total urban housing demand is

$$H_D = h_D N \qquad \text{(8-2)}$$

Total housing supply in equilibrium is

$$H_S^* = B p^{\beta_1} W^{\beta_2} \qquad \text{(8-3)}$$

The actual stock of urban housing adjusts as

$$H_S / H_{S\text{-}1} = (H_S^* / H_{S\text{-}1})^{\lambda} \qquad \text{(8-4)}$$

In each year, price clears the market

$$H_S = H_D \qquad \text{(8-5)}$$

The complete notation is:
Endogenous variables
h_D = housing demand per urban household
H_D = total demand for urban housing
P = urban housing price per dwelling
H_S^* = equilibrium urban housing stock supply
H_S = actual urban housing stock
Exogenous variables
y = real income per urban household
N = number of urban households
w = construction cost, a weighted average of real wage rates
  and real materials prices
Predetermined variables
$H_{S\text{-}1}$ = lagged urban housing stock
Parameters
A = scale parameter in demand equation
α_1 = price elasticity of housing demand
α_2 = income elasticity of housing demand
B = scale parameter in supply equation
β_1 = price elasticity of supply

β_2 = supply elasticity with respect to construction cost

λ = percent of housing stock disequilibrium adjusted in one year

Equation 8-1 shows how housing demand per urban household depends on housing price and on income. Equation 8-2 indicates that total urban housing demand is demand per household multiplied by the number of urban households. Equation 8-3 shows how the equilibrium housing stock depends on housing price and on construction cost. Equation 8-4 says that the urban housing stock adjusts by 100λ percent per 1 percent by which the stock is out of equilibrium. Equation 8-5 says that, each year, price adjusts to equate demand to the actual housing stock.

H_S^* in (8-3) is unknown since there are no observations on the equilibrium housing stock. If we substitute the right side of (8-3) for H_S^* in (8-4) and the right side of (8-1) for h_D in (8-2), and take natural logarithms of all variables, the result is:

$$lnH_D = lnA + \alpha_1 lnp + \alpha_2 lny + lnN \qquad (8\text{-}6)$$

and

$$lnH_S = \lambda lnB + \lambda\beta_1 lnp + \lambda\beta_2 lnw + (1-\lambda)lnH_{S\text{-}1} \qquad (8\text{-}7)$$

The fact that H_D and H_S are equal, from (8-5), implies that (8-6) and (8-7) are two simultaneous equations in the two endogenous variables lnH_S and lnp, and in all the exogenous and predetermined variables in the model. Equations 8-6 and 8-7 were estimated by two stage least squares from the data in appendix Table A-8-2. There are only 14 annual observations, covering the years 1962 to 1975, so great accuracy of estimated coefficients cannot be expected.

The estimated equations are:

$$ln\,H_D = 5.375 - 0.134\,lnp + 0.027\,ln\,y + 1.157\,lnN$$
$$ (1.504)(-0.240) \quad\ (0.046) \quad\ (5.87)$$
$$R^2 = 0.969 \qquad\qquad\qquad\qquad\qquad (8\text{-}8)$$

and

$$\ln H_S = 3.959 + 0.283 \ln p - 0.377 \ln w + 0.755 \ln H_{S-1}$$
$$(0.447)\ (0.860)\quad -(0.352)\qquad (1.929)$$
$$R^2 = 0.955 \tag{8-9}$$

All estimated coefficients have the signs indicated by economic theory and common sense. The demand equation, (8-8), indicates that urban housing demand increases with income and urban population and decreases as housing price increases. The supply equation, (8-9), indicates that housing supply increases with housing price and with lagged supply, and decreases as construction cost increases.

The price and income elasticities of demand in (8-8) are surprisingly small. Few studies have found these elasticities to be less than 0.5 in other countries. The small number of degrees of freedom available means that the estimated coefficients are not particularly reliable, and the true elasticities may be substantially larger. In addition, government constraints on housing supply are likely to cause downward bias to the estimate of income elasticity of demand. According to (8-6), the coefficient of $\ln N$ in (8-8) should be about +1. The estimated coefficient differs from +1 by less than one standard deviation.

The supply elasticities in (8-7) can be calculated from (8-9). The coefficient of $\ln H_{S-1}$ is $(1-\lambda)$, so the estimate of λ is 0.245. Then the price and construction cost elasticities of supply are the coefficients in (8-9) divided by λ. The complete set of estimates is

$$\lambda = 0.245$$
$$\beta_1 = 1.155$$
$$\beta_2 = -1.539$$

The estimated value of λ implies that supply adjustments eliminate about 25 percent of housing disequilibrium each year. This is a plausible estimate. It is also plausible that the housing supply adjustment coefficient should be larger than the adjustment coefficient in the density gradient, Equation 6-5 in Chapter 6. The housing stock can be adjusted by building, demolishing, or altering relatively few structures, whereas adjusting the density gradient requires alteration of most structures in the urban area.

The estimate of 1.155 for β_1, the price elasticity of housing supply, indicates that housing supply is quite responsive to housing price, much more responsive than one would conclude if one looked merely at the coefficient of lnp in (8-9). The coefficient of lnp in (8-9) is much smaller than the supply elasticity because of the effect of λ.

The estimate of –1.539 for β_2 indicates that housing supply is also quite responsive to housing construction cost. Table A-8-2 indicates an erratic but substantial decline in the real value of the housing construction cost index from 1960 to 1975. That seems surprising at first, in view of the rapid rise of housing prices. But the appendix data are in real terms; that is, they record construction costs relative to the overall price level. The decline in the index undoubtedly results from the use of better tools, more highly skilled and experienced labor, more machinery, and better designs in construction. The downward trend will probably continue as construction techniques continue to improve.

In the 1970s, urban housing demand has risen greatly. The urban population has grown an average of 6 percent per year; real income per capita has increased 6.9 percent per year; and the relative price of housing has fallen 3.4 percent per year. These trends imply that the stock of housing has fallen below its equilibrium level. In the model, the equilibrium housing stock is the level to which the stock would tend if the exogenous variables remained unchanged for an indefinite time. The equilibrium stock can be calculated by putting $H_S = H_{S-1}$ in (8-9) and solving (8-8) and (8-9) simultaneously for H_S and p. Performing this calculation for 1975 values of the exogenous variables indicates that the 1975 equilibrium housing stock was about 6 percent greater than the actual stock. This means that, if urban population, real income, and construction cost remained at their 1975 levels, the urban housing stock would eventually settle at a level 6 percent greater than its 1975 level. Most of the 6-percent growth would take place during the first few years after the adjustment started.

It may be wondered why we have not included land values in our construction cost index, w, which appears in the supply equation, (8-3), even though land costs are about half of housing cost in Korea. The reason is that land costs are unlikely to have an independent influence on housing prices. Land supply in and near urban areas is fixed. In addition, most rural land converted to urban uses is for housing. As an urban area expands, it drives up the price of the fixed land supply. But the increased housing demand is the cause of rising land prices. It is not that rising land prices deter construction. If housing demand had risen less, land prices would have risen less. If land supply is completely inelastic, land price is entirely determined by housing demand, not vice versa. The only way rising land prices could deter housing construction would be if the cause were an increase in demand for non-housing uses of land. For example, an increase in agricultural demand would raise land prices to the housing sector and deter construction. But the evidence analyzed in Chapter 7 suggests that it is urban growth that has driven up urban land values, not the growth of non-urban demand for land. Our view is supported by the very large R^2's in our regression equations, (8-8) and (8-9), which do not include land prices as explanatory variables. These remarks about relationships between land values and housing demand are unaffected by the fact, recognized in Chapter 7, that land values are in part speculations about future land productivity. Such speculations are themselves a function of the trend of land values, not an exogenous influence on land values.

In concluding this section, we must emphasize the tentative nature of our findings. We believe our procedure is sound. But much more research is needed to produce a model of housing in which great faith is justified. The demand equation needs to be improved by inclusion of other prices, for example, of food, by inclusion of variables that represent the size and quality of dwellings as well as the number, and in other ways. The supply and demand equations need variables to represent financial conditions. Above all, more observations are needed, presumably by formulating the model so that individual urban areas can be used as sample observations. Several alternative specifications to (8-6) and (8-7) were estimated. In particular, the model was estimated in first differences, but the result was not more satisfactory in any way.

HOUSING FINANCE

Demand studies, including the one reported in the previous section, show that the fraction of income spent on housing declines as income rises. In very poor countries, food takes more than half of income and housing most of the remainder. In very rich countries, food takes less than 20 percent of income and housing between 10 and 15 percent. Consumer durables and services take increasing proportions of income as income rises.

In Korea, the percentage of income spent on food has fallen substantially during the recent period of very rapid economic growth. The percentage of income spent on housing, however, seems to have risen between the early 1960s and the early 1970s. At least that is the conclusion of students of Korean housing problems. Our doubts on the subject stem from the fact that our data employed in the last section show a declining relative price of housing since 1972, and an inelastic demand with respect to both price and income. These facts imply a decreasing share of income going to housing. Only housing expenditure studies that account for capital gains in housing can settle the matter.

Estimating housing expenditure is not a simple matter, mainly because rents include varying costs of household operation and because the opportunity cost of foregone return on the owner-occupier's equity must be imputed. In Korea, estimation is made even more difficult by the tradition of *chŏnse*, a deposit frequently made by the renter to the landlord at the beginning of his tenure and returned at the end of his tenure. A substantial part of Korean housing expenditure is imputed interest on *chŏnse*. The most careful estimate of housing expenditures as a percentage of income, for various income classes, has been made by Song and Struyk, and is presented in Table 32. According to this estimate, the average Seoul resident spent 19.4 percent of his income on housing in 1974. The percentage decreases as income rises, from 29.8 percent in the lowest income group to 15.7 percent in the highest group. According to the data in Table 32, owner-occupiers spend a larger percentage of income on housing than renters in the high-income groups, but a somewhat smaller percentage in the low-income groups. The authors conjecture that the estimates are too low, especially for owner-occupiers, because of omission of utilities, taxes, and repairs. In addition, costs for owner-occupiers are overstated because of the omission of capital gains, which were shown in Chapter 7 to be large. Many urban dwellings appreciate 15 or 20 percent per year in Korea, which is comparable to total costs of ownership shown in Table 32. Such rapid appreciation makes housing virtually costless for owner-occupiers.

Renters normally finance housing by periodic payments from current income. Those who purchase homes for owner-occupancy must pay the full price of the home at time of purchase. In many countries, mortgages permit people to purchase homes with small initial assets and to pay for the home over many years. Basically, a mortgage market enables those with capital to lend it to people who wish to buy homes with little capital. In practice, those with assets tend to be owner-occupiers. But in principle there is no necessary connection between dwelling tenure and asset position. Those without assets may be able to borrow enough to become owner-occupiers. And those with assets may choose to invest them in assets other than owner-occupied homes and be renters. The latter situation

TABLE 32 Housing Expenditures as a Percentage of Income for Seoul Households, 1974

| Monthly Income | Owner-Occupant Households | Renting Households | | | All Households |
		Chŏnse Only	Chŏnse and Monthly Payment	All Rental Units Combined	
All Income Classes	21.1	15.9	18.0	16.6	19.4
Under 28,000 wŏn	29.1	27.1	36.2	30.4	29.8
28,000 – 35,999 wŏn	20.8	20.8	30.0	22.6	21.7
36,000 – 51,999 wŏn	23.2	16.4	20.2	17.3	20.6
Over 52,000 wŏn	16.6	13.9	10.9	13.6	15.7

Source: Byung-Nak Song and Raymond J. Struyk, "Korean Housing," p. 5.

is institutionalized in the form of *chŏnse* in Korea. *Chŏnse* means that the tenant deposits money with the landlord, the income from which pays all or part of the rent. The principle is returned to the tenant at the end of his tenancy, but he accumulates no equity. *Chŏnse* is a form of rental rather than ownership with a perpetual mortgage because the landlord retains the benefits and risks of ownership.

In a society with a rich set of financial institutions, people might in principle be indifferent to investing their assets in their housing or in other ways. In practice, home ownership is the main form of asset accumulation for people of modest means in many countries. One reason is that there are income tax advantages to owner-occupancy in some countries. A second reason is that owner-occupiers receive the returns from maintenance and improvements in their homes and are therefore motivated to invest their labor and money in these ways. There is evidence that owner-occupiers take better care of their homes than renters. A third reason is that, in countries with at least some inflation of house prices, investment in owner-occupied homes is the best investment available to people with only modest assets. In such countries, homes are excellent collateral, and mortgage rates are much lower than other borrowing rates. The inflation of house prices provides a substantial return on the owner-occupier's equity, whereas other high-return investments are unavailable to those with modest assets.

The last two of the above reasons for owner-occupancy must apply with special force in Korea. The data in Chapter 7 on land appreciation suggest strongly that housing must have been one of the best investments in Korea during the 1960s and 1970s. In addition, real incomes and assets have risen rapidly, so people have both funds and incentives to invest in owner-occupied housing. Yet the share of owner-occupied housing has fallen, especially in urban areas.

One reason for this anomalous situation undoubtedly is that the national government has taken steps to channel funds into industrial investments and away from housing investments, because of the urgent need to industrialize the Korean economy. The mechanisms have been for the government to allocate little money for housing through the Korea Housing Bank and, probably more important, to control interest rates for housing at artificially low levels. The result has been that the main institutional source of borrowed funds for housing has been the informal or "curb" market. Since this market is partly illegal, investments are risky and interest rates are extremely high, often about 3 percent per month. Moreover, the curb market is a source only of short-term funds.

The effect of this situation can be seen in Table 33, showing data from a recent survey of sources of funds for home purchases. Of the purchases surveyed, less than 12 percent of the houses' cost was financed by loans. Less than 5 percent was financed by loans from lending institutions, almost all the remainder of the loans coming from employers and the curb markets. It is also interesting to observe that loans are a smaller proportion of purchase costs in large cities than in small.

ILLEGAL HOUSING

In most poor and rapidly urbanizing countries, groups of poor people settle illegally on urban land and take up residence there. Frequently referred to as squatters, they mostly settle on public land, but sometimes also on private land. Often they settle on river banks or flood plains, but they also settle in parks and other open spaces. They build more or less permanent and substantial dwellings, depending on the resources and materials at hand and on the prospect of being tolerated by the authorities.

Little is known about these illegal residents, or squatters, in many countries. Many, but by no means all, squatters are recent migrants to cities from the countryside. Some are long-term urban residents who have been unable to increase their incomes enough to afford conventional housing. When tolerated by the authorities, some are long-term urban residents whose incomes

TABLE 33 Sources of Finance for Home Purchase, 1974
(%)

	Large Cities	Other Cities	All Cities
Personal Sources	92.1	84.4	88.4
Savings	46.1	37.4	42.0
Liquidation of other assets	24.1	16.9	20.7
Security[a]	11.6	18.0	14.6
Others[b]	10.3	12.1	11.1
Loans	7.9	15.6	11.6
Private loan	4.1	8.2	6.1
Employer	0.1	1.2	0.6
Bank & Similar Institutions	3.3	5.5	4.4
Others	0.4	0.7	0.5

Source: Korea Industrial Development Research Institute, *Study on Housing Policy Formulation*, 1974, p. 8.

Notes: Sample survey only for those who purchased the house in recent 5 years.
[a]Deposit money for rented housing.
[b]Others include donation, retirement allowance, and other sources.

have risen gradually but who have remained in their illegal housing, gradually improving it, because it provides inexpensive housing in familiar surroundings.

Whether poor or not, squatters almost never have housing that is considered adequate. It is almost always extremely small and crowded and provides inadequate protection against cold and precipitation. It usually lacks adequate water supply and waste disposal. Much squatter housing is marked by hazards from fire, injury, and sickness.

Korea has long had an illegal housing sector. During the prosperous 1970s, the number of illegal houses seems to have decreased. A government estimate[3] is that there were 218,000 illegal households in 1973. Not all these households are squatters; some hold title to the land, but live in houses that do not meet standards. More than 70 percent of the illegal households were in Seoul; 22 percent were in Pusan, Taegu, and Inch'ŏn; the remainder were in other cities. The same source estimates that there had been 31,000 more illegal households in 1972 than in 1973. The 218,000 illegal households represent about 4 percent of the country's population and about 8 percent of the urban population.

Seoul's squatters are mostly on river banks or on high hills where water supply is inadequate. They appear to be unusually varied in socio-economic composition. Some live in permanent housing, having long been tolerated by government; others live in shacks made from scrap materials. Although many are recent migrants, surprising numbers have been in Seoul for many years, having been unable to increase their incomes, having fallen on hard times, or merely choosing to remain in illegal housing in order to spend their incomes on other things.

Squatters represent serious problems for governments. Squatter settlements are illegal, unhealthy, dangerous, ugly, and sometimes they occupy land needed for other high-priority public purposes. Government policies toward squatters can be classified into three categories, all of which have been tried in Korea.

First, governments may remove squatters, using bulldozers, wrecking crews, and policemen. This policy obviously worsens squatters' problems. It destroys their abodes and only assets, and forces them into worse accommodations. Frequently, they squat elsewhere, or in the same places after an interval. The only thing to be said for a policy of vigorous removal is that it is a deterrent to those contemplating this form of illegal behavior.

Second, governments frequently try to relocate squatters, usually in public housing built for the purpose. Building new housing and subsidizing it enough so that very poor people can afford to live in it is very expensive, and governments in poor countries can afford to do it for only a few people. Furthermore, in Korea and elsewhere, the housing is often in places and of kinds that do not meet the needs of the very poor. Transportation may be expensive or inadequate to get them to places of work. Finally new and highly subsidized housing for squatters is seen by others as a reward for illegal behavior. Low-income people living in legal housing resent the fact that squatters end up with more satisfactory housing than theirs. They and others may thereby be motivated to become squatters.

Third, squatter settlements may be legalized. The Korean government has recently begun to try this approach in a carefully controlled way. Squatters are permitted to buy their land, usually on favorable payment terms, if the lot and house meet minimum standards and if residents collectively provide roads and other facilities, usually with government help. This policy builds on the ingenuity and resourcefulness of squatters, motivating them to improve their housing by enabling them to gain title to the fruits of their labor. Legalization programs have two dangers. If financial terms or lot, building, and infrastructure standards are too high, squatters cannot meet them on their meager incomes. Alternatively, if standards are too low, the health and other hazards of squatter settlements are not removed. Also, financial terms that are too favorable become rewards for illegal behavior. This is unfair to those who have struggled to maintain legal housing on equally meager incomes. A proposal designed to cope with these dangers has been put forward by Song and Struyk[4].

Legalization proposals are self-defeating unless accompanied by rigorous action against those who continue to squat illegally. Many people will not make the great effort required to take part in legalization programs if illegal land continues to be available free.

Ideally, the solution to the squatter problem is an adequate welfare program. If Korea had an adequate negative-income-tax program or some other program to transfer purchasing power to the needy, the case for special assistance to squatters would be greatly weakened. Economists mostly favor assistance to the poor by providing them purchasing power instead of providing or subsidizing particular goods and services. This permits the poor to use their incomes to purchase whatever best meets their particular needs, just as others do. As a matter of social policy, it is better to provide assistance on the basis of need than to help particular groups of poor such as squatters. Any program of assistance to squatters carries the implications of rewarding illegal behavior in comparisons with groups of equally needy, but law-abiding citizens.

An adequate welfare program must be a long-term solution to the squatter problem. In the meantime, controlled legalization programs appear to provide the best hope of solving this serious social problem.

URBAN LAND DEVELOPMENT POLICIES

As urban areas grow and decentralize, land must be converted from rural to urban uses. It is inevitable that governments become involved in this process because of the need to provide infrastructure in the form of roads, schools, sanitary facilities, and so on. In fact, governments frequently become deeply involved in deciding what land is to be converted, when, and to exactly what set of urban uses.

In Korea, the main government program for rural-urban land conversion is the Land Readjustment Project. Under this program, undeveloped sites near the urban fringe are designated as development sites. Development sites may be chosen by an 80-percent vote of the landowners, but mostly they are designated by a city government or by the national government or Korea Housing Corporation. Once a site is designated, a development plan is prepared. The essence of the Land Readjustment Project is that public sector infrastructure costs are financed by a tax under which part of the land on the site is paid to the government. The land so seized consists of two parts: one part on which infrastructure is built and a second part taken by government and later resold to private developers. The revenues received are intended to cover the cost of building the infrastructure. Usually, about half the land on a site is taken by government for the two purposes.

The Land Readjustment Project has been used extensively in the period of rapid urbanization. The best study of the program[5] reports that more than one-quarter of Seoul has been developed under this program. The program is made viable by the fact that inclusion in a project causes land values to rise substantially. Thus, the 50 percent of their land left to landowners is worth considerably more after completion of infrastructure than the 100 percent of their land before designation as a development site.

The basic attraction of the program is that it imposes on landowners the cost of the infrastructure needed if their land is to be urbanized in satisfactory fashion. This solves a problem common in urbanizing countries of imputing to urban residents infrastructure costs incurred on their behalf. This means, for example, that it is not necessary to tax old urban residents to pay for the infrastructure needed by newcomers, a common source of serious conflict in many countries.

Serious analysis of the program must take account of the fact that it provides two things: a method of financing infrastructure and permission to develop land. In Korea, for the most part, it is not legal to develop land for urban uses without being included in a Land Readjustment Project. Thus, one reason that inclusion in a project raises land values is that infrastructure is supplied, but another reason is that development permission is itself scarce and therefore valuable.

William A. Doebele in his World Bank draft report is concerned that land in readjustment projects becomes so valuable that low-income housing cannot be built on it. He proposes increasing the tax to more than 50 percent of the land in the project so that the extra land tax can be used to finance low-income housing there or elsewhere. But, if land values rise by more than the value of the infrastructure, it is because development land is kept scarce by permitting too few projects. The way to keep urban land values down is to increase the supply of urban land, that is, to approve more projects. In fact that is the best thing that government could do for low-income urban residents. It is simply not viable to build new housing for very-low-income people. If the supply of readjustment projects were increased, low-income residents would be helped two ways. First, land values would rise less rapidly. Second, the supply of housing would increase more rapidly, thus increasing the speed with which decent housing would filter down to low-income residents, as middle-income residents move to better housing.

CONCLUSIONS

Korea started the period of modernization after 1953 with a terrible legacy of inadequate housing. In Korea, as in Japan a few years earlier, it was decided as a matter of national policy to place primary emphasis on industrialization and secondary emphasis on improvement and expansion of the housing stock. Industrialization and related forces brought rapid urbanization. The result was a relatively under-utilized rural housing stock and a crowded, expensive, and inadequate urban housing stock. By the mid-1970s, somewhat more emphasis was being placed on housing, and the stock was improving.

Real construction costs have fallen during the late 1960s and early 1970s as the construction industry has become more productive. But urbanization and rising incomes have forced land values up in urban areas, and housing takes a large fraction of the incomes of poor urban residents. Nevertheless, housing quality for squatters and other low-income urban residents has improved during the first half of the 1970s.

The national government exercises severe control over conversion of land from rural to urban uses near large cities. The fiscal profitability of Land Readjustment Projects shows that developable land is kept scarce, and therefore expensive, by government controls. The most important single step the government could take to improve urban housing would be to relax controls on land-use conversion. The next most important step would be to facilitate the entry of mortgage money into urban housing investment.

NINE

Urban Transportation

As Chapter 1 noted, the economic function of an urban area is to provide proximate locations for large numbers of people and businesses. Thus, economic activities can take place at efficient scales and can locate close to workers, customers, and suppliers. The urban transportation system moves people and goods among the highly interconnected activities in an urban area. In almost all countries, urban transportation is a complex interaction between government and private decisions. Government must build and maintain road systems; it must build and operate, or closely regulate, subway, bus, and other public transit modes. But private decisions determine whether cars, trucks, motorcycles, or bicycles are used on the roads and whether public transit is patronized.

Choices of transportation systems are among the most important that governments make in influencing urban development.

Large sums of money are invested in building and operating road, bus, and subway systems. And the wisdom with which choices are made greatly affects the efficiency of the entire urban system. Basic urban transportation decisions are almost always controversial because measurement of benefits and costs is difficult. If the government builds a subway system, some of the benefits accrue to its passengers; it is difficult to measure the benefits they receive from the system. But some of the benefits accrue to non-users who travel on less congested roads than if the subway system had not been built; their benefits are even harder to measure. In addition, governments sometimes observe that people refrain from using a public transit system even though it appears that they would benefit from doing so.

Most discussions of urban transportation concentrate unduly on the trip to work. Although commuting is the single most important kind of trip, it is a minority of all urban travel. Furthermore, goods movement is an important part of urban transportation. Although people can be moved by subway or by public or private modes on streets, goods can be moved only on trucks, carts, and people's backs on streets. Thus, there are more options for the movement of people than of goods, and data are more plentiful on movement of people than of goods.

In most countries, controversy regarding urban transportation centers on a small set of issues. What kinds and amounts of public transit should be provided and on what terms should it be used? And to what extent should people be permitted or encouraged to use cars in large urban areas?

THE PATTERN OF KOREAN
URBAN TRANSPORTATION

Most available urban transportation data refer to movement of people in Seoul and Pusan. This is unfortunate, because transportation problems are somewhat different in small cities from those in the large cities. Seoul and Pusan have, and can justify, elaborate public transit systems. Small cities may have only rudimentary systems, and it is unclear what systems can be justified. Nevertheless, we must restrict our attention to the large cities.

Table 34 compares commuting modes in the two largest Korean cities with those in Japanese cities and U.S. metropolitan areas. The table shows that, whereas U.S. metropolitan

TABLE 34 Commuting Modes in Korean and Japanese Cities and in U.S. Metropolitan Areas

| Mode | Percent Distribution | | | |
| | Seoul | Pusan | Japanese Cities | U.S. Metropolitan Areas |
	(1973)	(1973)	(1970)	(1970)
Car	6.0	9.3	14.5	78.3
Train, Bus, Streetcar	59.7	62.0	46.0	12.1
Walking	33.7	27.8	23.4	6.4
Other	0.5	1.0	16.1	3.2
Total	100.0	100.0	100.0	100.0

Sources: Korean data are from Han'guk Kwahak Kisul Yŏn'guso, *Sŏul [Seoul] T'ŭkpyŏlsi t'onghaeng silt'ae chosa,* 1974, and "Pusan-si kyot'ong kibon kyehoek," 1974; Japanese and U.S. data are from Mills and Ohta.

commuting is automobile-based, Korean urban commuting, even more than Japanese, relies on public transit. Furthermore, nearly all Korean urban public transportation is by bus, whereas most Japanese urban public transit passengers go by train and subway. Cars are of minor importance in Korean urban commuting. It is also of note that fully one-third of the workers in Seoul and more than one-fourth of those in Pusan walk to work.

Table 35 shows modal choice data in detail for all trips in Seoul in 1973. Of all trips, 56.8 percent were by bus and 33.7 percent were by foot. Thus, 90 percent of all trips were by bus or foot and fully 85.7 percent of all vehicular trips were by bus. Seoul does indeed have a bus-based transportation system! Although more than half the trips are by bus for almost all

TABLE 35 Purpose of Trips by Transportation Modes, Seoul, 1973
(%)

Purposes	Modes						
	Commercial Bus	Commercial Taxi	Private Autos	Train	Walk	Other	Total
School	49.2	0.2	0.8	0.3	48.2	1.3	100.0
Work	64.3	4.9	4.7	0.5	19.3	6.4	100.0
Shopping	55.4	4.6	1.1	0.3	34.9	3.6	100.0
Business	52.5	14.9	11.2	0.5	15.7	5.2	100.0
Recreation	69.1	8.4	3.3	0.4	18.4	0.5	100.0
Home	57.4	2.3	2.2	0.4	34.7	3.0	100.0
Travel	53.2	18.9	3.5	12.6	11.9	0.0	100.0
Other	60.0	9.5	4.2	0.5	23.2	2.5	100.0
Average	56.8	3.0	2.8	0.4	33.7	3.3	100.0

Source: Han'guk Kwahak Kisul Yŏn'guso, Sŏul [Seoul] T'ŭkpyŏlsi t'onghaeng silt'ae chosa, 1974.

purposes, buses are even more important for work trips than for others. Perhaps most surprising, buses are most predominant in recreational trips, 69.1 percent of such trips being by bus. Only travel (presumably out-of-town trips) and business trips are less than 80 percent by bus and walking. Buses account for nearly 86 percent of all vehicular trips, and for less than 80 percent only for business and travel trips.

Table 36 shows the phenomenal growth of public transit in Korea's two largest cities from 1955 to 1974. During the 20-year period, total public transit trips increased by an average compound rate of 11.1 percent per year in Seoul and 10.3 percent in Pusan. Streetcars were phased out in both cities by 1970. Taxis show the highest growth rate during the two decades in both cities, but their share of total trips has stabilized or fallen since 1970 in both. Bus travel grew by an average of more than 13 percent per year in both cities, having reached more than 12 times its 1955 level by 1974. Furthermore, the growth of bus travel has shown no sign of slackening in recent years.

Bus companies are numerous and privately owned in Seoul. Fares are regulated and companies buy and sell franchises to operate particular routes. Bus companies are not subsidized, and their diesel fuel is taxed at only 40 percent and sells at less than 0.60 dollars per U.S. gallon (in contrast with gasoline which is subject to a 300-percent tax and sells at between 1.60 and 1.90 dollars per U.S. gallon, about the same price as in Japan and Western Europe). Relatively free entry is permitted to bus companies, and many competing companies operate in large cities.

Seoul's first subway line started operation in mid-1974. It consists of 9.5 kilometers of double track running from the main Seoul railroad station northeast to Ch'ŏngnyang-ni. Data are not yet available in the mid-1970s that would permit operating comparisons with other transportation modes. In late 1974, the subway carried about 170,000 passengers per day, about 2.5 percent of all person-trips in Seoul. Fares cover about 74 percent

TABLE 36 Trends and Shares of Transportation
Modes in Seoul and Pusan, 1955–1974

City	Year	Bus	Taxi	Streetcar	Total
Seoul	1955	100(53)	100(4)	100(43)	100(100)
	1960	192(65)	149(4)	113(31)	156(100)
	1965	381(70)	460(6)	154(24)	286(100)
	1967	486(73)	790(9)	151(18)	353(100)
	1970	859(81)	2,629(19)	-(-)	557(100)
	1973	1,124(77)	4,510(23)	-(-)	771(100)
	1974	1,289(82)	3,748(18)	-(-)	828(100)
Pusan	1955	100(48)	100(5)	100(47)	100(100)
	1960	192(54)	477(14)	112(32)	168(100)
	1965	381(56)	1,477(23)	152(21)	328(100)
	1967	486(54)	2,537(29)	150(17)	431(100)
	1970	747(67)	3,493(33)	-(-)	531(100)
	1973	1,104(76)	3,287(24)	-(-)	691(100)
	1974	1,203(80)	2,932(20)	-(-)	720(100)

Source: Ministry of Transportation, *Statistics Yearbook of Transportation, 1963, 1968, 1974.*

Notes: 1955 is the base year. 1955 = 100 for each mode.
Figures in parentheses indicate modal share.

of operating costs, but none of capital cost. The deficit is made up by general funds from the national government. The government intends to extend the subway systems to 113.4 kilometers in the 1980s.[1] At that time the subway will be a major component of Seoul's transportation system.

Table 37 shows data on motor vehicle ownership in several developed and developing countries.[2] In the United States there are more than 50 vehicles per 100 people, whereas in Japan and Western Europe the number varies between 20 and 30 per hundred. The Korean figure of 0.5 vehicles per 100 people is small, not only relative to the developed world, but also relative

TABLE 37 International Comparisons of Road Transportation, 1972

	Vehicle Ownership (1,000s)	Vehicles per 100 population	Vehicles per Sq. Km. of Land	Vehicles per Km. of Road Length
U. S. A.	109,300	52.8	11.7	1.82
Japan	20,430	19.5	55.2	19.72
U. K.	13,790	24.8	60.0	4.09
West Germany	16,820	28.4	67.6	4.03
France	15,020	29.3	27.3	1.90
Italy	12,340	22.8	41.0	4.30
Taiwan[a]	1,365	8.8	37.9	85.89
Korea[a]	171	0.5	1.7	3.92

Sources: Taiwan: Republic of China/Economic Planning Council, *Taiwan Statistical Data Book, 1974*. Korea: Sŏul [Seoul] T'ŭkpyŏlsi, *Sŏul [Seoul] t'onggye yŏnbo, 1974*. Other Countries: Mills and Ohta.

Note: [a]Data refer to 1973.

to such developing countries as Taiwan and the Philippines. Korea also has few vehicles relative to its road length and road area compared with other countries. But the number of motor vehicles is increasing much more rapidly in Korea than in most countries. Vehicle ownership grew about 15 percent per year from 1963 to 1974.

Growth is not unduly concentrated in Seoul, where concern with congestion is focused. Table 38 presents data on motor vehicle registration in Seoul from 1968 to 1974. Although the growth during the 6-year period was 13.8 percent per year, close to the national average, much of the growth was during the early years covered by the table. Furthermore, truck registration grew most rapidly during the period, followed by cars and then buses. Automobile registrations, many of them taxis, are increasing rapidly in Seoul, but the data do not suggest that automobile congestion will become a serious problem during the next few years. That will happen only if large numbers of people want to commute by private car instead of by bus or subway; there is as yet no evidence of this.

Many vehicles used in Korea are imported. Domestic production has grown rapidly from about 1,000 vehicles in 1964 to about 44,000 vehicles in 1974. Most recent growth in production has been concentrated in trucks and private automobiles. Few private cars were being imported by the mid-1970s. Bus production has not increased rapidly during the 1970s because many buses for expressway use have been imported.

THE OUTLOOK
FOR URBAN TRANSPORTATION

Our judgment is that it was good urban planning to rely on the development of a large bus system as the backbone of the transportation system in Korea's large cities during the post-Korean War period. Large cities need a high quality system of paved roads for trucks, taxis, and automobiles. Given that, it is not much more expensive to construct the road system so that it can move large numbers of people by bus. It is economical to use a transportation mode that can share the right-of-way with other modes. Bus systems are inexpensive, in that capital costs for the vehicles and for required additional investment in roads are not large. Fuel and personnel operating costs are also small.

TABLE 38 Number of Motor Vehicles Registered, Seoul, 1968–1974

	Total		Car		Bus		Truck		Others	
	Number	Annual Rate of Increase	Number	Annual Rate of Increase	Number	Annual Rate of Increase	Number	Annual Rate of Increase	Number	Annual Rate of Increase
1968	35,135		19,938		3,809		11,388			
1969	49,628	41.3	29,111	46.0	4,475	17.5	14,333	25.9	1,709	
1970	60,442	21.8	34,870	19.8	4,805	7.4	19,325	34.8	1,442	-15.6
1971	67,275	11.3	39,054	12.0	5,518	14.8	20,923	8.3	1,780	23.4
1972	68,492	1.8	40,573	3.9	5,546	0.5	20,463	-2.2	1,910	7.3
1973	76,303	11.4	45,331	11.7	5,957	7.4	22,922	12.0	2,093	9.6
1974	80,248	5.2	44,768	-1.2	6,315	6.0	26,854	17.2	2,311	10.4

Source: Sŏul [Seoul] T'ŭkpyŏlsi, Sŏul [Seoul] t'onggye yŏnbo, 1975.

Subways, by contrast, require an expensive separate right-of-way and expensive vehicles. Buses have the added great advantage that vehicles can be shifted quickly and cheaply from one route to another as the city grows, as traffic patterns change, and as modal shifts occur. Buses can carry many times the passengers per lane of roadway as cars.

But bus-based urban transportation systems are likely to become inadequate for a combination of three reasons.

First, roads may become so congested with buses and other vehicles that travel becomes intolerably slow. In the absence of large numbers of cars on the roads, this is almost impossible in U.S. metropolitan areas, because roads occupy about 20 or 25 percent of the land area. Road space is thus adequate for almost any conceivable amount of non-automobile traffic. But congestion has developed in large Japanese cities where roads are less than 10 percent of the land area. In Seoul and Pusan, roads are also less than 10 percent of the land area, and less than half the road surface is paved. It would not require a great increase in the numbers of buses, autos, and trucks on Seoul's roads to make much bus travel very slow indeed.

Second, as a metropolitan area becomes very large, buses simply cannot compete with subways and trains in travel speed, at least for long commuting trips. In Tokyo, many people commute to the central business district from suburbs 40 to 60 kilometers away. At these distances, fixed rail systems become advantageous because the time lost in suburban collection can be made up by the time saved on the main line haul.

Third, if residential densities are low, jobs are dispersed, and incomes are high, buses may not be able to compete with private autos as commuting modes. This is the United States pattern. A combination of plentiful land, high incomes, cheap cars, and cheap fuel has created very-low-density residential areas, as shown in Chapter 6. This means that buses must collect passengers over large residential areas to obtain an economical load. Many stops and much travel not in the direction of the destination are needed. In addition, many of the same reasons have increasingly caused jobs to be dispersed around the metropolitan area instead of being concentrated in the central business district. Thus, additional time is lost in distributing people to dispersed job sites. These facts provide great advantages to automobiles, which are self-scheduled and go directly from origin to destination. High incomes have also placed a premium on fast travel. Finally, autos and fuel have been cheap in the United States. The result has been substantial replacement of bus travel by autos since World War II in U.S. metropolitan areas.

It appears that only the first two reasons above are likely to be relevant in Korea during the remainder of this century. In Chapter 6, we concluded that Korean cities are likely to continue to disperse, but high land values will continue to cause densities to be high relative to those in U.S. urban areas. Even at very high income levels, it is inconceivable that Korean residential densities would be even close to the low levels typical in U.S. metropolitan areas. Thus, we do not believe that the feasibility of bus-based urban transportation will be jeopardized by very-low-density residential areas in Korea.

The first of the above three reasons will certainly become important during coming decades. As Seoul and Pusan continue to grow, employment will increase near city centers, and the numbers of buses, trucks, and cars on the roads will continue to increase. To avoid serious congestion, it will be necessary to extend, pave, and otherwise improve the road system.

The second reason will also become important. A rail-based transportation network, underground near the center and at ground level on the outskirts, is justified in a very large and high-density metropolitan area unless incomes are very low. Seoul is at about the size and structure at which a subway system becomes justified, and it has probably been a wise decision to begin construction. It also seems likely that a more extensive system will be justified during the next decade or two. The subway system will curtail the need for a bus system, but will not eliminate it. A substantial bus system will be needed to provide service on routes not served by the subway system and to provide feeder services to subway stops. Thus, we foresee a gradual shift of emphasis from buses to subways. It should be added that justification of an expanded subway system depends crucially on the continued growth of the Seoul metropolitan area. We believe that Seoul should continue to grow, but the justification for a large subway system would be greatly reduced if the government were to decide firmly to stop further growth in the Seoul region.

Other metropolitan areas will be able to justify subway systems in future years as they approach the size and income level of Seoul. Given the stability in the rank order of Korean city populations that was found in Chapter 4, Pusan will undoubtedly be the next metropolitan area to reach the size at which a subway system is justified. Without careful study of the cities involved, it is not possible to say when subway systems will be justified in Pusan and other cities.

As for the likely future role of the automobile in Korean cities, experience in the United States, Europe, Japan, and elsewhere has shown that people place great value on auto travel as incomes rise. In Japan, for example, auto use has risen rapidly despite high purchase prices, high registration costs, high fuel costs, congested roads, and inadequate storage space. People make modal choices carefully because much time and money are involved. People tend to use cars only if they are the most satisfactory form of transportation available. In Japan, people tend not to use autos for commuting when satisfactory public transit is available. Cars are used for commuting in small towns where public transit is inadequate, by those who live and work in metropolitan suburbs where public transit is unavailable, and by those who must use cars to get to suburban transit stops. Otherwise, cars are used for shopping, business, and recreational trips.

We do not believe that Korean cities are imminently threatened with a surge of auto use. But as incomes rise during the remainder of the century, increasing numbers of people will want to own cars. There is no reason not to accommodate the growth of auto demand, provided users pay the full social costs of their driving. Beyond a doubt, additional investment in road and traffic systems will be required, and some additional congestion will have to be tolerated. But the Japanese experience suggests that people will continue to use public transit for work trips if it is available on advantageous terms. Thus, continued emphasis on development of a high-quality public transit system is the best way to prevent overuse of autos in Korean cities.

CONCLUSIONS

An efficient and elaborate bus-based transportation system has been developed in large Korean cities. Buses are probably the best mode to constitute the backbone of the transportation system in Korean conditions. A subway system has been started in Seoul and should grow during coming years, provided the government permits continued growth in the Seoul area.

It is certain that road use by public and private vehicles will continue to increase rapidly in Korean cities as urbanization proceeds and cities grow. This will necessitate large government investments in new and improved road systems. It will also necessitate large private investments in buses, trucks and other vehicles.

As incomes continue to rise, automobile use will spread in Korean cities. Even modest increases in urban auto use will produce considerable congestion in many cities. Provided public transit continues to be an advantageous alternative to automobile use, there is no reason to expect a large switch from present transportation modes to automobiles in the foreseeable future.

TEN

Environmental Quality

In this chapter we survey briefly the available data on environmental quality in Korea, and compare problems and possible solutions with those in other countries. Some people use the term "environmental quality" broadly to include not only air and water quality but also a variety of aesthetic and social problems. For example, people often include in discussions of the environment comments on the aesthetic quality of buildings, on crime, on litter, and on other issues. We use the term in a narrow and precise sense to refer to the quality of the ambient air over cities and the quality of the water in streams and estuaries in and near cities.

All economic activity removes materials from the environment, processes them into forms usable by people, and returns them to the environment after their usefulness has been depleted by consumption. For example, agriculture removes materials from the environment by harvesting crops. The manufacturing sector processes them for human use, and the wholesaling and retailing sectors deliver them to consumers. Materials are returned to the environment at every stage of the process. Some materials are returned to the environment by the agricultural sector in the form of unused parts of crops, animal wastes, fertilizer, and so forth. Food-processing plants return large amounts of unwanted materials to the air and water environment. Wholesalers and retailers return more materials to the environment because of spoilage and additional processing. Consumers return materials to the environment because of spoilage, food preparation, and human wastes. The same thing is true in other industries, although the kinds and amounts of materials, and the forms of discharges to the environment vary greatly from one industry to another.

The materials balance says that all materials removed from the environment must eventually be returned. In terms of weight and bulk, most materials removed from the environment are returned in the form of solid waste. Although solid wastes cause environmental problems, they are less serious and less well studied than other environmental discharges. Materials not returned to the environment as solid wastes are discharged to the atmosphere and to water bodies. Although relatively small in quantity, materials discharged to air and water are the causes of the worst environmental degradation or pollution.

Discharges to water bodies are conveniently classified as organic and inorganic. Organic discharges come from such industries as food processing and organic chemicals, and from municipal sewage systems. Organic wastes are gradually degraded by natural processes in water bodies, reducing the oxygen dissolved in the water as degradation occurs. Dissolved oxygen is necessary in water bodies to support fish and other life and to enable the water to purify itself. Large volumes of organic wastes overload water bodies' capacity to degrade wastes, making the water devoid of oxygen, or anaerobic, and thus making it putrid. If sewage and other organic wastes contaminate public water supplies, the result is intestinal disorders that are endemic in developing countries.

Although smaller in volume and less studied than organic discharges, substantial amounts of inorganic materials are discharged to water bodies. Inorganic discharges do not degrade and may thus build up in the water body over long periods of time. In Japan, there have been well-documented cases of heavy metals discharges which were ingested by humans after working their way up the food chain. The result has been peculiarly horrible disabilities and many deaths.

Airborne discharges are small in quantity, but important for two reasons. First, humans are sensitive to even small concentrations of some substances discharged to the air. Particulates and sulfur oxides in the air cause and exacerbate respiratory problems. Carbon monoxide is toxic in large quantities and causes loss of mental acuity at low concentrations. Hydrocarbons and nitrous oxides are instrumental in causing smog. Most effects of air pollutants are chronic, taking place over many years, and are therefore extremely difficult to measure precisely. Second, people have fewer ways to avoid polluted air than polluted water. We can choose places to swim and withdraw drinking water, but we must be able to breathe the air everywhere we go. Most airborne discharges come from burning fossil fuels, but some come from a variety of industrial processes.

Every society has many options in dealing with polluting discharges. All involve some cost, and some are very costly. Most simply, wastes can be discharged to air and water at times and places at which they do little harm. For example, thermoelectric plants can be built away from population centers, or food-processing plants can store organic wastes until times when water pollution is slight. More important, wastes can be discharged to the environment in harmless solid form instead of being discharged to air and water. Most organic wastes can be disposed of in sanitary landfills instead of being brushed into the nearest stream. Finally, the most sophisticated and costly option is treatment of wastes before discharge to convert them to relatively harmless substances. The conventional municipal treatment plant is the best known example of this option. It converts sewage to a relatively harmless discharge and into a solid sludge that can be used as organic fertilizer. Auto emission control devices used in the United States, Japan, and elsewhere, both reduce the fuel consumed through more efficient combustion and also convert airborne discharges to harmless substances.

Environmental data are of two basic types: discharge quantities and ambient air and water concentrations. Discharge data are important only because discharges cause pollution of the ambient environment. The relationships between discharges and ambient concentrations are complex, depending on detailed characteristics of the atmosphere and of water bodies. Discharge data are the more plentiful because they can be inferred from the content of materials used. If a ton of coal is burned, the entire content except for the ash remaining in the incinerator must be discharged to the air. There is no other place for it to go. Thus, discharges can be calculated from the content of the coal and the remaining ash and from the characteristics of the combustion process. Not only are ambient concentrations difficult to infer from discharge quantities, but also they are difficult to meter directly. All ambient pollutant concentration data should be treated with healthy skepticism.

DISCHARGES AND
AMBIENT CONCENTRATIONS

In Korea, as elsewhere, environmental data have improved greatly since the late 1960s. It is now possible to obtain as complete environmental data as in most countries, but comparisons covering more than a few years are impossible.

We start with air pollution, on which the data are remarkably rich. Table 39 shows estimates of total airborne discharges and discharges per square kilometer of land area in Korea and the United States. Total tons of U.S. discharges seem very large

TABLE 39 Comparison of Air Pollution Emissions in Korea and the United States by Area

(tons)

	Area (km²)	1965		1969		1971		1974	
		Total	per km²	Total	per km²	Total	per km²	Total	per km²
Korea	98,757	516,000	5.2	1,123,500	11.3	1,431,000	14.4	1,437,200	14.5
Seoul	613	148,608	242.0	303,210	494.6	375,000	611.0	-	-
U.S.A.	9,246,213	125,000,000	13.5	-		215,800,000	23.3	198,400,000	21.5

Source: Ch'ŏr-hwan Ch'a, "Tosi kaebal kwa hwan'gyŏng munje," and Proceedings of the National Conference on Human Environment - National Development and Human Environment in Korea. Sponsored by the Korea Atomic Energy Research Institute and Graduate School of Environmental Studies, Seoul National University, December 1975.

relative to the Korean total, but the two are in about the same ratio to the countries' GNPs at that time. Total U.S. discharges are so much greater than Korean that discharges per square kilometer of land area are greater in the United States, despite the fact that Korean population density is 15 times greater. Ambient quality is strongly correlated with discharges per unit of land area, averaging over an entire country. Korean discharges nearly tripled between 1965 and 1974, growing just slightly faster than real GNP. As the second line of the table shows, polluting discharges are heavily concentrated in urban areas, discharges per unit of land area being between 40 and 50 times the national average.

Table 40 displays total emissions by source for years between 1965 and 1973. The most striking thing about Table 40 is the relative unimportance of the transportation sector as an emission

TABLE 40 Estimated National Air Pollution Emissions
          by Source
                        (1,000 ton/year)

Sources	Year			
	1965	*1967*	*1969*	*1973*
Transportation	105.5(20)	163.2(24)	272.7(24)	254.4(16.3)
Industry	58.0(12)	111.3(17)	348.7(31)	637.0(40.8)
Power Stations	105.0(20)	91.2(13)	102.6(9)	194.0(12.4)
Housing	247.7(48)	312.6(46)	399.5(36)	476.4(30.5)
Total	516.2(100)	678.3(100)	1,123.5(100)	1,561.8(100)

Source: Ch'ŏr-hwan ch'a, "Tosi kaebal kwa hwan'gyŏng munje."

source. In 1973, it accounted for only 16.3 percent of emissions, whereas it accounts for more than half in Japan and the United States. Although total emissions have grown rapidly in the transportation sector, they are a small part of the total because many Korean vehicles are diesel-engine trucks and buses, which have much smaller emissions than cars with internal-combustion engines. Emissions from industry have grown rapidly as Korea has industrialized. About 30 percent of emissions originate in homes, virtually all from burning fuels for heating and cooking. Coal briquettes are the predominant fuel. Korean home-heating systems generate large discharges of sulfur oxides and carbon monoxide, but little improvement is possible without massive investments in improved home-heating systems.

Unfortunately, a classification of national emissions by substance is not available. Table 41 shows a classification of emissions by substances emitted in Seoul for 1965 and 1970,

TABLE 41 Estimated Future Air Pollutant of Seoul,
1965–1980

(1,000 ton)

		Substance			
Year	Total Pollutant	Sulfur Oxide	Nitrous Oxide	Carbon Monoxide	Hydro- carbons
1965	140.7	26.4	18.0	66.6	9.6
1970	347.4	94.4	50.1	141.4	26.5
1975[a]	530.1	135.9	79.6	215.9	56.0
1980[a]	618.4	156.9	81.9	260.3	71.3

Source: Suk-p'yo Kwŏn, "Sŏul [Seoul] T'ŭkpyŏlsi taegi oyŏm paech'ullyang" in Bulletin of the Korea Pollution Control Association, 1972.

Note: [a]Estimates based on the trends of fuel consumption.

with projections for 1975 and 1980. The tonnages for the four pollutants do not add to the total because certain pollutants, notably particulates and aerosols, have been omitted from the detail. In terms of tonnage, carbon monoxide is the largest pollutant in the table. Most carbon monoxide comes from motor vehicles, home heating, and industrial processes. Next highest are sulfur oxides, coming mostly from burning coal and oil in power plants, industry, and homes. Nitrous oxides and hydrocarbons are smaller in total quantity.

In respect to ambient concentrations of air pollutants, Table 42 shows concentrations of sulfur oxides in parts of Seoul

TABLE 42 Sulfur Oxide Concentrations in Seoul by Land-Use Zone and Year[a]
(p.p.m.)

Land use	Year						
	1968	1969	1970	1971	1972	1973	1974
Industrial & semi-industrial	0.042	0.052	0.061	0.068	0.067	0.060	0.065
Commercial	0.019	0.049	0.054	0.063	0.062	0.050	0.069
Residential	0.022	0.041	0.047	0.046	0.049	0.042	0.046
Green	0.015	0.027	0.029	0.028	0.029	0.027	0.042
From the core of CBD:							
5 km	-	-	-	0.047	-	-	-
5 – 10 km	-	-	-	0.058	-	-	-
10 – 15 km	-	-	-	0.063	-	-	-

Source: Sŏul [Seoul]-si Pogŏn Yŏn'guso, *Yŏn'gu pogoso*, 1974, and Sŏul [Seoul] T'ŭkpyŏlsi, *Sijŏng Kaeyo*, 1975, p. 372.

Note: [a]Average observed bimonthly from April to December of each year.

classified by land use from 1968 to 1974. It is evident that concentrations vary considerably from place to place, as is typical of air pollutants. In each kind of area, the concentration was up sharply from 1968 until sometime in the interval 1970–1972. Each series peaked in that interval and then fell somewhat, though three of the four 1974 figures are above the 1973 levels. The decreasing trend since 1972 reflects the gradual substitution of oil and electricity for coal briquettes for household heating and cooking, the major source of sulfur oxide concentrations in Korea.

In Japan, by comparison, sulfur oxide concentrations in large cities peaked in the late 1960s and have declined since then. Japanese concentrations were mostly higher than those in Table 42 during the late 1960s, but have fallen below the Korean levels in the 1970s. Averages in U.S. cities are mostly in the range 0.02 to 0.03 p.p.m., below those in Japan and Korea. We have seen no studies of the effect of sulfur oxide concentrations on respiratory problems in Korea. But studies in the United States, Japan, and Europe have concluded that concentrations at levels shown in Table 42 cause and exacerbate respiratory problems. It is also of interest that Table 42 indicates that sulfur oxide concentrations rise with distance from the center of Seoul. The finding of rising pollutant concentrations with distance from the city center is contrary to the usual assumption made for U.S. metropolitan areas, that pollution is worst in the poor, central parts of metropolitan areas. Evidence for the assumed U.S. pattern relates mainly to automobile emissions, and does not extend to sulfur oxides. In the United States, sulfur oxides result mainly from discharges from thermoelectric and manufacturing plants, and concentrations may not follow the pattern of those from automobile discharges. In Korea, sulfur oxide concentrations depend heavily on home heating systems, so concentrations are greatest in distant parts of metropolitan areas where residences are predominantly located.

Table 43 shows similar ambient concentration data for nitrous oxides. The table shows phenomenal increases in all land-use

TABLE 43 Nitrous Oxide Concentrations in Seoul
by Land-Use Zone and Year
(p.p.m.)

Land use	Year			
	1965	*1967*	*1968*	*1969*
Industrial & semi-industrial	0.040	0.189	0.229	0.346
Commercial	0.058	0.164	0.129	0.157
Residential	0.029	0.089	0.100	-
Green	0.024	0.079	0.032	-

Source: Suk-p'yo Kwŏn, "Hwan'gyŏng pojŏn ŭi tangmyŏn kwaje wa chŏnmang,"
Research Report of Yonsei University Pollution Research Institute, 1974.

categories during the short period covered, presumably resulting in part from the rapid increase in motor vehicles. Concentrations recorded in the table for 1968 and 1969 are well above comparable levels in Japanese and U.S. cities in the late 1960s and early 1970s. As with sulfur oxide levels, we have seen no studies of health effects of nitrous oxide concentrations in Korea. But the growth and levels of nitrous oxide concentrations recorded in the table suggest that some adverse health effects must have resulted. It is unfortunate that the data-collection program seems to have been discontinued.

We turn now to water pollution, for which data are fragmentary. As in most countries, data are limited to organic discharge estimates and a few dissolved oxygen records for major streams through large metropolitan areas. Table 44 shows sources of organic discharges to the Han River in Seoul, the percentage contribution of each source of pollution for 1973, and an advance estimate for 1975. The estimate of 1.06 million tons a day of sewage discharge is less than 300 million gallons a day, which is a typical return flow from a U.S. metropolitan area of less than half Seoul's population. Not only is water use per person greater in the United States than in Korea, but also only 90 percent of Seoul's population is sewered. For the

TABLE 44 Amount of Discharges and Percentage Contributions to Pollution in the Han River in Seoul (10,000 ton/day)

	1973		1975[a]	
	Amounts	*Contribution to Pollution*	*Amounts*	*Contribution to Pollution*
Sewage	106	45.5%	134	77%
Excrement	0.19	30.5	0.15	15.5
Industrial Waste Water	24	24.0	26	17.5
Total	134	100.0	160	100.0

Source: Sŏul [Seoul] T'ŭkpyŏlsi, *Sijŏng Kaeyo*, 1974, p. 466.

Note: [a]Figures for 1975 are estimates.

remainder, sewage is collected in tanks and hauled away to be dumped directly into the river. The projected growth in the share of sewage as a pollution source reflects the gradual extension of Seoul's sewage system and the corresponding reduction of direct discharges of excrement to the river.

The small contribution of industrial waste water to pollution in the Han River is in contrast with United States experience. In a large U.S. metropolitan area, industry contributes more organic waste to nearby water bodies than the municipal sewage system does. The contrast stems only partly from the fact that industrial output, and therefore waste generation, is greater per capita in U.S. than Korean metropolitan areas. It also reflects in part the high level of treatment of municipal wastes in large U.S. metropolitan areas.

Massive amounts of organic wastes are discharged to the Han River and its tributaries. The traditional means of disposal of human wastes was collection of night soil and its use as fertilizer. That is now rare in Seoul. About 90 percent of city residents are served with piped water and sewage systems. The first sewage treatment plant, serving about 1.3 million people, opened in 1976, but most raw sewage is returned to the Han

River. A second treatment plant is under construction. Thus, the main function of the sewage system is to dilute the wastes with other waste waters. Table 45 shows minimum, maximum, and average dissolved oxygen levels for two tributaries of the Han River in Seoul. The tributaries are highly polluted. Most

TABLE 45 Dissolved Oxygen in Two Main Streams
Leading to the Han River in Seoul
(p.p.m.)

	Average (Minimum, Maximum)			
	1969	*1970*	*1971*	*1972*
Ch'ŏnggye Stream	0.65 (0, 2)	0.4 (0, 0.8)	0.9 (0, 1.8)	0.1 (0, 1.0)
Anyang Stream	0.9 (0, 4.1)	0.6 (0.2, 1.2)	1.5 (0.8, 3.5)	0.0 (0, 0)

Source: Inch'ŏn-si, *Han-gang sujil oyŏm chosa pogosŏ* (December 1973), p. 108–109. Surveys for 1969, 1970, and 1971 were conducted by the Seoul Metropolitan Government Board of Health, and surveys for 1972 by Yonsei University Pollution Research Institute.

Note: Ch'ŏnggye Stream runs through the downtown and Anyang Stream the southwestern industrial part of Seoul.

fish life requires 4–6 p.p.m. of dissolved oxygen. Only once, early in the four years covered by the table, did one of the tributaries reach that range. The zero minimum and low average and maximum records imply that the tributaries are anaerobic during large parts of the year. During such times the streams stink and merely carry organic wastes downstream without substantially degrading them.

Seoul withdraws municipal water from five places on the Han, two above places where organic wastes are discharged to the river and three—providing more than half the total water—below the areas where large volumes of waste are discharged to the river. Water quality is adequate near the upstream withdrawals, but is unacceptably low at downstream withdrawals. Water is treated before use, but waterborne diseases are common.

However, the incidence of typhoid fever has fallen substantially as a result of investments in Seoul's water system since the early 1970s.

GOVERNMENT ENVIRONMENTAL POLICIES

There are two main components of government environmental policies. One is government investment in water supply and waste disposal systems, and the other is government controls on private waste discharges. The former is important only for water pollution control whereas the latter is important for both air and water pollution control.

In developing, even more than in developed, countries, there is serious debate as to how much of the society's scarce resources should be invested in pollution control. All measures to control pollution require the commitment of resources that have valuable alternative uses. In Korea and elsewhere, the debate has been put in the context of investment in industry versus investment in environmental improvement. Any society whose industrialization has advanced to the point at which large urban areas emerge needs to make investment adequate to ensure high-quality municipal water supply and at least minimum sewage treatment. Otherwise, human welfare and productivity are impaired by high incidence of waterborne diseases. Likewise, at least minimum amounts of industrial waste treatment are called for. Air pollution is more difficult to deal with. Large Korean cities are now reaching air pollution levels at which some health damage is almost inevitable. Home heating systems are the source of 25 to 50 percent of most air pollutants in Korea. It is clearly not possible to convert them to cleaner systems quickly or cheaply. Vehicles are the source of more than half the carbon monoxide in Seoul, and they will grow as a percentage source of most air pollutants in coming years. Diesels are inherently clean engines and can be kept clean by careful periodic maintenance. Internal combustion engines are dirtier, but about 50 percent abatement from uncontrolled cars can be obtained cheaply; 95 percent abatement, at which U.S. and Japanese government policies aim, is expensive.

Until recently, government expenditures on water and sewage facilities were very small. The Third Five-Year Plan calls for expenditure of 54 billion wŏn, only 0.5 percent of total investments.[1] In the early 1970s government expenditure to increase the quantity and quality of water supply, especially in Seoul, began to increase rapidly. The Fourth Five-Year Plan 1977–1981, calls for a tripling of expenditures on water supply and sewage treatment, to 1.0 percent of total investment. It is planned to concentrate investments on improving water supplies in large cities and on construction of sewage-treatment plants.

Korea has had an anti-pollution law, permitting regulation of private discharges, since 1963. The 1963 law was amended and extended in 1971. The 1971 law, and regulations issued pursuant thereto, give the Minister of Health and Social Affairs and local governments broad authority to regulate industrial air and water discharges and to require relocation of offending firms. At least some abatement has been required of both air and water discharges. Newspaper stories tell of cases undertaken and directives issued by public officials. New cars are required to have devices that abate discharges. But no data appear to have been published that permit measurement of the effects of the new law on discharges and ambient concentrations.

ELEVEN

Conclusions

This book has been concerned with urbanization in Korea from 1945 to 1975 and with the problems that have accompanied urbanization. Large-scale and prolonged urbanization is a complex process, involving massive changes in living standards, political processes, and social interactions. It inevitably entails conflict, competition, and friction. In some countries, Korea being a notable example, it works much better than in others. Previous chapters have discussed specific aspects of Korean urbanization, and have pointed to particular areas in which Korean experience should enable other developing countries to avoid or solve similar problems. In this concluding chapter, we attempt to step back and speculate on broad implications of the Korean experience for urbanization in developing countries.

Urbanization and economic development are intimately related in several ways. The most fundamental and important relationship is that economic development is the primary cause of rapid urbanization. Economic development consists in substantial degree of rising real income per capita and of a related shift of labor and other productive resources from primary to secondary and tertiary activities. Secondary and tertiary activities are largely and for good economic reasons concentrated in urban areas. Although the correlation between urbanization and economic development is by no means mechanical or perfect, it is strong and pervasive. Although difficult to measure, the benefits of urbanization in developing countries are great. Urbanization provides ease of transportation and communication between highly interactive sectors whose growth is a major component of economic development. It also facilitates communication among people in business, government, education, and other sectors in which innovation and exchange of ideas are important sources of growth and efficient allocation of resources. There are many things government can do to channel and influence urbanization, but to oppose large-scale urbanization is in large part to oppose economic development and modernization. Attempts by national governments to limit urbanization severely are likely to slow down economic development and prevent realization of its benefits.

It is trite to say that rapid economic growth alleviates many problems. Economic growth enables people to improve their living standards, protect their health, provide security, and avoid the most brutal kinds of work. But it is sometimes forgotten that, although rapid economic growth promotes rapid urbanization, it also provides the resources to alleviate many of the problems that accompany urbanization. Korea is a prime example of this point. Rapid urbanization invariably creates problems of scarcity and cost of housing, congested and inadequate transportation, and strains on most kinds of public services. But, despite the speed of urban migration and the growth of cities, none of these problems has been as severe in Korea as in other countries in which growth has been less rapid. Take as an example urban squatter settlements, the symbol of urban discontent and frustration in many countries. Korean cities have had illegal squatters throughout the period since the Korean War. But the numbers of squatters have decreased, apparently steadily, during the early and mid-1970s. This progress has resulted in part from government programs to remove or help squatters. But the most important reason for the decreasing importance of the problem has been rapid economic growth. Rapid growth has enabled most urban migrants to obtain legal housing. And most of those that resorted to illegal housing have, within relatively short periods of time, been able to earn enough to afford legal housing. In contrast, in many other countries in South Asia, South America, and Africa, squatters have been a larger and more persistent problem. Urbanization is somewhat less rapid in less rapidly growing countries, but squatter settlements are larger and persist longer the less rapid the country's economic growth.

Rapid economic growth promotes rapid urbanization, but, the more rapidly a country develops, the less serious are most economic problems, urban and otherwise. Put this way, the conclusion is almost trite. But it has relevance to many actions of governments in developing countries. Governments frequently see urbanization as a spontaneous or exogenous cause of urban problems such as unemployment, congestion, and scarce housing. But urbanization does not occur spontaneously or frivolously. It is the response of people trying to improve their lives in changing circumstances. People migrate to cities because economic and other prospects are better there for them and their children. Almost invariably, urbanization is the response of people to the release of resources from agriculture and their transfer to industry and services. It is a normal and desirable concomitant of economic growth. The role of government should be to facilitate and encourage the transfer of resources, treating urbanization as an opportunity to promote economic growth. Governments should do what they can to promote productive employment opportunities for urban migrants, helping create jobs that will promote economic growth. That is a difficult and challenging task, whose discussion is beyond the scope of this book. But it is a much more productive and appropriate task, and perhaps even easier, than trying to curtail urbanization.

What will be the future pattern of urbanization in Korea and other developing countries? Developing countries follow a typical curve of urbanization. Very poor countries are mostly only 15–20 percent urban. As a country develops, it urbanizes. Even countries that develop only slowly show substantial urbanization, but rapidly developing countries urbanize rapidly. The pace of urbanization typically slows down after the country is 60 to 70 percent urban. Urbanization then proceeds more slowly until the country is 70 to 80 percent urban, the stage reached by the most developed countries in the 1970s. After that, urbanization proceeds very slowly indeed. Korea has gone through a quarter century of extremely rapid urbanization and is approaching the state at which deceleration of the urbanization process is likely. But urbanization will almost certainly continue at a brisk pace during the remainder of the twentieth century, if economic growth continues at a rapid pace. Assuming continuation of peace and prosperity, Korea may be 70 percent urban by the end of the twentieth century. That would represent rapid urbanization during the last quarter of the century, but at a somewhat slower pace than during the third quarter.

Korea's recent urbanization has been extremely rapid, but mainly because its growth has been rapid. There is no reason to believe that Korea has urbanized significantly more rapidly than will other developing countries that grow at Korea's pace during the remainder of the century. Most developing countries were no more than 25 percent urban in the mid-1970s. That percentage will grow during the remainder of the century, although much more rapidly in some countries than in others. The world average percentage urban was just under 40 in the mid-1970s. It seems almost certain that half the world's population will be urban by the end of the century.

Predicting the size distribution and structure of cities is much more difficult. We saw in Chapter 4 that there is some tendency for primacy to decline as a country develops. It seems likely that natural forces and government policy will combine to continue that trend in Korea during the remaining years of the century. It is less likely that the same trend will characterize other developing countries. Primacy sometimes increases during early stages of development, and many countries may pass through that stage in coming years. As a poor country develops and urbanizes rapidly, it is economical to concentrate secondary and tertiary activites in a small number of large urban areas to economize on scarce transportation, communication, and port facilities. This process can result in increasing primacy. As economic growth enables such facilities to be duplicated in several urban areas, primacy tends to decrease. Large countries tend to be less primate than small countries because long distances prevent single urban centers from serving most of the urban needs in a large country.

As incomes have risen, urban transportation improved, and cities grown, Korean cities have decentralized. Population density functions have flattened and, in some cases, average density has declined. The implication is that more urban land is required per urban resident, hastening the conversion of land from rural to urban uses and intensifying the conflict between rural and urban residents. We have no reason to believe Korea is atypical of developing countries in this respect, although studies of urban structures have not been made in other developing countries. In many developing, and indeed developed, countries there are inadequate means of resolving conflicting rural and urban demands for land near the peripheries of cities. Our study suggests that the pressure for conversion of land from rural to urban uses is overwhelming as cities grow and decentralize in developing countries. Governments resist this trend because they want to preserve rural values and because they are concerned about inadequate food supplies. But urbanization rarely entails decreases in agricultural output in developing countries. Normally, workers and land are released from agriculture because agricultural productivity is rising as part of economic growth. Rising productivity in agriculture permits increasing amounts of food to be grown on constant or shrinking amounts of land. In fact, in many developing countries governments tilt the competition for land in favor of agriculture by price supports and subsidies for the agricultural sector.

Excessive population density is thought to be a serious urban problem in many developing countries, especially in Asia. Urban decentralization is the response of people trying to reduce crowding as rising incomes permit them to do so. Modest reductions in population density by urban decentralization are an important component of improved well-being in developing countries. When governments impose stringent controls on land conversion from rural to urban uses they prevent an important component of increased well-being from being realized. In most Asian countries, extremely high land values provide a stringent market control on urban decentralization. Even in the absence of government controls on urban expansion, Asian cities will continue to have very high densities and urban uses will occupy only a small part of total land area. Government attempts to control land prices at artificially low levels prevent markets from performing an important function in limiting the demand for urban uses of land.

Korean urbanization has been a great success story during the third quarter of the twentieth century. The basic reason is that the national government has focused its efforts on promotion of economic growth instead of on controls on urban growth and structure. Even though government investments in urban infrastructure have been modest, rapid economic growth has made available resources—some government, but mostly private—to solve or ameliorate urban problems that have become endemic sources of frustration and conflict in less rapidly developing countries.

Appendixes

Appendix Tables

TWO   *Statistical Data on Urbanization in Korea*

1. Employment and Industrialization in Korea, 1911–1970
2. Population, Area, and Density by Region and Major Regional Centers, 1960–1973
3. Regional Distribution of Urban and Rural Population, 1955–1973
4. Share of Urban and Rural Population by Region, 1955–1975
5. Employment by Industry and Region, 1970
6. Employment by Industry and Region, 1966
7. Income, Employment, and Family Size in Cities, 1974

THREE   *Statistical Data on Urban Growth*

1. Major Economic Indicators, 1953–1975
2. Data for Development Processes in Korea
3. Data for Sectoral Growth in Korea

FOUR   *Statistical Data on Primacy and City Size Distribution*

1. Urban Population by Cities (Si) and Towns (Ŭp), 1949–1975
2. Area and Administrative Unit by Province, 1974
3. Status of Industrial Estates in Korea, 1976
4. Industrial Estates Development Plan, 1977–1981
5. Structure of Employment by Urban Areas

FIVE   *Statistical Data on Migration*

1. Pattern of Urban and Rural Migration in Korea, 1965–1970
2. Intra- and Inter-Provincial Migration in Korea, 1967–1974
3. Migration Statistics for the Seven Largest Cities, 1974
4. Characteristics of Migration to Seoul
5. Total Fertility Rates of Urban and Rural Areas in Korea

SIX   *Statistical Data on Structure of Cities*

1. Data for Density Gradients
2. Urban Density Functions for 12 Cities (Quadratic Form)
3. Andong
4. Pusan
5. Ch'ŏnan
6. Ch'ŏngju
7. Taegu
8. Taejŏn
9. Kangnŭng
10. Kwangju
11. Inch'ŏn
12. Samch'ŏnp'o
13. Seoul
14. Suwŏn

SEVEN   *Statistical Data on Land Values*

1. Status of Land Use in Korea, 1972
2. Pattern of Land Use by Region, 1973
3. Pattern of Land Use in the Seoul Metropolitan Region, 1973
4. Average Land Value Index for Major Cities
5. Land Value Index for Major Cities (Commercial and Residential Land)
6. Land Values—Seoul
7. Land Values—Pusan
8. Land Values—Taegu
9. Land Values—Suwŏn

EIGHT   *Statistical Data on Housing*

1. Major Economic Indicators Concerning Korean Housing
2. Data for the Housing Model
3. Population, Households, and Housing by Region, 1970 and 1975
4. Housing Tenure and Shortage by Region, 1970
5. Dwelling Sizes, 1970
6. Proportion of Urban and Rural Housing by Age, 1970
7. Proportion of Housing by Age in Seoul
8. Construction of Public Sector Housing by Size and Constructors, 1973

TABLE A-2-1 Employment and Industrialization in Korea, 1911–1970

| | Labor Force (1,000s) | | | | | Non-agriculture L in Total L (NAL/L) | MMCL in Total L (MMCL/L) | Manufacturing L in NAL (ML/NAL) | Agricultural L in Total L (AL/L) |
	Agriculture (AL)	Non-agriculture (NAL)	Manuf. Mining Const. (MMCL)	Manuf. (ML)	Total (L)				
1911	3,859	554	52	52	4,413	0.1255	0.0118	0.0939	0.8745
1920	7,268	678	117	117	7,946	0.0853	0.0147	0.1726	0.9147
1925	7,835	941	144	144	8,776	0.1072	0.0164	0.1530	0.8928
1930	7,886	1,083	143	143	8,969	0.1207	0.0159	0.1320	0.8793
1935	7,622	1,263	169	169	8,885	0.1421	0.0190	0.1338	0.8579
1947	4,995	1,389	243	195	6,384	0.2176	0.0381	0.1404	0.7824
1949	6,360	1,601	300[a]	266	7,961	0.2011	0.0374	0.1610	0.7938
1960	6,775	1,746	497	427	8,521	0.2049	0.0583	0.2446	0.7951
1965	4,810	3,396	1,089	772	8,206	0.4138	0.1327	0.2273	0.5862
1970	4,916	4,829	1,679	1,284	9,745	0.4955	0.1723	0.2659	0.5045

Source: Chōsen Sōtokufu tōkei nenpō 1923, 1932, 1936; EPB, Korea Statistical Yearbook, 1952, 1970, 1975.

Note: [a]Construction excluded.
Chosŏn ch'ongdokpu Statistics include Mining and Construction in Manufacturing.

TABLE A-2-2 Population, Area, and Density by Region and Major Regional Centers, 1960–1973

Region	Area (km²)		Population			
	Total	Arable	1960	%	1966	%
	(1973)	(1973)				
Whole Country	98,757.7	22,412.5	24,989,241	100.0	29,192,762	100.0
Seoul Region	11,696.6	3,077.0	5,194,167	20.8	6,911,167	23.7
Seoul	627.9	81.7	2,445,402	9.8	3,803,360	13.0
Kyŏnggi province	11,068.7	2,995.3	2,748,765	11.0	3,107,807	10.6
(Inch'ŏn)	(166.4)	-	(401,473)	(1.6)	(525,827)	(1.8)
(Suwŏn)	(83.7)	-	(90,801)	(0.4)	(127,733)	(0.4)
Pusan Region	12,333.0	2,673.3	4,182,042	16.7	4,606,412	15.8
Pusan	375.1	29.9	1,163,671	4.7	1,430,011	4.9
S. Kyŏngsang province	11,957.9	2,643.4	3,018,371	12.1	3,176,401	10.9
(Masan)	(196.9)	-	(158,010)	(0.6)	(154,600)	(0.5)
(Ulsan)	(174.3)	-	-	-	(112,848)	(0.4)
Kangwŏn province	16,784.7	1,559.2	1,636,767	6.5	1,832,519	6.3
(Ch'unch'ŏn)	(56.3)	-	(82,526)	(0.3)	(100,033)	(0.3)
(Wŏnju)	(111.7)	-	(76,990)	(0.3)	(103,810)	(0.4)
N. Ch'ungch'ŏng province	7,436.6	1,766.9	1,369,780	5.5	1,550,009	5.3
(Ch'ŏngju)	(65.0)	-	(92,093)	(0.4)	(123,666)	(0.4)
S. Ch'ungch'ŏng province	8,752.2	2,918.0	2,528,133	10.1	2,905,275	10.0
(Taejŏn)	(88.1)	-	(228,987)	(0.9)	(314,991)	(1.1)
N. Kyŏngsang province	19,802.0	3,830.7	3,848,424	15.4	4,476,625	15.3
(Taegu)	(178.3)	-	(676,692)	(2.7)	(845,189)	(2.9)
(P'ohang)	(52.9)	-	(59,536)	(0.2)	(65,927)	(0.2)
N. Chŏlla province	8,057.7	2,493.4	2,395,224	9.6	2,522,964	8.6
(Chŏnju)	(105.8)	-	(188,216)	(0.8)	(220,432)	(0.8)
S. Chŏlla province	12,074.9	3,607.0	3,553,041	14.2	4,050,461	13.9
(Kwangju)	(214.8)	-	(314,420)	(1.3)	(403,495)	(1.4)
Cheju Island	1,820.0	487.0	281,663	1.1	337,330	1.2
(Cheju)	(252.3)	-	(68,090)	(0.3)	(87,369)	(0.3)

TABLE A-2-2 (continued)

Region	Population 1970	%	Population 1973	%	Density	Households
Whole Country	31,465,654	100.0	33,250,248	100.0	337	6,056,239
Seoul Region	8,893,747	28.3	9,959,396	30.0	851	1,903,646
Seoul	5,535,725	17.6	6,289,556	18.9	10,017	1,215,538
Kyŏnggi province	3,358,022	10.7	3,669,840	11.0	332	693,108
(Inch'ŏn)	(634,046)	(2.0)	(714,246)	(2.1)	(4,292)	(142,053)
(Suwŏn)	(167,201)	(0.5)	(191,676)	(0.6)	(2,290)	(37,999)
Pusan Region	4,999,573	15.9	5,274,032	15.9	428	927,957
Pusan	1,879,904	6.0	2,071,950	6.2	5,524	405,904
S. Kyŏngsang province	3,119,669	9.9	3,202,082	9.6	268	567,053
(Masan)	(186,890)	(0.6)	(303,807)	(0.9)	(1,543)	(54,691)
(Ulsan)	(157,088)	(0.5)	(186,907)	(0.6)	(1,072)	(37,553)
Kangwŏn province	1,866,494	5.9	1,852,456	5.6	110	339,751
(Ch'unch'ŏn)	(120,517)	(0.4)	(135,271)	(0.4)	(2,403)	(26,118)
(Wŏnju)	(110,188)	(0.4)	(128,037)	(0.4)	(1,146)	(23,273)
N. Ch'ungch'ŏng province	1,481,263	4.7	1,518,681	4.6	204	261,919
(Ch'ŏngju)	(141,074)	(0.4)	(167,018)	(0.5)	(2,570)	(31,292)
S. Ch'ungch'ŏng province	2,860,213	9.1	2,923,039	8.8	334	493,951
(Taejŏn)	(406,910)	(1.3)	(462,834)	(1.4)	(5,254)	(82,077)
N. Kyŏngsang province	4,559,092	14.5	4,780,997	14.4	241	886,180
(Taegu)	(1,063,553)	(3.4)	(1,200,273)	(3.6)	(6,732)	(251,045)
(P'ohang)	(77,690)	(0.2)	(108,854)	(0.3)	(2,058)	(22,252)
N. Chŏlla province	2,433,577	7.7	2,452,648	7.4	304	416,037
(Chŏnju)	(257,530)	(0.8)	(285,660)	(0.9)	(2,700)	(51,136)
S. Chŏlla province	4,006,265	12.7	4,098,549	12.3	339	692,461
(Kwangju)	(493,634)	(1.6)	(552,432)	(1.7)	(2,572)	(97,800)
Cheju Island	365,430	1.2	390,450	1.2	215	84,337
(Cheju)	(104,493)	(0.3)	(117,585)	(0.4)	(466)	(25,594)

Sources: Han'guk Ŭnhaeng, *Chiyŏk Kyŏngje t'onggye,* June, 1975.
MHA, *Municipal Yearbook of Korea, 1974.*
Kyŏngsang-namdo, *Kyŏngnam t'onggye yŏnbo,* 1974.

TABLE A-2-3 Regional Distribution of Urban and Rural Population, 1955–1973

	1955		1960		1966		1970		1973	
	Urban	*Rural*	*Urban*	*Rural*	*Urban*	*Rural*	*Urban*	*Rural*	*Urban*	*Rural*
Whole Country	100.0	100.0	100.0	100.0	100.0	100.0	100.0	100.0	100.0	100.0
Seoul Metropolitan Region	37.4	12.1	41.9	12.5	46.2	12.3	49.8	11.9	49.8	12.1
Seoul	29.8	0.0	34.9	0.0	38.8	0.0	40.7	0.0	40.4	0.0
Kyŏnggi province	7.6	12.1	7.0	12.5	7.4	12.3	9.1	11.9	9.8	12.1
Pusan Metropolitan Region	26.3	14.7	22.5	14.5	20.3	13.5	18.8	13.7	19.0	13.1
Pusan	19.9	0.0	16.6	0.0	14.6	0.0	13.8	0.0	13.2	0.0
S. Kyŏngsang province	6.4	14.7	5.9	14.5	5.7	13.5	5.0	13.7	5.8	13.1
Taegu Region	12.4	16.7	12.3	16.6	11.4	17.3	11.1	17.1	11.0	17.4
Kwangju Region	9.1	16.3	8.6	16.4	7.6	17.0	6.5	17.5	6.2	17.8
Kangwŏn province	3.7	8.0	3.1	7.9	3.4	7.7	4.0	7.4	3.7	7.2
N. and S. Ch'ungch'ŏng provinces	4.8	19.4	5.6	19.5	6.0	19.9	5.8	20.0	5.6	20.3
N. Chŏlla province	5.2	11.4	4.9	11.4	4.1	10.9	3.4	11.0	3.9	10.5
Cheju Island	1.1	1.4	1.0	1.2	0.9	1.3	0.8	1.5	0.8	1.6

Sources: EPB, *Korea Statistical Yearbook, 1971,* pp. 40–41.
Chŏlla-namdo, *Chŏlla-namdo t'onggye yŏnbo, 1974.*

TABLE A-24 Share of Urban and Rural Population by Region, 1955–1975
(%)

	1955		1960		1966		1970		1975	
	Urban	Rural	Urban	Rural	Urban	Rural	Urban	Rural	Urban	Rural
Whole country	25.0	75.0	28.1	71.9	34.1	65.9	43.1	56.9	50.9	49.1
Seoul	100.0	0.0	100.0	0.0	100.0	0.0	100.0	0.0	100.0	0.0
Pusan	100.0	0.0	100.0	0.0	100.0	0.0	100.0	0.0	100.0	0.0
Kyŏnggi province	16.9	83.1	17.9	82.1	27.2	72.8	34.9	65.1	46.5	53.5
Kangwŏn province	13.1	86.9	17.4	82.6	22.9	77.1	29.1	70.9	31.7	68.3
N. Ch'ungch'ŏng province	11.1	88.9	11.8	88.2	13.2	86.8	19.9	80.1	24.5	75.5
S. Ch'ungch'ŏng province	7.8	92.2	9.1	90.0	13.3	86.7	17.3	82.7	20.5	79.5
N. Chŏlla province	12.8	87.2	14.4	85.6	15.9	84.1	21.0	79.0	28.0	72.0
S. Chŏlla province	15.4	84.6	16.9	83.1	18.5	81.5	22.1	77.9	26.1	73.9
N. Kyŏngsang province	6.6	93.4	23.8	76.2	25.0	75.0	33.0	67.0	36.8	63.2
S. Kyŏngsang province	14.2	85.8	12.0	88.0	17.7	82.3	21.6	78.4	32.5	67.5
Cheju Island	20.7	79.3	24.0	76.0	26.0	74.0	29.2	70.8	45.8	54.2

Sources: EPB, *Korea Statistical Yearbook, 1975* and *Report on Population and Housing Census, 1960, 1966, 1970, 1975.*

Note: Urban population is defined as popualtion of si (cities) or ǔp (towns) which have populations over 50,000.

TABLE A-2-5 Employment by Industry and Region, 1970

(1,000s)

	Whole Country	Urban		Rural
		Si (Cities) (over 50,000)	*Up* (Towns) (20,000–50,000)	
	10,153 (100.0) (100.0)	3,742 (100.0) (36.9)	875 (100.0) (8.6)	5,536 (100.0) (54.5)
A. Agri., Forest., Fishery	5,157 (50.8) (100.0)	278 (7.4) (5.4)	381 (43.6) (7.4)	4,498 (81.3) (87.2)
B. Mining	100 (1.0) (100.0)	14 (0.4) (14.0)	25 (2.9) (25.4)	60 (1.1) (60.6)
C. Manufacturing	1,448 (14.3) (100.0)	1,039 (27.8) (71.8)	116 (13.3) (8.0)	293 (5.3) (20.3)
D. Electricity & Water	31 (0.3) (100.0)	24 (0.7) (78.6)	3 (0.4) (10.0)	4 (0.06) (11.4)
E. Construction	462 (4.6) (100.0)	325 (8.7) (70.3)	36 (4.1) (7.8)	101 (1.8) (21.9)
F. Wholesale & Retail	1,280 (12.6) (100.0)	913 (24.4) (71.3)	140 (16.0) (10.9)	227 (4.1) (17.8)
G. Transport. & Comm.	329 (3.2) (100.0)	237 (6.3) (72.0)	37 (4.3) (11.3)	55 (1.0) (16.7)
H. Banking & Real Estate	97 (1.0) (100.0)	84 (2.2) (86.7)	6 (0.7) (6.2)	7 (0.1) (7.2)
I. Other Services	1,222 (12.0) (100.0)	812 (21.7) (66.4)	120 (14.7) (10.5)	282 (5.1) (23.1)
J. Unclassifiable	21 (0.2) (100.0)	12 (0.3) (57.0)	2 (0.2) (7.7)	7 (0.1) (35.3)

TABLE A-2-5 (continued)

	Seoul Region			Pusan Region		
	Seoul	Kyŏnggi Province	Total	Pusan	S. Kyŏngsang Province	Total
	1,622 (100.0)(16.0)	1,048 (100.0)(10.3)	2,670 (100.0)(26.3)	535 (100.0)(5.3)	1,056 (100.0)(10.4)	1,592 (100.0)(15.7)
A. Agri., Forest., Fishery	34 (2.0)(0.6)	512 (48.9)(9.9)	544 (20.4)(10.6)	19 (3.5)(0.4)	715 (67.7)(13.9)	734 (46.1)(14.2)
B. Mining	6 (0.4)(6.6)	8 (0.8)(8.1)	15 (0.6)(14.7)	1 (0.3)(1.4)	6 (0.5)(5.7)	7 (0.5)(7.1)
C. Manufacturing	458 (28.3)(31.7)	145 (13.8)(10.0)	603 (22.6)(41.7)	185 (34.6)(12.8)	111 (10.5)(7.7)	296 (18.6)(20.5)
D. Electricity & Water	11 (0.7)(36.1)	4 (0.4)(12.4)	15 (0.6)(48.5)	3 (0.5)(9.4)	2 (0.2)(7.7)	5 (0.3)(17.0)
E. Construction	160 (9.9)(34.7)	48 (4.6)(10.4)	209 (7.8)(45.2)	42 (7.8)(9.0)	31 (3.0)(6.8)	73 (4.6)(15.8)
F. Wholesale & Retail	423 (26.1)(33.1)	128 (12.3)(10.0)	512 (19.2)(40.0)	127 (23.7)(9.9)	80 (7.6)(6.3)	207 (13.0)(16.2)
G. Transport. & Comm.	92 (5.7)(28.1)	43 (4.1)(13.1)	136 (5.1)(41.2)	42 (7.9)(12.8)	21 (2.0)(6.5)	64 (4.0)(19.3)
H. Banking & Real Estate	51 (3.2)(53.2)	7 (0.7)(7.6)	59 (2.2)(60.8)	8 (1.6)(8.7)	3 (0.3)(3.3)	12 (0.7)(12.1)
I. Other Services	375 (23.1)(30.7)	151 (14.4)(12.3)	526 (19.7)(43.0)	105 (19.6)(8.6)	84 (7.9)(6.8)	188 (11.8)(15.4)
J. Unclassifiable	7 (0.5)(34.9)	1 (0.1)(3.6)	8 (0.3)(38.6)	2 (0.5)(11.5)	2 (0.2)(10.3)	5 (0.3)(21.7)

TABLE A-2-5 (continued)

	Kangwŏn Province	N. Ch'ungch'ŏng Province	S. Ch'ungch'ŏng Province	N. Chŏlla Province
	616 (100.0) (6.1)	497 (100.0) (4.9)	943 (100.0) (9.3)	824 (100.0) (8.1)
A. Agri., Forest., Fishery	371 (60.2) (7.2)	368 (74.1) (7.1)	621 (65.8) (12.0)	563 (68.4) (10.9)
B. Mining	36 (5.9) (36.2)	6 (1.3) (6.4)	9 (0.9) (8.6)	4 (0.5) (4.3)
C. Manufacturing	36 (5.9) (2.5)	29 (5.8) (2.0)	93 (9.9) (6.4)	80 (9.7) (5.5)
D. Electricity & Water	3 (0.5) (9.0)	1 (0.1) (1.8)	2 (0.2) (5.3)	1 (0.2) (4.3)
E. Construction	19 (3.1) (4.1)	12 (2.4) (2.6)	29 (3.1) (6.3)	27 (3.3) (5.9)
F. Wholesale & Retail	62 (10.1) (4.9)	34 (6.9) (2.7)	84 (8.9) (6.5)	59 (7.2) (4.6)
G. Transport. & Comm.	17 (2.8) (5.2)	9 (1.9) (2.8)	21 (2.2) (6.4)	16 (2.0) (5.0)
H. Banking & Real Estate	3 (0.5) (3.0)	2 (0.4) (2.0)	4 (0.5) (4.5)	3 (0.4) (3.4)
I. Other Services	68 (11.1) (5.6)	34 (6.9) (2.8)	79 (8.4) (6.5)	68 (8.2) (5.5)
J. Unclassifiable	- (0.1) (1.9)	1 (0.2) (5.0)	1 (0.2) (7.1)	1 (0.1) (3.6)

TABLE A-2-5 (continued)

	S. Chŏlla Province		N. Kyŏngsang Province		Cheju Island	
	1,379		1,499		135	
	(100.0)	(13.6)	(100.0)	(14.8)	(100.0)	(1.3)
A. Agri., Forest., Fishery	993		867		98	
	(72.0)	(19.3)	(57.8)	(16.8)	(72.1)	(1.9)
B. Mining	9		13		-	
	(0.7)	(9.4)	(0.9)	(12.8)	(0.4)	(0.5)
C. Manufacturing	96		207		6	
	(7.0)	(6.7)	(13.8)	(14.3)	(4.3)	(0.4)
D. Electricity & Water	2		2		-	
	(0.1)	(6.4)	(0.1)	(6.6)	(0.2)	(1.0)
E. Construction	33		55		5	
	(2.4)	(7.2)	(3.7)	(11.8)	(3.7)	(1.1)
F. Wholesale & Retail	104		167		11	
	(7.6)	(8.2)	(11.2)	(13.1)	(7.8)	(0.8)
G. Transport & Comm.	27		35		4	
	(2.0)	(8.3)	(2.3)	(10.5)	(3.1)	(1.3)
H. Banking & Real Estate	5		8		1	
	(0.4)	(5.2)	(0.5)	(8.3)	(0.6)	(0.9)
I. Other Services	105		143		10	
	(7.6)	(8.6)	(9.5)	(11.7)	(7.7)	(0.9)
J. Unclassifiable	2		2		-	
	(0.2)	(10.8)	(0.2)	(10.5)	(0.1)	(0.8)

Source: EPB, *Report on Population and Housing Census, 1970*, Vol. 2, 10% Sample Survey, No. 4-1 Economic Activity, Seoul, 1973.

Note: Due to round-up, numbers may not add up to total.

TABLE A-2-6 Employment by Industry and Region, 1966

(1,000s)

	Whole Country	Urban	Rural	Seoul	Kyŏnggi province	Total
				Seoul Region		
	7,963 (100.0)(100.0)	2,364 (100.0)(29.7)	5,599 (100.0)(70.3)	834 (100.0)(11.1)	801 (100.0)(10.1)	1,684 (100.0)(21.2)
A. Agri., Forest, Fishery	4,553 (57.2)(100.0)	258 (10.9)(5.7)	4,295 (76.7)(94.3)	26 (3.0)(0.6)	437 (54.5)(9.6)	463 (27.5)(10.2)
B. Mining	91 (1.1)(100.0)	12 (0.5)(13.1)	79 (1.4)(86.9)	6 (0.7)(6.7)	6 (0.7)(6.2)	12 (0.7)(13.0)
C. Manufacturing	958 (12.0)(100.0)	612 (25.9)(63.8)	346 (6.2)(36.2)	233 (26.3)(24.3)	83 (10.3)(8.6)	315 (18.7)(32.9)
D. Electricity & Water	25 (0.3)(100.0)	19 (0.8)(77.8)	5 (0.1)(22.2)	10 (1.1)(39.8)	2 (0.3)(9.7)	12 (0.7)(49.4)
E. Construction	191 (2.4)(100.0)	120 (5.1)(62.6)	72 (1.3)(37.4)	60 (6.8)(31.2)	16 (2.1)(8.6)	76 (4.5)(39.8)
F. Wholesale Retail	797 (10.0)(100.0)	493 (20.8)(61.8)	304 (5.4)(38.2)	195 (22.1)(24.5)	81 (10.1)(10.1)	276 (16.4)(34.7)
G. Transport. & Comm.	166 (2.1)(100.0)	115 (4.9)(69.3)	51 (0.9)(3.1)	40 (4.5)(23.9)	18 (2.2)(10.8)	57 (3.4)(34.7)
H. Banking & Real Estate	40 (0.5)(100.0)	35 (1.5)(87.7)	5 (0.1)(12.3)	21 (2.4)(52.9)	2 (0.3)(5.8)	24 (1.4)(58.7)
I. Other Services	1,141 (14.3)(100.0)	700 (29.6)(61.4)	440 (7.9)(33.6)	292 (33.1)(25.6)	156 (19.5)(13.7)	448 (26.6)(39.3)
J. Unclassifiable	1 (0.02)(100.0)	– (0.02)(31.9)	1 (0.02)(68.1)	– (0.02)(13.0)	– (0.02)(9.4)	– (0.02)(22.5)

TABLE A-2-6 (continued)

	Pusan Region					
	Pusan	S. Kyŏngsang province	Total	Kangwŏn Province	N. Ch'ungch'ŏng Province	S. Ch'ungch'ŏng Province
	346 (100.0) (4.3)	831 (100.0) (11.1)	1,227 (100.0) (15.4)	461 (100.0) (5.8)	452 (100.0) (5.7)	804 (100.0) (10.1)
A. Agri., Forest., Fishery	23 (6.7) (0.5)	626 (71.0) (13.7)	649 (52.9) (14.1)	275 (59.5) (6.0)	337 (74.4) (7.4)	533 (66.3) (11.7)
B. Mining	1 (0.3) (1.2)	4 (0.4) (4.3)	5 (0.4) (5.5)	38 (8.2) (41.7)	9 (2.0) (10.1)	8 (1.0) (8.7)
C. Manufacturing	113 (32.7) (11.8)	77 (8.7) (8.0)	190 (15.5) (19.8)	34 (7.4) (3.5)	25 (5.4) (2.6)	71 (8.0) (7.4)
D. Electricity & Water	3 (0.8) (11.6)	1 (0.1) (4.3)	4 (0.3) (15.9)	2 (0.5) (8.5)	1.6 (2.5)	1 (0.2) (5.2)
E. Construction	14 (4.0) (7.3)	16 (1.9) (8.5)	30 (2.5) (15.8)	9 (1.9) (4.7)	6 (1.4) (3.4)	14 (1.8) (7.5)
F. Wholesale Retail	71 (20.6) (8.9)	63 (7.1) (7.9)	134 (10.9) (16.8)	39 (8.5) (4.9)	27 (6.1) (3.4)	71 (8.8) (8.9)
G. Transport. & Comm.	22 (6.2) (13.0)	14 (1.5) (8.3)	35 (2.9) (21.3)	9 (2.0) (5.7)	5 (1.1) (2.9)	12 (1.6) (7.5)
H. Banking & Real Estate	4 (1.1) (9.8)	2 (0.2) (5.0)	6 (0.5) (14.9)	0.9 (0.2) (2.3)	0.9 (0.2) (2.2)	2 (0.1) (5.5)
I. Other Services	95 (27.5) (8.3)	79 (8.9) (6.9)	174 (14.2) (15.2)	54 (11.8) (4.8)	40 (9.0) (3.5)	91 (11.3) (8.0)
J. Unclassifiable	— (0.006) (1.4)	— (0.003) (2.2)	— (0.004) (3.6)	— (0.009) (2.9)	— (0.009) (2.9)	— (0.02) (13.0)

TABLE A-2-6 (continued)

	N. Chŏlla Province	S. Chŏlla Province	N. Kyŏngsang Province	Cheju Island
	707 (100.0) (8.9)	1,231 (100.0) (15.5)	1,285 (100.0) (16.2)	112 (100.0) (1.4)
A. Agri, Forest., Fishery	498 (70.4) (10.9)	896 (72.8) (19.7)	815 (63.4) (17.9)	88 (78.6) (1.9)
B. Mining	2 (0.3) (2.0)	8 (0.7) (9.3)	8 (0.7) (9.4)	0.2 (0.2) (0.3)
C. Manufacturing	55 (7.8) (5.8)	111 (9.0) (11.6)	151 (11.7) (15.8)	6 (5.1) (0.6)
D. Electricity & Water	1 (0.2) (5.5)	1 (0.1) (5.0)	2 (0.1) (7.3)	0.2 (0.2) (0.7)
E. Construction	10 (1.5) (5.4)	17 (1.4) (8.7)	26 (2.0) (13.4)	2 (2.1) (1.2)
F. Wholesale & Retail	53 (7.4) (6.6)	75 (6.1) (9.4)	117 (9.1) (14.7)	5 (4.4) (0.6)
G. Transport. & Comm.	9 (1.3) (5.4)	15 (1.2) (9.0)	21 (1.6) (12.6)	2 (1.4) (1.0)
H. Banking & Real Estate	1 (0.1) (2.6)	3 (0.2) (6.2)	3 (0.2) (7.3)	0.2 (0.2) (0.4)
I. Other Services	77 (10.9) (6.8)	104 (8.5) (9.2)	143 (11.1) (12.5)	9 (7.8) (0.8)
J. Unclassifiable	- (0.04) (20.3)	- (0.03) (28.3)	- (0.007) (6.5)	- - -

Source: EPB, *Report on Population and Housing Census, 1966*, Vol. 1–12, Seoul.

Note: Due to rounding, numbers may not add up to total

TABLE A-2-7 Income, Employment, and Family Size in Cities, 1974

	Number of households (1,000s)	Average family size (persons)	Average monthly income per household (1,000s)	Economically active population (1,000s)	Employment ratio (%)
Whole country	6,350	5.1	48	12,038	94.7
Total cities	3,130	4.8	55	5,071	90.7
Seoul	1,300	4.8	61	2,085	90.6
Pusan	460	4.8	54	747	89.5
Inch'ŏn	150	4.9	49	241	90.1
Suwŏn	41	4.9	49	68	90.6
Sŏngnam	45	4.8	37	72	87.5
Uijŏngbu	21	4.8	49	36	89.9
Anyang	24	4.7	48	40	91.4
Puch'ŏn	14	4.8	45	24	89.9
Ch'unch'ŏn	27	4.8	42	39	90.3
Wŏnju	26	4.8	42	38	93.1
Kangnŭng	16	4.9	48	26	94.6
Sokch'o	15	5.0	37	23	93.5
Ch'ŏngju	34	5.0	57	51	92.3
Ch'ungju	19	5.2	45	29	90.8
Taejŏn	90	5.1	48	144	91.2
Ch'ŏnan	16	5.3	44	27	92.5
Chŏnju	55	5.2	46	89	91.3
Kunsan	27	5.1	44	45	83.5
I-ri	20	5.3	45	38	95.2
Kwangju	113	4.9	47	166	92.0
Mokp'o	38	4.8	33	55	89.3
Yŏsu	23	5.3	50	46	92.3
Sunch'ŏn	18	5.4	41	33	92.0
Taegu	249	4.8	52	425	89.1
P'ohang	26	4.6	50	42	94.0
Kyŏngju	19	4.9	44	38	96.9
Kimch'ŏn	13	4.9	53	22	95.0
Andong	18	4.9	51	27	93.2
Masan	69	4.9	56	120	91.5
Chinju	28	5.2	46	46	93.0
Ch'ungmu	12	5.0	43	20	91.3
Chinhae	20	4.8	49	32	91.8
Samch'ŏnp'o	11	5.3	34	19	93.9
Ulsan	48	4.7	52	76	93.9
Cheju	25	4.7	49	44	97.6

Source: Retabulated from EPB, *Special Labor Force Survey Report, 1974.*

Appendix to Chapter 3
Statistical Data on Urban Growth

TABLE A-3-1 Major Economic Indicators, 1953–1975

Year	Population as of Mid-Year (1,000s)	Area (km²)	Density	Share of Urban Population (%)	Share of Agricultural Population (%)	GNP (in billion 1970 wŏn)
1975	33,459	98,758	339	50.9	40.2	4,107.71
1974	32,905	98,758	333	49.1	44.5	3,825.50
1973	32,360	98,758	329	47.2	45.3	3,522.72
1972	31,828	98,484	323	45.9	46.2	3,023.63
1971	31,298	98,477	318	43.9	46.1	2,826.82
1970	30,738	98,477	312	42.3	50.7	2,589.26
1969	30,171	98,477	306	38.6	52.7	2,400.49
1968	29,541	98,477	300	36.7	54.4	2,087.12
1967	28,962	98,477	294	40.1	54.5	1,853.01
1966	28,327	98,477	288	33.9	55.8	1,719.18
1965	27,678	98,491	281	33.4	56.2	1,529.70
1964	26,987	98,434	274	33.1	56.6	1,441.99
1963	26,231	98,434	267	32.3	57.6	1,328.31
1962	25,498	98,454	259	30.7	56.9	1,220.98
1961	24,695	98,434	251	28.1	59.0	1,184.48
1960		98,434	244	28.3	58.9	1,129.72
1959	24,003	98,434	237	26.3	58.9	1,108.33
1958	23,331	98,434		24.4		1,067.15
1957	22,677			24.3		1,014.44
1956	22,042					942.21
1955	21,424					938.24
1954	20,823					890.18
1953	20,239					843.52

TABLE A-3-1 (continued)

	Share of GNP by Agriculture (%)	Per capita GNP (in current U.S. dollars)	Parity Exchange Rate	Wholesale Price Index	Seoul Consumer Price Index	Farm Price Index	
						Received	Paid
1975	22.2	501		238.0	202.2	267.5	237.9
1974	22.8	376		188.2	160.1	215.6	192.5
1973	25.2	304		132.4	129.5	164.2	143.1
1972	26.5	275	392.9	123.8	125.6	147.9	130.5
1971	28.0	242	360.3	108.6	112.3	121.4	114.4
1970		208	342.6	100.0	100.0	100.0	100.0
1969	30.5	168	325.3	91.6	88.7	84.8	86.8
1968	31.1	143	316.3	85.8	80.6	74.3	78.8
1967	34.3	126	299.8	79.4	72.5	63.5	65.8
1966	38.9	106	282.5	74.6	65.4	55.4	58.1
1965	39.4	102	268.0	68.5	58.4	52.2	51.8
1964	42.6	98	249.1	62.3	51.4	50.2	44.8
1963	40.0	87	185.0	46.3	39.7	40.1	35.3
1962	40.3	83	153.6	38.4	32.9	27.1	31.8
1961	44.1	81	139.9	35.1	30.9	24.6	28.7
1960	41.3	83	123.4	31.0	28.6		
1959	42.6	81	111.6	28.0	26.4		
1958	44.8	74	109.2	27.3	25.3		
1957	44.4	66	118.3	29.2	26.1		
1956	43.8	66	104.5	25.1	21.2		
1955	46.7	70	82.1	19.1	17.3		
1954	48.0	67	45.6	10.5	10.3		
1953	47.1		35.4	8.2	7.5		

TABLE A-3-1 (continued)

	Industrial Production Index		Employment			Foreign Trade		Real Economic Growth Rate
	Total	Manuf.	Total (1,000s)	Share of Agriculture	Share of Manuf.	Exports (in $ million)	Imports (in $ million)	
1975	267.8	283.6	11,830	48.2	18.6	5,081.0	7,274.4	7.4
1974	225.0	237.5	11,586	50.0	17.4	4,460.4	6,851.8	8.6
1973	176.4	183.8	11,139	50.6	15.9	3,225.0	4,240.3	16.5
1972	132.2	135.7	10,559	48.4	13.7	1,624.1	2,522.0	7.0
1971	115.4	116.6	10,066	50.4	13.3	1,067.6	2,394.3	9.2
1970	100.0	100.0	9,745		13.2	835.2	1,984.0	7.9
1969	89.7	89.6	9,414	51.3	13.1	622.5	1,823.6	15.0
1968	74.8	74.3	9,155	52.4	12.8	455.4	1,462.9	12.6
1967	57.1	54.7	8,717	55.2	11.7	320.2	996.2	7.8
1966	45.1	42.2	8,423	57.9	9.9	250.3	716.4	12.4
1965	36.8	33.9	8,206	58.6	9.4	175.1	463.4	6.1
1964	34.3	31.8	7,799	61.9	8.2	119.1	404.4	8.6
1963	31.7	29.6	7,662	63.1	8.0	86.8	560.3	8.8
1962	28.1	26.2				54.8	421.8	3.1
1961	24.0	22.4				40.9	316.1	4.8
1960	22.7	21.5				32.8	343.5	1.9
1959	20.8	20.4				19.8	303.8	3.9
1958	18.1	18.3				16.5	378.2	5.2
1957	16.5	16.5				22.2	442.2	7.7
1956	14.3	14.7				24.6	386.1	0.4
1955	11.7	12.2				18.0	341.4	5.4
1954	9.8	10.1				24.2	243.3	5.5

Sources: BOK, Economic Statistics Yearbook, 1976, and National Income in Korea, 1973, 1975.

TABLE A-3-2 Data for Development Processes in Korea
(billion wǒn at current prices)

	1953	1954	1955	1956	1957	1958
GNP deflator in Korea (1970=100)	5.7	7.5	12.4	16.2	19.5	19.4
GNP deflator in the U.S. (1960=100)	85.52	86.78	87.97	91.00	94.39	96.82
Population (in thousands)	20,239	20,823	21,424	22,042	22,677	23,331
GNP at 1970 constant factor cost	803.25	846.24	887.89	886.91	953.81	1,001.78
GDP at current factor cost	45.97	63.00	110.24	145.64	187.40	193.42
Expenditure on GDP	47.61	66.24	114.68	151.05	196.35	205.76
Accumulation Processes						
Gross domestic investment	7.69	7.78	13.81	14.41	30.26	26.73
Exports of goods & nonfactor services	0.95	0.73	1.92	2.11	2.97	4.23
Imports of goods & nonfactor services	4.67	4.89	11.43	19.98	23.73	22.12
Government revenue	2.76	5.16	8.16	10.59	17.54	20.63
Tax revenue	2.33	4.56	7.12	9.06	14.79	17.53
Education expenditure by government	0.51	1.97	4.00	4.55	6.73	7.52
Resource Allocation Processes						
Private consumption	39.86	55.84	100.28	140.63	165.50	170.77
Government consumption	3.78	6.78	10.10	13.88	21.35	26.15
Food consumption	22.96	39.96	59.46	90.14	102.93	103.19
Value added by sector						
Agriculture, forestry & fishery	22.66	26.74	51.75	71.61	88.39	84.75
Mining & quarrying	0.53	0.64	1.22	1.75	2.89	3.27
Manufacturing	3.55	6.39	10.89	14.61	17.68	20.77
Construction	1.01	1.72	3.47	4.35	6.86	6.61
Electricity, gas & water	0.20	0.27	0.53	0.38	1.06	1.66
Transportation, storage & communication	0.74	1.31	3.34	4.91	7.71	7.20
Wholesale & retail trade	5.37	7.44	13.07	16.51	18.90	18.81
Banking, insurance & real estate	0.33	0.32	0.72	0.88	1.66	2.35

TABLE A-3-2 (continued)

	1953	1954	1955	1956	1957	1958
Ownership of dwellings	5.96	7.74	8.89	10.29	12.34	13.99
Public administration & defense	2.81	4.85	6.42	7.45	11.95	13.65
Services	2.81	5.58	9.94	12.90	17.96	20.36
Merchandise share of total exports	0.7521	0.7507	0.4330	0.6838	0.4051	0.2691
Manufactures share of all merchandise						
Demographic & Distributional Processes						
Total labor force (in thousands)						
Primary labor						
Industry labor						
Services labor						
Urbanization (%)					24.1	24.4

TABLE A-3-2 (continued)

	1959	1960	1961	1962	1963
GNP deflator in Korea (1970=100)	19.9	21.8	25.1	28.6	36.8
GNP deflator in the U.S. (1960=100)	98.43	100.00	101.29	102.41	103.76
Population (in thousands)	24,003	24,695	25,498	26,231	26,987
GNP at 1970 constant factor cost	1,036.33	1,053.40	1,107.67	1,135.34	1,233.19
GDP at current factor cost	203.44	226.06	276.39	319.29	455.13
Expenditure on GDP	219.54	244.53	294.30	345.71	485.21
Accumulation Processes					
Gross domestic investment	23.72	26.80	38.79	45.47	90.26
Exports of goods & nonfactor services	5.88	8.22	15.76	17.98	23.76
Imports of goods & nonfactor services	22.40	31.02	43.83	59.11	79.45
Government revenue	25.10	31.90	39.23	48.99	58.31
Tax revenue	22.21	25.19	28.42	37.74	43.12
Education expenditure by govenment	9.34	19.51	10.01	12.11	13.30
Resource Allocation Processes					
Private consumption	181.49	207.26	245.44	293.79	403.31
Government consumption	30.85	35.54	40.06	49.62	54.74
Food consumption	101.48	114.20	141.66	164.33	235.55
Value added by sector					
Agriculture, forestry & fishery	76.07	90.24	118.83	127.03	204.97
Mining & quarrying	3.86	5.23	5.51	6.97	8.14
Manufacturing	24.61	27.27	34.30	40.40	62.49
Construction	7.54	7.97	9.46	11.46	14.48
Electricity, gas & water	1.35	1.64	2.95	3.94	4.29
Transportation, storage & communication	8.98	10.34	12.87	15.71	18.20
Wholesale & retail trade	21.82	21.64	24.65	33.15	50.14
Banking, insurance & real estate	2.79	3.41	3.75	4.79	6.18

TABLE A-3-2 (continued)

	1959	1960	1961	1962	1963
Ownership of dwellings	14.89	16.01	16.25	17.92	20.96
Public administration & defense	16.56	17.42	20.40	26.54	28.08
Services	24.97	24.89	27.42	31.38	37.20
Merchandise share of total exports	0.2721	0.4108	0.3333	0.3962	0.6239
Manufactures share of all merchandise		0.182	0.219	0.270	0.517
Demographic & Distributional Processes					
Total labor force (in thousands)					7,662
Primary labor					4,894
Industry labor					803
Services labor					1.965
Urbanization (%)	26.3	28.3	28.1	30.7	32.3

TABLE A-3-2 (continued)

	1964	1965	1966	1967	1968	1969
GNP deflator in Korea (1970=100)	48.6	52.6	60.1	68.5	76.6	86.7
GNP deflator in the U.S. (1960=100)	105.38	107.33	110.31	113.84	118.40	124.12
Population (in thousands)	27,678	28,327	28,962	29,541	30,171	30,738
GNP at 1970 constant factor cost	1,343.25	1,416.92	1,589.88	1,700.03	1,902.08	2,182.80
GDP at current factor cost	662.09	750.61	946.78	1,149.35	1,427.62	1,859.65
Expenditure on GDP	694.95	797.67	1,019.07	1,248.00	1,574.86	2,056.49
Accumulation Processes						
Gross domestic investment	102.24	121.98	224.48	280.97	427.87	620.70
Exports of goods & nonfactor services	42.06	68.61	106.81	144.61	209.30	287.81
Imports of goods & nonfactor services	96.44	127.79	207.82	279.42	416.81	541.86
Government revenue	70.64	94.67	141.55	195.83	293.30	378.54
Tax revenue	50.55	69.27	100.34	152.12	228.71	311.91
Education expenditure by government	14.49	15.81	23.69	31.81	45.55	56.10
Resource Allocation Processes						
Private consumption	586.31	668.80	805.18	985.97	1,204.44	1,493.65
Government consumption	61.95	76.02	104.82	132.17	175.28	222.69
Food consumption	375.63	398.92	449.73	534.74	630.33	788.02
Value added by sector						
Agriculture, forestry & fishery	319.74	307.75	363.44	398.05	454.07	595.71
Mining & quarrying	12.04	14.70	16.33	20.45	20.28	23.40
Manufacturing	99.88	130.08	166.66	205.68	267.15	346.18
Construction	19.95	27.29	37.49	48.73	77.64	119.46
Electricity, gas & water	5.62	8.57	11.87	14.81	19.31	27.00
Transportation, storage & communication	22.00	29.80	46.25	64.79	90.11	109.25
Wholesale & retail trade	72.28	99.10	131.27	169.87	205.06	278.41
Banking, insurance & real estate	8.16	9.82	12.55	16.84	25.34	33.90

TABLE A-3-2 (continued)

	1964	1965	1966	1967	1968	1969
Ownership of dwellings	24.58	27.20	32.38	42.55	47.17	52.18
Public administration & defense	33.64	39.94	53.84	67.15	85.64	107.28
Services	44.20	56.36	74.70	100.43	135.85	166.88
Merchandise share of total exports	0.6575	0.6774	0.6358	0.6263	0.6425	0.6594
Manufactures share of all merchandise	0.515	0.623	0.624	0.701	0.773	0.790
Demographic & Distributional Processes						
Total labor force (in thousands)	7,799	8,206	8,423	8,717	9,155	9,414
Primary labor	4,878	4,887	4,956	4,905	4,913	4,939
Industry labor	820	1,010	1,042	1,280	1,486	1,569
Services labor	2,101	2,309	2,425	2,532	2,756	2,906
Urbanization (%)	33.1	33.4	33.9	35.2	36.7	38.6

TABLE A-3-2 (continued)

	1970	1971	1972	1973	1974
GNP deflator in Korea (1970=100)	100.0	111.5	127.7	139.9	177.2
GNP deflator in the U.S. (1960=100)	130.93	136.85	141.47	149.39	164.69
Population (in thousands)	31,298	31,828	32,360	32,905	33,459
GNP at 1970 constant factor cost	2,337.88	2,536.78	2,697.99	3,117.91	3,372.41
GDP at current factor cost	2,325.98	2,857.40	3,533.90	4,542.86	6,339.78
Expenditure on GDP	2,577.36	3,153.81	3,875.32	4,965.66	6,844.74
Accumulation Processes					
Gross domestic investment	704.66	805.35	805.48	1,292.29	2,125.88
Exports of goods & nonfactor services	381.23	514.21	813.81	1,577.72	2,071.19
Imports of goods & nonfactor services	642.44	865.95	1,013.52	1,739.64	2,923.28
Government revenue	497.14	593.63	653.79	784.22	1,194.64
Tax revenue	393.69	480.17	519.66	650.13	1,016.84
Education expenditure by government	77.93	95.14	120.83	138.51	200.66
Resource Allocation Processes					
Private consumption	1,884.25	2,337.32	2,844.45	3,359.55	4,734.32
Government consumption	281.81	355.96	438.24	479.35	741.90
Food consumption	1,015.95	1,278.15	1,564.42	1,777.87	2,590.48
Value added by sector					
Agriculture, forestry & fishery	723.91	909.85	1,093.14	1,277.45	1,713.07
Mining & quarrying	30.35	33.72	37.57	47.82	79.05
Manufacturing	444.19	541.22	741.12	1,105.30	1,603.06
Construction	148.05	164.23	176.01	234.00	297.46
Electricity, gas & water	37.75	44.06	66.17	72.76	84.44
Transportation, storage & communication	128.96	156.02	199.09	266.53	359.20
Wholesale & retail trade	354.66	442.46	558.04	787.09	1,167.76
Banking, insurance & real estate	46.47	62.48	71.11	83.45	127.81

TABLE A-3-2 (continued)

	1970	1971	1972	1973	1974
Ownership of dwellings	58.89	68.57	69.31	78.04	100.13
Public administration & defense	138.07	168.02	199.46	214.36	289.36
Services	214.68	266.77	322.88	376.07	518.44
Merchandise share of total exports	0.7188	0.7656	0.8091	0.8256	0.8810
Manufactures share of all merchandise	0.836	0.860	0.877	0.882	0.902
Demographic & Distributional Processes					
Total labor force (in thousands)	9,745	10,066	10,559	11,139	11,586
Primary labor	5,027	4,968	5,400	5,616	5,634
Industry labor	1,568	1,684	1,837	2,145	2,462
Services labor	3,150	3,414	3,322	3,378	3,490
Urbanization (%)	42.3	43.9	45.9	47.2	49.8

Sources: BOK, *National Income in Korea, 1975.*
EPB, *Annual Report on the Economically Active Population, 1974.*

TABLE A-3.3 Data for Sectoral Growth in Korea

(million wŏn at 1970 constant prices)

	1953	1954	1955	1956	1957	1958
GNP at 1970 constant price (in billion wŏn)	843.52	890.18	938.24	942.21	1,014.44	1,067.15
Population (in millions)	20.2	20.8	21.4	22.0	22.7	23.3
Per capita GNP (in 1960 dollars)	102.7	105.2	107.8	105.3	109.9	112.6
Share of primary exports in GNP						
Share of manufactured exports in GNP						
Share of gross fixed capital formation in GNP	0.061	0.073	0.079	0.084	0.090	0.082
Value Added in Manufacturing						
Food	10,922	13,864	15,204	17,316	18,555	20,874
Beverage	7,377	5,740	10,905	13,398	11,750	13,734
Tobacco	5,958	6,380	6,888	6,987	7,164	7,643
Textiles	9,879	12,589	15,450	19,702	23,795	24,153
Footwear and wearing apparel	2,808	3,916	4,938	5,588	6,717	7,033
Wood and cork products	1,284	1,971	2,084	2,355	3,100	2,374
Furniture and fixtures	1,079	1,314	1,929	1,980	2,032	1,985
Paper and paper products	506	681	765	715	670	1,266
Printing and publishing	2,486	2,862	3,445	3,542	3,265	4,291
Leather and leather products	595	735	889	1,166	1,141	1,302
Rubber products	787	1,053	966	975	1,439	1,584
Chemicals and chemical products	1,557	1,817	2,123	2,342	2,560	2,836
Coal products	354	411	486	697	823	1,001
Clay, glass and stone products	978	1,410	1,747	2,146	2,319	3,102
Basic metal industries	264	309	418	653	952	1,210
Metal products	780	933	1,052	1,066	1,257	1,401
Machinery	1,306	1,652	1,747	2,213	1,892	2,449
Electrical machinery	351	440	303	799	908	855
Transport equipment	1,180	1,592	1,974	2,371	2,729	2,686

TABLE A-3-3 (continued)

	1959	1960	1961	1962	1963
GNP at 1970 constant price (in billion wŏn)	1,108.33	1,129.72	1,184.48	1,220.98	1,328.31
Population (in millions)	24.0	24.7	25.5	26.2	27.0
Per capita GNP (in 1960 dollars)	113.6	112.5	114.2	114.6	121.0
Share of primary exports in GNP		0.0111	0.0138	0.0150	0.0148
Share of manufactured exports in GNP		0.0025	0.0039	0.0056	0.0158
Share of gross fixed capital formation in GNP	0.084	0.086	0.088	0.109	0.126
Value Added in Manufacturing					
Food	21,370	22,587	23,225	23,552	28,947
Beverage	16,420	18,167	19,352	14,980	14,870
Tobacco	7,946	7,848	8,528	9,712	10,754
Textiles	24,845	24,484	22,555	25,707	29,084
Footwear and wearing apparel	8,279	9,438	9,343	12,450	13,800
Wood and cork products	3,054	3,210	2,282	3,275	4,097
Furniture and fixtures	1,748	1,711	1,471	1,693	1,697
Paper and paper products	1,312	1,759	2,240	3,115	4,084
Printing and publishing	4,533	5,799	5,087	6,558	7,228
Leather and leather products	1,061	1,027	1,188	1,229	1,131
Rubber products	2,584	2,601	2,433	2,656	3,048
Chemicals and chemical products	3,270	4,166	4,970	7,197	10,998
Coal products	1,254	1,621	1,822	2,191	3,304
Clay, glass and stone products	3,618	3,786	4,050	5,316	6,134
Basic metal industries	1,428	2,248	2,161	3,177	4,317
Metal products	1,682	2,028	2,333	2,669	3,185
Machinery	2,564	3,279	4,336	6,256	5,443
Electrical machinery	1,233	1,292	1,728	2,864	3,944
Transport equipment	2,671	2,946	4,417	5,073	7,518

TABLE A-3-3 (continued)

	1964	1965	1966	1967	1968	1969
GNP at 1970 constant price (in billion wŏn)	1,441.99	1,529.70	1,719.18	1,853.01	2,087.12	2,400.49
Population (in millions)	27.7	28.3	29.0	29.5	30.2	30.7
Per capita GNP (in 1960 dollars)	128.0	132.9	145.8	154.4	169.9	192.3
Share of primary exports in GNP	0.0191	0.0217	0.0246	0.0214	0.0191	0.0191
Share of manufactured exports in GNP	0.0203	0.0359	0.0409	0.0500	0.0651	0.0719
Share of gross fixed capital formation in GNP	0.107	0.128	0.171	0.193	0.239	0.266
Value Added in Manufacturing						
Food	31,569	34,265	37,647	43,724	51,692	64,455
Beverage	15,072	19,605	23,068	28,810	28,996	35,608
Tobacco	12,947	17,115	20,707	25,764	31,360	36,482
Textiles	28,555	33,574	36,989	44,193	55,141	68,147
Footwear and wearing apparel	12,255	14,258	16,508	20,505	24,259	27,501
Wood and cork products	3,977	5,063	6,667	8,021	12,138	13,361
Furniture and fixtures	1,332	1,539	1,549	1,910	2,896	3,296
Paper and paper products	4,772	5,351	6,414	7,232	8,623	10,203
Printing and publishing	8,581	10,023	11,486	12,345	13,020	13,374
Leather and leather products	1,302	1,318	1,428	1,556	1,872	1,637
Rubber products	3,526	4,332	5,052	4,971	6,437	7,789
Chemicals and chemical products	10,886	10,877	13,435	19,344	32,665	37,368
Coal products	7,449	12,021	14,849	17,654	28,469	38,088
Clay, glass and stone products	8,357	9,733	10,855	13,930	18,200	22,495
Basic metal industries	4,185	5,274	5,961	7,462	9,629	11,955
Metal products	2,902	3,882	4,440	5,057	6,252	6,606
Machinery	5,653	6,648	6,407	8,687	9,265	8,767
Electrical machinery	4,961	5,594	8,307	10,388	14,625	21,042
Transport equipment	6,028	8,619	12,397	17,316	24,018	31,716

TABLE A-3-3 (continued)

	1970	1971	1972	1973	1974
GNP at 1970 constant price (in billion wŏn)	2,589.26	2,826.82	3,023.63	3,522.72	3,825.50
Population (in millions)	31.3	31.8	32.4	32.9	33.5
Per capita GNP (in 1960 dollars)	203.4	218.6	229.5	263.3	280.8
Share of primary exports in GNP	0.0173	0.0175	0.0210	0.0312	0.0263
Share of manufactured exports in GNP	0.0883	0.1073	0.1497	0.2330	0.2424
Share of gross fixed capital formation in GNP	0.251	0.241	0.218	0.242	0.246
Value Added in Manufacturing					
Food	71,709	81,883	93,668	102,373	104,713
Beverage	43,340	52,694	52,690	63,009	71,058
Tobacco	46,972	56,447	61,865	61,781	72,407
Textiles	82,582	96,383	123,350	152,169	154,124
Footwear and wearing apparel	33,594	50,676	73,305	130,671	172,649
Wood and cork products	14,309	16,188	18,546	22,274	19,358
Furniture and fixtures	3,308	3,153	3,394	3,323	3,358
Paper and paper products	11,248	13,719	15,559	20,183	23,201
Printing and publishing	14,226	15,030	15,910	16,642	18,375
Leather and leather products	1,827	3,350	5,775	12,952	27,825
Rubber products	7,304	8,645	9,915	13,889	16,621
Chemicals and chemical products	47,643	57,321	62,945	76,072	89,692
Coal products	50,916	60,043	61,706	74,346	70,383
Clay, glass and stone products	27,098	31,854	32,250	44,286	47,692
Basic metal industries	13,600	15,066	17,866	27,260	36,503
Metal products	7,029	7,231	6,669	10,355	12,460
Machinery	8,408	7,850	9,029	13,781	13,000
Electrical machinery	23,407	27,712	35,388	70,296	106,940
Transport equipment	28,339	28,097	29,982	42,566	71,424

Source: BOK, National Income in Korea, 1975.

Appendix to Chapter 4
Statistical Data on Primacy and
City Size Distribution

TABLE A-4-1 Urban Population by Cities (Si) and Towns (Ŭp), 1949–1975
(1,000s)

	1975	1973	1972	1971	1970	1969	1968	1967	1966	1965
1. Si (cities)										
Seoul	6,889	6,299	6,076	5,851	5,536	4,777	4,335	3,868	3,805	3,471
Pusan	2,454	2,072	2,015	1,944	1,881	1,676	1,552	1,463	1,430	1,420
Inch'ŏn	800	714	690	671	646	578	556	536	529	486
Suwŏn	224	192	183	176	171	161	142	131	128	123
Sŏngnam	272	191	166	–	–	–	–	–	–	–
Ŭijŏngbu	108	105	101	95	96	87	83	78	75	70
Anyang	135	111	105	–	–	–	–	–	–	–
Puch'ŏn	109	65	61	–	–	–	–	–	–	–
Ch'unch'ŏn	141	135	133	126	123	113	107	104	100	101
Wŏnju	120	128	116	114	112	108	106	104	104	95
Kangnŭng	85	82	79	77	74	71	69	67	65	65
Sokch'o	71	76	74	73	73	73	71	67	63	60
Ch'ŏngju	193	167	159	155	144	133	131	127	124	121
Ch'ungju	105	96	95	92	88	84	83	81	80	79
Taejŏn	507	463	452	437	415	365	352	330	316	307
Ch'ŏnan	97	85	82	79	78	73	72	72	71	69
Chŏnju	311	286	277	272	263	243	234	224	220	217
Kunsan	154	136	133	116	112	106	107	103	102	100
I-ri	117	91	88	86	87	81	80	79	78	77
Kwangju	607	552	538	520	503	480	461	433	404	366
Mokp'o	193	192	187	182	178	168	168	166	162	157
Yŏsu	131	123	119	116	114	106	107	103	102	98
Sunch'ŏn	108	104	101	97	91	82	82	81	79	78
Taegu	1,311	1,200	1,164	1,133	1,083	1,034	962	887	847	811
P'ohang	134	109	93	85	79	76	72	68	66	66
Kyŏngju	108	98	96	94	92	90	89	86	86	86
Kimch'ŏn	67	67	66	63	62	60	59	57	57	57
Andong	95	87	83	79	76	73	71	66	64	62
Masan	372	304	211	195	191	177	173	165	155	159
Chinju	155	143	130	126	122	114	111	109	107	104

TABLE A-4-1 (continued)

	1975	1973	1972	1971	1970	1969	1968	1967	1966	1965
Ch'ungmu	67	63	59	56	55	53	52	51	51	52
Chinhae	104	100	93	94	92	88	85	83	81	77
Samch'ŏnp'o	60	57	56	56	55	55	55	55	54	54
Ulsan	253	187	165	160	159	143	131	122	113	97
Cheju	135	118	114	110	106	98	94	90	88	84
Total	16,794	14,988	14,359	13,529	12,955	11,625	10,850	10,158	9,729	9,267
2. Ŭp (towns)[a]										
Tongduch'ŏn	60	60	56	55	60	61	59	59	59	54
P'yŏngt'aek	51	53	53	52	52					
Songt'an	57									
Sindo	59									
Yŏngch'ŏn	51	53	52	51	50					
Sangju	53	56	56	54	53	52	51	50	–	53
Mukho	55	57	57	57	56	55	54	53	50	51
Changsŏng	56	51	53	103	103	100	95	94	87	83
Hwangji	61	50								
Chech'ŏn	74	68	67	65	62	59	53	51	50	50
Namwŏn	51	51	50							
Chŏngju	55	55	53	52	50	55	50			
Yŏngju	71	67	65	63	59					
Kimhae	56	50	50							
Sŏgwi	53	54	51							
Munsan		53	53							
Anyang				102	92	76	65	60	54	51
Sosa				58	57	50				
Total	865	779	715	711	693	508	427	365	300	341
3. Total Si (cities) and Ŭp (towns)	20,429	18,631	17,100	16,401	15,809			12,848	12,369	11,891
4. Urban population	17,658	15,767	15,074	14,240	13,012	12,133	11,277	10,523	10,029	9,608
5. Total population	34,709	32,905	32,360	31,828	31,435	30,738	30,171	29,541	29,160	28,327

TABLE A-4-1 (continued)

	1964	1963	1962	1961	1960	1959	1958	1957	1955	1949
1. Si (cities)										
Seoul	3,424	3,255	2,983	2,577	2,445	2,094	1,756	1,666	1,575	1,418
Pusan	1,400	1,351	1,270	1,164	1,164	1,087	1,045	1,019	1,049	471
Inch'ŏn	465	445	430	397	401	361	319	301	318	257
Suwŏn	122	118	113	87	91	79	76	74	81	53
Sŏngnam										
Ŭijŏngbu	65	62	57[b]	24[b]	25[b]	38[b]	31[b]	27[b]	26[b]	22[b]
Anyang										
Puch'ŏn										
Ch'unch'ŏn	94	91	86	80	83	74	72	63	68	55[b]
Wŏnju	86	83	77	75	77	64	59	55	76	34[b]
Kangnŭng	62	60	57	55	59	53	52	51	51	30[b]
Sokch'o	59	56	51[b]	42[b]	46[b]	34[b]	31[b]	29[b]	28[b]	
Ch'ŏngju	119	118	112	91	92	82	78	77	81	65[b]
Ch'ungju	77	76	71	65	69	59	56	56	51[b]	41[b]
Taejŏn	303	290	268	234	229	200	184	176	173	127
Ch'ŏnan	68	66	63[b]	44[b]	44[b]	40[b]	38[b]	37[b]	34[b]	27[b]
Chŏnju	212	204	194	185	188	163	157	157	124	101
Kunsan	101	95	92	87	90	86	87	88	86	74
I-ri	74	71	68	63	66	69	69	62	62	47
Kwangju	343	334	313	318	315	306	261	248	233	159
Mokp'o	154	150	143	127	130	129	122	108	114	111
Yŏsu	95	94	89	86	87	80	71	71	73	179
Sunch'ŏn	77	75	72	70	69	64	64	61	62	53
Taegu	788	762	717	693	676	647	614	609	457	313
P'ohang	66	64	62	60	60	51	49	49	46	51
Kyŏngju	85	82	80	75	76	68	67	64	65	36[b]
Kimch'ŏn	57	55	53	51	51	47	45	45	41	48
Andong	60	59	56[b]	53[b]	53[b]	52[b]	44[b]	45[b]	46[b]	41[b]
Masan	156	158	152	152	158	155	152	121	130	91
Chinju	102	98	93	86	87	103	84	84	78	77

TABLE A-4-1 (continued)

	1964	1963	1962	1961	1960	1959	1958	1957	1956	1949
Ch'ungmu	53	52	48	46	48	43	50	52	61	–
Chinhae	76	76	71	64	67	55	54	51	68	–
Samch'ŏnp'o	54	53	51	50	50	51	50	51	50[b]	–
Ulsan	94	92	85	30[b]	30[b]	27[b]	26[b]	26[b]	26[b]	–
Cheju	82	79	73	68	68	63	62	61	60	58[b]
Total	9,074	8,733	8,153	7,300	7,139	6,522	5,925	5,685	5,496	4,039
2. Ŭp (towns)										
Tongduch'ŏn										
P'yŏngt'aek										
Songt'an										
Sindo										
Yŏngch'ŏn										
Sangju	52									
Mukho		50								
Changsŏng	83	89	82	67	67	51				
Hwangji	50									
Chech'ŏn										
Namwŏn										
Chŏngju										
Yŏngju										
Kimhae										
Sŏgwi										
Munsan										
Anyang										
Sosa										
Total	185	139	82	67	67	51				
3. Total Si (cities) and Ŭp (towns)	11,641	11,253	10,923	9,582	9,472	8,613	7,943	7,481	7,288	5,675
4. Urban population	9,259	8,872	8,817	7,180	7,013	6,344	5,705	5,427	5,249	3,712
5. Total population	27,678	26,987	26,231	25,498	24,954[c]	22,866	22,505	22,329	21,502[c]	20,167[c]

Sources: MHA, *Municipal Yearbook of Korea, 1969, 1972, 1974;* EPB, *Report on Population and Housing Census, 1975.*

Notes: [a] Ŭp with population over 50,000.   [b] Population before these urban areas became si.   [c] Census data.

TABLE A-4-2 Area and Administrative Unit by Province, 1974

	Area		Ku	Si	Kun	Ŭp	Tong	Myŏn	I	Pan
	Km²	Share	(Borough)	(City)	(County)	(Town)	(Precinct)	(Township)	(Village)	(Neighborhood)
Whole Country	98,758	100.0	28	33	138	122	1,483	1,348	31,351	253,061
Seoul	658	0.6	11	–	–	–	468	–	–	49,202
Pusan	375	0.4	6	–	–	–	161	–	–	18,980
Kyŏnggi province	11,069	11.2	4	6	18	14	143	181	4,002	25,407
Kangwŏn province	16,785	17.0	–	4	15	15	72	98	2,179	14,322
N. Ch'ungch'ŏng province	7,437	7.5	–	2	10	8	35	96	2,435	12,525
S. Ch'ungch'ŏng province	8,752	8.9	–	2	15	21	55	158	4,237	22,510
N. Chŏlla province	8,058	8.2	–	3	13	8	70	153	1,580	2,517
S. Chŏlla province	12,075	12.2	2	4	22	17	127	214	6,229	23,052
N. Kyŏngsang province	19,802	20.1	5	5	24	22	187	229	5,538	46,537
S. Kyŏngsang province	11,958	12.1	–	6	19	14	151	209	4,964	34,098
Cheju Island	1,820	1.8	–	1	2	3	14	10	187	3,911

Source: EPB, *Korea Statistical Yearbook, 1975.*

TABLE A-4-3 Status of Industrial Estates in Korea, 1976

Location	Type	Area (1,000s p'yŏng)		No. of firms	Export (in 1975, $1,000s)	Employees (1,000s)
		Developed	Occupied			
(Local Gov't Estates)	Local	2,899	2,235	551	228,366	57.7
Inch'ŏn	,,	362	292	39	14,052	2.4
Sŏngnam	,,	484	368	129	60,119	19.0
Ch'unch'ŏn	,,	149	112	20	5,410	2.5
Wŏnju	,,	120	70	16	1,496	1.0
Ch'ŏngju	,,	224	115	34	32,810	4.4
Taejŏn	,,	145	106	41	2,626	3.9
Chŏnju	,,	509	401	47	31,795	4.6
Kwangju	,,	436	356	45	1,746	2.7
Mokp'o	,,	159	82	14	3,975	1.6
Taegu	,,	331	293	166	74,337	15.2
(Private Estates)		1,120	851	155	12,341	8.7
Yŏngdŭngp'o	Machinery					
	Synthetic Resin	45	34	68	2,409	2.8
Inch'ŏn	Machinery	99	79	47	1,512	1.5
P'ohang	Iron & Steel	976	738	40	8,420	4.2
(Export-Oriented Special Estates)		6,653	3,966	654	823,742	140.4
Masan	Free Export	284	150	103	174,803	25.0
Kuro	Export	1,129	853	344	545,039	97.0
Kumi	Export (Electronics)	3,170	1,504	100	101,312	14.2
I-ri	Free Export	431	156	66	1,975	3.0
Ch'angwŏn	Export (Machinery)	2,070	1,303	41	613	1.2

Source: Kongŏp Tanji Kwallich'ŏng, *Kongŏp tanji ŭi hyŏnhang,* I, II, (March 1976)
Note: 1 p'yŏng = 3.3058 m² = 0.00317 acre

TABLE A-4-4 Industrial Estates Development Plan, 1977-1981

Location	Type	Area of Estates (km^2)		Development Period	Budget (billion wŏn)	
		Completed	To be Completed		Total	FFYP
Ch'angwŏn	General machinery	1,598	5,279	1974-1981	90.7	66.0
Yŏch'on	General chemical	1,969	4,580	1974-1981	303.7	125.6
Onsan	Oil refining & non-ferrous metals	110	4,760	1969-1981	120.5	93.3
Okp'o	Shipbuilding	–	951	1974-1977	26.8	7.9
Chukto	,,	378	584	1974-1981	14.3	8.8
Anjŏng	,,	–	1,054	1974-1979	20.4	20.4
P'ohang	Integrated iron & steel	1,212	5,600	1968-1981	112.3	69.2
Mip'o	Shipbuilding	836	836	1962-1981	6.3	3.3
Pukp'yŏng	Cement & mining machines	–	3,200	1978-1981	90.0	74.6

Source: Kŏnsŏlbu, *Kukt'o mit sanŏp ipchi pumun kyehoek, 1977-1981*, Seoul, 1976.

Note: All industrial estates except Pukp'yŏng are located in the southeastern coastal region.

TABLE A-4-5 Structure of Employment by Urban Areas

	Total Employment		Agriculture, Forestry & Fishery		Mining & Manufacturing		Service & Others	
	Number	*%*	*Number*	*%*	*Number*	*%*	*Number*	*%*
Whole country	11,453,690	100.0	5,484,994	47.9	1,958,584	17.1	4,010,112	35.0
Total cities	4,605,463	100.0	212,143	4.6	1,469,174	31.9	2,924,146	63.5
Seoul	1,889,247	100.0	12,714	0.7	658,632	34.9	1,217,901	64.4
Pusan	670,263	100.0	19,529	2.9	252,211	37.6	398,623	59.5
Inch'ŏn	216,800	100.0	17,869	8.2	70,403	32.5	128,528	59.3
Suwŏn	61,973	100.0	4,706	7.6	20,600	33.2	36,667	59.2
Sŏngnam	62,628	100.0	6,528	10.4	22,813	36.4	33,287	53.2
Ŭijŏngbu	32,444	100.0	2,369	7.3	6,271	19.3	23,804	73.4
Anyang	36,812	100.0	4,021	10.9	15,048	40.9	17,743	48.2
Puch'ŏn	21,395	100.0	1,734	8.1	10,045	47.0	9,616	44.9
Ch'unch'ŏn	35,212	100.0	3,223	9.2	5,143	14.6	26,846	76.2
Wŏnju	35,385	100.0	4,309	12.2	6,671	18.9	24,405	68.9
Kangnŭng	24,172	100.0	5,580	23.1	3,470	14.4	15,122	62.7
Sokch'o	21,783	100.0	11,016	50.6	3,161	14.5	7,606	34.9
Ch'ŏngju	46,779	100.0	5,160	11.0	11,062	23.6	30,557	65.3
Ch'ungju	26,567	100.0	5,449	20.5	6,603	24.9	14,515	54.6
Taejŏn	131,184	100.0	5,866	4.5	37,099	28.3	88,219	67.2
Ch'ŏnan	25,197	100.0	4,684	18.6	6,355	25.2	14,158	56.2
Chonju	81,511	100.0	18,557	22.8	16,849	20.7	46,105	56.5
Kunsan	39,481	100.0	6,139	15.5	12,205	30.9	21,137	53.5
I-ri	36,199	100.0	10,252	28.3	8,379	23.1	17,568	48.5
Kwangju	152,948	100.0	18,198	11.9	29,259	19.1	105,491	69.0
Mokp'o	49,183	100.0	6,516	13.2	10,670	21.7	31,997	65.1

(*continued*)

TABLE A-4-5 (continued)

	Total Employment		Agriculture, Forestry & Fishery		Mining & Manufacturing		Service & Others	
	Number	*%*	*Number*	*%*	*Number*	*%*	*Number*	*%*
Yŏsu	41,859	100.0	13,035	31.1	6,128	14.6	22,696	54.2
Sunch'ŏn	30,250	100.0	8,850	29.3	2,991	9.9	18,409	60.8
Taegu	378,727	100.0	13,589	3.6	135,105	35.7	230,033	60.7
P'ohang	39,358	100.0	5,254	13.3	10,905	27.7	23,199	58.9
Kyŏngju	36,737	100.0	16,206	44.1	3,239	8.8	17,292	47.1
Kimch'ŏn	21,351	100.0	5,052	23.7	4,945	23.2	11,354	53.2
Andong	24,914	100.0	4,588	18.4	3,774	15.1	16,552	66.4
Masan	109,688	100.0	13,301	12.1	35,777	32.6	60,610	55.3
Chinju	42,729	100.0	6,921	16.2	10,605	24.8	25,203	59.0
Ch'ungmu	17,877	100.0	4,412	24.7	4,157	23.3	9,308	52.0
Chinhae	29,152	100.0	5,294	18.2	7,007	24.0	16,851	57.8
Samch'ŏnp'o	17,884	100.0	9,069	50.7	2,780	15.5	6,035	33.7
Ulsan	71,334	100.0	15,434	21.6	24,531	34.4	31,369	44.0
Cheju	43,490	100.0	16,819	38.7	4,330	10.0	22,341	51.3

Source: EPB, *Special Labor Force Survey Report, 1974.*

Appendix to Chapter 5
Statistical Data on Migration

TABLE A-5-1 Pattern of Urban and Rural Migration in Korea, 1965–1970
(1,000s)

| Origin | Destination | | | | | |
| | Urban | | | | Rural | Total |
	Seoul	Pusan	Others	Total		
Urban	369.0	94.9	206.0	669.9	377.8	1,047.7
Seoul		22.4	83.9	106.3	141.6	247.9
Pusan	57.2		37.9	95.1	32.3	127.4
Others	311.8	72.5	84.2	468.5	203.9	672.4
Rural	813.3	213.8	817.4	1,844.5	297.1[a]	2,141.6
Total	1,182.3	308.7	1,023.4	2,514.4	674.9	3,189.3

Source: Yae-yŏng Kim, and Hyo-gu Yi, *Uri nara in'gu idong ŭi t'ŭkching 1965–1970*,
    KDI Working Paper No. 76–01, Korea Development Institute, May, 1976,
    p. 36.
Note: [a]Inter-provincial migration only.

TABLE A-5-2 Intra-and Inter-Provincial Migration in Korea, 1967–1974
(1,000s)

| | Total Migrants | | Intra-Province | | Inter-Province | |
	Persons	%	Persons	%	Persons	%
1967	3,762	12.8	2,831	9.6	931	3.2
1968	3,678	12.4	2,672	9.0	1,005	3.4
1969	2,529	8.3	1,675	5.5	854	2.8
1970	4,047	13.1	2,780	9.0	1,266	4.1
1971	4,210	13.5	2,878	9.2	1,332	4.3
1972	3,688	11.7	2,619	8.3	1,069	3.4
1973	4,860	15.1	3,436	10.7	1,425	4.4
1974	5,298	16.1	3,709	11.3	1,589	4.8

Source: EPB, *Yearbook of Migration Statistics, 1974*, p. 7.

TABLE A-5-3 Migration Statistics for the Seven Largest Cities, 1974

	Seoul		Pusan		Inch'ŏn		Taejŏn		Chŏnju		Kwangju		Taegu	
	In	Out	In	Out	In	Out	In	Out	In	Out	In	Out	In	Out
Total	(2,050)	(1,820)	(681)	(554)	(170)	(145)	(98)	(96)	(57)	(59)	(165)	(147)	(329)	(277)
	100.0	100.0	100.0	100.0	100.0	100.0	100.0	100.0	100.0	100.0	100.0	100.0	100.0	100.0
Seoul	73.8	83.1	3.3	5.5	10.7	12.5	5.7	13.7	4.7	18.0	3.4	8.7	2.9	5.6
Pusan	1.5	1.2	65.6	80.7	1.2	1.9	1.0	2.4	0.5	2.4	0.5	1.7	1.9	3.1
Kyŏnggi province	5.2	8.2	1.4	1.2	72.6	76.1	2.1	3.0	1.0	2.7	0.9	1.7	0.9	1.2
Kangwŏn province	2.1	0.9	1.0	0.4	1.6	0.9	0.9	0.7	0.4	0.4	0.4	0.5	0.8	0.4
N. Ch'ungch'ŏng province	1.9	0.6	0.7	0.2	1.6	0.6	5.9	3.5	0.2	0.2	0.3	0.1	0.5	0.3
S. Ch'ungch'ŏng province	3.0	1.4	1.1	0.4	4.3	2.3	76.3	70.9	1.3	1.6	0.5	0.6	0.7	0.4
N. Chŏlla province	2.9	0.9	1.4	0.3	1.9	0.7	3.3	1.6	88.1	69.6	2.6	1.4	0.5	0.2
S. Chŏlla province	3.4	1.2	2.7	0.8	2.5	1.1	1.5	0.8	2.9	2.5	90.4	83.6	0.5	0.2
N. Kyŏngsang province	3.3	1.5	5.9	2.9	2.1	2.1	2.2	2.1	0.5	1.4	0.5	0.7	79.8	85.9
S. Kyŏngsang province	2.2	0.9	14.6	7.4	1.4	1.7	1.0	1.2	0.3	1.1	0.4	0.8	3.9	2.6
Cheju Island	0.4	0.1	0.3	0.2	0.1	0.1	0.1	0.1	0.1	0.1	0.1	0.2	0.1	0.1
Overseas & Others	0.3	–	2.0	–	0.0	–	–	–	–	–	–	–	7.5	–

Source: EPB, *Yearbook of Migration Statistics, 1974*, pp. 210–222.

Note: Numbers in parentheses are migrants in thousands.

TABLE A-5-4 Characteristics of Migration to Seoul

Time		Age of Migrants		Origin of Migrants		Destination in Seoul	
Month	%	Age	%	Province	%	Ku (Borough)	%
Oct	9.3	0 – 4	10.2	Pusan City	3.2	Chŏngno	4.4
Nov	4.4	5 – 9	7.1 (58.3)a	Kyŏnggi	29.3	Chung	1.9
Dec	4.1	10 – 14	8.8 (63.5)	Kangwŏn	6.9	Tongdaemun	14.3
Jan	4.7	15 – 19	20.3 (69.2)	N. Ch'ungch'ŏng	6.9	Sŏngdong	11.2
Feb	6.7	20 – 24	14.0 (64.2)	S. Ch'ungch'ŏng	16.4	Sŏngbuk	12.7
Mar	12.2	25 – 29	13.0 (57.9)	N. Chŏlla	9.0	Tobong	11.1
Apr	10.0	30 – 34	8.1 (56.1)	S. Chŏlla	10.5	Sŏdaemun	13.2
May	8.0	35 – 39	5.3 (58.3)	N. Kyŏngsang	9.4	Map'o	3.3
Jun	5.7	40 – 44	3.7 (60.8)	S. Kyŏngsang	7.2	Yongsan	4.0
Jul	6.9	45 – 49	2.6 (62.6)	Cheju Island	0.6	Yŏngdŭngp'o	15.4
Aug	12.4	50 – 54	2.1 (65.0)	Foreign country	0.5	Kwanak	8.7
Sep	15.5	55 – 59	1.6 (65.1)				
		Over 60	2.7				

TABLE A-5-4 (continued)

Purpose of Migration	%	Status after Migration	%	Type of Movement	%	Monthly Average Income after Movement	%	Level of Education of Migrants — School	%
Job seeking	18.6	Employed	38.4	Single	19.1	Below W 5,000	10.9	Grade dropout	11.5 (59.9)
Employed	10.9	Home affairs	20.7	With family (part)	17.7	5,000 – 10,000	25.0	Graduate	33.0 (62.7)
Movement of job	7.7	Education	17.7	All family	59.2	10,000 – 20,000	28.8	Junior high dropout	3.5 (63.6)
Study	11.2	Unemployed	5.1	Other	4.1	20,000 – 30,000	17.4	Graduate	18.7 (63.1)
Joining family	47.0	Other	18.1			Over 30,000	16.4	Senior high dropout	2.7 (66.9)
Other	4.7					Family related worker	1.6	Graduate	13.0 (60.9)
								College dropout	2.3 (78.0)
								Graduate	5.5 (60.2)
								No Education	9.7 (58.3)

Source: Sŏul [Seoul] T'ŭkpyŏlsi, Sŏul [Seoul] t'ongye yŏnbo, 1974, pp. 42–47.

Note: Data based on analysis of 249,000 migrants during the period of Oct. 1, 1972 –Sept. 30, 1974.
[a]Numbers within parentheses indicate Seoul's share of total migrants.

TABLE A-5-5 Total Fertility Rates of Urban and Rural Areas in Korea

	KIFP		*Lee Jay Cho*		
	Urban	*Rural*	*Urban*	*Rural*	*Korea*
1975					
1974					
1973	3,265	4,700			
1972	3,410	5,385			
1971	4,000	5,690			
1970	3,550	5,530	3,465		
1969	3,465	5,225	3,309	4,730	3,898
1968	3,730	5,330	3,563	4,820	3,855
1967			3,344	5,362	4,169
1966			3,454	5,007	3,930
1965			3,356	5,822	4,334
1964			4,118	5,414	4,183
1963			4,562	5,579	4,877
1962			4,738	6,156	5,407
1961			4,935	6,191	5,507
1960			5,380	6,610	5,786

Sources: Korean Institute for Family Planning, *A Study on National Family Planning and Fertility,* 1974; Lee Jay Cho, *Estimates of Current Fertility for the Republic of Korea and Its Geographical Subdivisions: 1959–1970,* Yonsei University Press, 1974, p. 19.

Appendix to Chapter 6
Statistical Data on Structure of Cities

TABLE A-6-1 Data for Density Gradients

Urban Area	Density Gradient, 1973	Density Gradient, 1970	Population, 1973 (1,000s)	Per Capita Income, 1974 (1,000s)
Seoul	0.186	0.223	6,290	152.5
Pusan	0.109	0.134	2,072	135.0
Taegu	0.666	0.739	1,200	130.0
Inch'ŏn	0.378	0.410	714	120.0
Kwangju	0.643	0.658	552	115.0
Taejŏn	0.622	0.703	463	113.0
Suwŏn	0.946	0.975	192	120.0
Ch'ŏngju	0.994	1.082	167	136.8
Andong	1.078	1.076	87	124.9
Samch'ŏnp'o	0.500	0.487	57	77.0
Kangnŭngo	0.617	0.616	82	117.6
Ch'ŏnan	0.937	0.937	85	99.6

Sources: Density gradients are from Table 21.
Data on income are from EPB, *Special Labor Force Survey Report*, 1974. Population data are from EPB, *Report on Population and Housing Census*, 1975. Per capita income is in thousands wŏn (Exchange rate; W/$ = 404.6 in 1974).

TABLE A-6-2 Urban Density Functions for 12 Cities (Quadratic Form)
$$[D(x) = D_o e^{-gx+hx^2}]$$

City		D_o		g		h		R^2
Seoul	1961	55,994	(26.2)	0.296	(2.3)	-0.348	(0.4)	0.748
	1965	51,740	(26.8)	0.200	(1.6)	-0.008	(1.1)	0.736
	1970	36,717	(28.3)	0.040	(0.4)	-0.012	(1.7)	0.616
	1973	28,999	(28.3)	0.059	(0.5)	-0.016	(2.3)	0.555
Pusan	1966	27,667	(15.2)	0.067	(0.3)	-0.012	(1.0)	0.576
	1970	32,403	(19.7)	0.187	(1.1)	0.003	(0.3)	0.355
	1973	32,338	(20.6)	0.172	(1.1)	0.004	(0.4)	0.290
Taegu	1966	195,438	(20.3)	1.272	(3.9)	0.058	(1.6)	0.810
	1970	135,131	(19.3)	0.993	(3.0)	0.030	(0.8)	0.783
	1972	132,986	(18.4)	0.984	(2.8)	0.0372	(0.9)	0.730
Kwangju	1966	160,974	(35.6)	1.770	(9.2)	0.118	(6.0)	0.923
	1970	159,213	(34.8)	1.654	(8.4)	0.105	(5.3)	0.918
	1973	140,365	(34.8)	1.561	(8.1)	0.097	(4.9)	0.915
Inch'ŏn	1966	64,216	(18.3)	0.553	(1.8)	0.009	(0.3)	0.681
	1970	52,313	(18.7)	0.358	(1.2)	-0.005	(0.2)	0.654
	1973	58,924	(19.0)	0.419	(1.4)	0.004	(0.1)	0.618
Taejŏn	1966	49,613	(30.4)	0.905	(2.9)	0.120	(0.2)	0.858
	1970	45,297	(28.9)	0.669	(2.1)	-0.006	(0.1)	0.784
	1973	39,616	(30.7)	0.507	(1.7)	-0.021	(0.4)	0.767
Ch'ŏngju	1966	54,447	(34.9)	1.97	(6.1)	0.189	(2.9)	0.897
	1970	49,712	(30.6)	1.75	(4.8)	0.143	(1.9)	0.869
	1973	50,970	(30.6)	1.671	(4.6)	0.146	(1.9)	0.849
Andong	1966	28,595	(29.5)	2.187	(4.5)	0.250	(2.4)	0.860
	1970	31,226	(29.1)	2.013	(4.1)	0.204	(1.9)	0.859
	1973	31,226	(29.3)	1.883	(3.8)	0.176	(1.7)	0.861
Suwŏn	1966	40,782	(17.6)	1.652	(2.7)	0.131	(1.0)	0.797
	1970	37,012	(17.6)	1.298	(2.1)	0.068	(0.5)	0.781
	1973	33,523	(18.0)	1.129	(1.9)	0.038	(0.3)	0.781
Ch'ŏnan	1966	43,174	(51.2)	2.507	(13.4)	0.034	(9.0)	0.940
	1970	46,490	(49.2)	2.458	(12.6)	0.287	(8.1)	0.937
	1973	48,485	(42.4)	2.426	(10.6)	0.282	(6.8)	0.916
Kangnŭng	1966	17,001	(22.0)	1.523	(4.6)	0.158	(2.9)	0.755
	1970	15,398	(22.9)	1.582	(4.9)	0.163	(3.1)	0.779
	1973	16,647	(23.7)	1.557	(4.9)	0.159	(3.1)	0.787
Samch'ŏnp'o	1960	43,434	(14.1)	1.759	(4.2)	0.156	(3.2)	0.747
	1966	46,444	(13.9)	1.747	(4.1)	0.155	(3.1)	0.738
	1970	51,072	(13.7)	1.772	(4.1)	0.155	(3.0)	0.744
	1973	56,444	(13.6)	1.776	(4.0)	0.154	(2.9)	0.745

Note: Numbers in parentheses are t statistics.

TABLE A-6-3 Andong

Tong (Precinct)	Distance (km)	Area (km²)	Population			
			1962	1966	1970	1972
Chunggu	0.1	0.11	2,671	2,685	2,934	2,888
Myŏngnyun	0.2	0.6	3,105	3,602	4,429	5,096
Ongnyul	0.5	0.251	2,498	2,905	3,373	3,423
Sinhŭng	0.8	1.218	4,694	5,224	6,232	6,123
Yongsŏng	2.5	3.315	4,115	4,871	6,534	7,980
Tonggu	0.5	0.718	2,992	3,154	3,805	3,912
Namgu	0.3	0.137	3,511	3,525	3,834	4,088
Taehŭng	0.6	0.147	3,879	3,961	4,531	5,242
Taesin	0.7	0.498	4,531	4,730	5,255	5,738
Tangbuk	0.9	0.466	1,891	2,184	2,885	3,064
T'aehwa	1.5	2.444	4,293	5,178	7,424	8,647
Hwasan	0.2	0.156	2,401	2,853	3,130	3,087
Pŏpsan	0.7	0.485	2,986	3,655	4,494	4,865
P'yŏnghwa	1.1	0.298	2,721	3,785	5,105	5,130
An'gi	1.2	2.323	3,109	3,431	4,182	4,927
Sŏnggok	3.5	6.35	867	933	1,003	1,087
Anmak	2.0	5.746	1,342	1,686	1,982	2,394
Oktong	4.0	4.373	979	1,236	1,415	1,467
Ich'ŏn	4.5	5.249	1,175	1,270	1,173	1,201
Noha	4.0	4.177	1,033	999	941	943
Songhyŏn	4.5	5.434	1,693	1,642	1,726	1,765

Source: Andong, *Andong-si t'ongsye yŏnbo*, 1963, 1967, 1971, 1973.

TABLE A-6-4 Pusan

Tong (Precinct)	Distance (km)	Area (km²)	Population 1966	Population 1970	Population 1973
Chungang	0.5	0.519	5,984	6,185	6,457
Yŏngju 2	1.5	0.355	22,826	13,262	14,540
Sŏdaesin 4	3.0	1.757	11,187	12,555	9,295
Nambumin 1	1.5	0.431	21,313	14,861	14,322
Hadan	6.0	2.658	3,896	5,668	7,422
Ch'oryang 2	2.3	0.380	15,246	14,612	14,286
Sujŏng 4	3.5	1.060	16,121	11,470	15,993
Pŏmil 3	5.0	0.570	13,976	15,838	15,386
Yŏngsŏn 2	1.7	0.231	17,870	20,674	22,492
Ch'ŏnghak 2	2.5	1.224	12,027	16,865	18,837
Yangjŏng 2	9.0	1.015	27,122	19,774	21,175
Kaya 1	6.0	1.200	7,604	17,579	18,132
Pŏmch'ŏn 4	6.0	1.241	18,321	24,367	25,812
Myŏngnyun	13.0	1.159	11,145	16,225	18,744
Yŏnsan 2	10.0	7.150	12,508	17,181	26,380
Pansŏng	17.0	7,617	784	18,691	29,376
Millak	10.5	1,377	3,959	8,531	11,564

Source: Pusan, *Pusan-si t'onggye yŏnbo, 1967, 1971, 1974.*

TABLE A-6-5 Ch'ŏnan

Tong (Precinct)	Distance (km)	Area (km²)	Population		
			1966	1970	1973
Taehŭng	0.3	0.27	3,888	3,766	3,685
Oryong	0.3	0.12	2,661	2,501	2,455
Munhwa	0.5	0.28	4,976	5,608	5,940
Sŏnghwang	1.0	0.39	4,787	5,891	5,983
Sajik	0.7	0.31	5,621	6,029	6,026
Yŏngsŏng	0.3	0.17	3,653	3,539	3,684
Wŏnsŏng	1.0	1.82	6,428	7,912	9,990
Wach'on	0.5	0.33	2,350	2,711	2,698
Sŏngjŏng	2.0	3.32	3,666	4,583	5,147
Pongmyŏng	1.5	1.46	4,082	5,288	6,384
Ssangyong	2.5	4.59	2,211	2,364	2,669
Paeksŏk	3.5	5.55	1,409	1,314	1,331
Taga	1.0	0.83	2,272	2,756	3,091
Yonggok	2.0	2.12	1,321	1,407	1,657
Sinbang	3.5	4.92	1,711	1,672	1,628
Ch'ŏngsu	1.3	0.66	1,629	1,979	2,412
Kusŏng	2.0	3.97	2,637	3,113	3,476
Samyong	3.2	4.05	1,536	1,660	1,766
Ch'ŏngdang	2.7	3.09	1,168	1,146	1,341
Sinbu	2.3	3.59	3,102	3,596	4,154
Yuryang	3.5	6.55	1,138	1,086	1,149
Pudae	4.2	3.60	817	817	795
Tujŏng	3.0	2.36	1,410	1,424	1,485
Sindang	5.5	3.43	1,107	1,028	1,022
Ŏpsŏng	5.5	2.23	1,406	1,258	1,297

Source: Ch'ŏnan, *Ch'ŏnan-si t'onggye yŏnbo, 1967, 1971, 1974.*

TABLE A-6-6 Ch'ŏngju

Tong (Precinct)	Distance (km)	Area (km²)	Population		
			1966	1970	1973
Yŏngdongbuk 2,3	1.0	0.54	12,901	12,401	13,020
Munhwabuk 1, Munhwanam 2	0.25	0.28	16,260	15,287	16,380
Sŏunnam 1	0.25	0.24	30,351	27,594	27,557
Sŏmun	0.5	0.20	19,790	20,199	21,472
Namju	0.5	0.15	33,380	30,586	30,490
Sŏkkyo	0.5	0.28	28,264	24,371	26,189
Sudong	1.2	1.36	7,360	8,212	8,342
Uam	2.0	1.68	5,582	8,473	10,949
Naedŏk, Yuryang, Sach'ŏn	3.5	11.25	1,275	1,551	1,944
Taptong, Taesŏng	0.75	0.8	10,585	13,023	14,416
Sajik, Sach'ang	2.0	2.91	3,965	4,908	5,435
Moch'ung	1.5	1.65	4,258	5,663	7,975
Yŏngun	1.75	0.77	6,266	7,863	8,972
Kŭmch'ŏn	1.5	1.30	2,554	3,627	4,894
Yongdam, Myŏngam	2.5	5.41	625	645	685
Unch'ŏn, Sinbong	2.8	3.14	838	1,079	1,315
Yongam, Yongjŏng	3.0	9.3	280	297	369
San, Mi, Pun, Sugok	3.0	6.98	535	409	837
Nongch'on, Kaesin	4.0	4.95	400	397	421
Kagyŏng, Pokt'ae	5.0	6.96	414	422	782
Pongmyŏng, Songjŏng	4.0	4.81	370	353	511

Source: Ch'ŏngju, Ch'ŏngju-si t'onggye yŏnbo, 1965, 1971, 1974.

TABLE A-6-7 Taegu

(Precinct)	Distance (km)	Area (km²)	Population		
			1966	1970	1972
Tongin 1,2	1.0	0.385	11,232	9,350	9,306
Samdŏk 3	1.25	0.369	10,118	10,029	9,469
Tongsŏnggu	0.5	0.379	14,927	12,246	11,567
Taesin	1.75	0.317	11,963	10,797	10,547
Sŏngdang	4.5	2.820	5,430	7,035	10,653
Naedang 4	2.5	0.240	16,778	16,662	16,658
Pisan 3	3.0	0.360	16,347	22,712	24,339
Sangjungni	5.25	6.320	3,575	4,101	4,124
Nogok	5.0	4.020	2,860	2,383	2,552
Sinam 1	3.0	0.651	11,346	15,550	18,900
Sinam 5	3.25	0.662	8,891	9,550	14,811
Sinch'ŏn 3	2.5	0.574	11,764	16,441	17,368
Manch'ŏn	4.5	2.777	1,532	2,985	4,149
Chisan	6.5	4.808	1,718	2,006	2,092
Chung	3.5	1.329	5,718	9,476	10,923
Pongmu	8.0	5.435	1,343	1,370	6,437
Ipsŏk	6.0	2.001	1,093	1,692	1,724
Tunsan	8.5	2.294	2,092	2,376	2,535
Namsan 1	1.25	0.387	13,920	12,442	12,126
Taebong 2	2.0	0.637	17,876	18,340	19,523
Ch'ilsŏng 1	1.0	0.216	10,485	7,799	7,620
San'gyŏk	2.75	1.723	6,856	12,845	14,121
Kŏmdan	5.5	4.129	2,212	2,584	2,848

Source: Taegu, *Taegu-si t'ongye yŏnbo, 1967, 1971, 1973.*

TABLE A-6-8 Taejŏn

Tong (Precinct)	Distance (km)	Area (km²)	Population		
			1966	1970	1973
Wŏn	0.7	0.193	3,743	4,014	3,475
In	1.2	0.446	9,650	10,023	9,492
P'anam	5.0	6.34	6,232	7,986	9,728
Taedong	2.0	0.682		20,515	22,811
Chayang	2.6	1.329		5,629	7,630
Soje	1.5	0.378	8,330	11,429	12,529
Sŏngnam	2.0	0.923	15,680	21,857	22,491
Hongdo	2.5	0.844	5,925	7,565	8,713
Samsŏng	1.2	1.306	20,234	14,411	14,242
Chŏng	1.0	0.328	5,703	6,208	7,311
Ŭnhaeng	0.2	0.227	8,268	8,760	8,280
Sŏnhwa	0.7	1.282	25,712	28,776	29,488
Chungch'on	2.5	1.15	2,900	5,318	6,657
Taehŭng	0.5	1.192	27,730	29,765	29,411
Munch'ang	1.8	0.414	15,357	18,663	17,576
Sŏkkyo	3.5	4.551	4,428	6,816	10,063
Pusa	2.2	1.146	7,373	10,253	12,135
Yongdu	1.5	0.864	14,162	17,811	19,752
T'aep'yŏng	3.2	1.806	5,715	9,213	12,386
Munhwa	3.0	3.803	7,006	12,635	15,501
Toma	5.3	7.882	6,884	10,804	16,588
Koejŏng	5.0	3.024	1,659	5,950	7,489

Source: Taejŏn, *Taejŏn-si t'onggye yŏnbo,* 1967, 1971, 1974.

TABLE A-6-9 Kangnŭng

Tong (Precinct)	Distance (km)	Area (km²)	Population 1966	1970	1973
Hongje	1.0	3.605	7,601	9,286	9,462
Nammun	0.1	0.255	3,452	3,559	3,564
Imdang	0.3	0.590	7,942	7,906	8,529
Sŏngnam	0.7	0.399	4,606	4,329	4,378
Okch'ŏn	1.5	1.016	4,894	6,692	7,303
Kyo	1.2	5.591	5,858	7,382	9,495
P'onam	4.0	3.405	2,516	2,637	3,567
Ch'odang	5.0	1.782	1,767	1,996	2,113
Songjŏng	4.0	4.197	2,170	2,203	2,031
Naegok	1.5	5.027	2,526	3,129	3,874
Changhyŏn	3.0	5.767	1,792	1,682	1,923
Noam	2.0	4.873	6,319	7,723	9,021
Wŏlhop'yŏng	4.0	3.430	1,281	1,178	1,483
Ibam	2.0	4.765	3,410	4,877	6,226
Tusan	4.0	4.095	2,695	2,219	2,219
Yuch'ŏn	4.0	5.680	1,491	1,302	1,341
Chukhŏn	4.0	7.088	1,801	1,549	1,553
Unjŏng	5.0	4.480	1,103	1,075	1,122
Chŏ	6.5	7.299	1,915	2,196	2,576

Source: Kangnŭng, *Kangnŭng-si t'ongye yŏnbo, 1967, 1971, 1974.*

TABLE A-6-10 Kwangju

Tong (Precinct)	Distance (km)	Area (km²)	Population 1966	1970	1973
Ch'ungsu	0.5	0.15	5,214	5,098	5,665
Ch'unggŭm	0.5	0.19	4,823	4,671	4,887
Namgŭm	0.75	0.25	9,410	9,982	10,843
Pangnim 1, 2	2.0	2.39	14,785	20,034	22,599
Chiwŏn	5.5	37.16	7,839	10,049	12,513
Tongmyŏng 1	1.25	0.28	11,999	12,680	3,453
Chisan	2.5	2.40	9,862	13,106	18,085
Kyerim 1,2,3	1.25	0.84	33,623	36,361	39,440
Munhwa	3.5	10.10	4,487	6,686	7,578
Changun	8.0	10.70	2,663	2,969	3,143
Ch'unghyo	8.0	21.36	2,873	2,444	2,712
Sŏdong 1, 2	1.2	0.34	11,675	14,132	15,026
Yangdong 1, 2, 3	1.5	1.80	24,288	31,943	35,069
Imdong	2.5	0.91	11,686	15,790	16,215
Numun	1.0	0.18	10,350	8,185	8,534
Tongun	4.5	7.40	4,188	4,850	5,191
Sangmu	4.5	8.93	7,691	10,663	11,970
Nongsŏng	2.5	1.18	4,021	6,151	7,968
Hyodŏk	5.0	8.94	3,013	2,837	2,943
Ponch'ŏn	8.0	14.00	7,502	7,879	8,468
Samso	10.0	8.80	3,514	3,650	3,678

Source: Kwangju, *Kwangju-si t'onggye yŏnbo, 1967, 1971, 1974.*

TABLE A-6-11 Inch'ŏn

Tong (Precinct)	Distance (km)	Area (km²)	Population 1966	Population 1970	Population 1972
Chungang, Haean, Hang, Kwan, Song, Hak	0.25	0.75	8,018	7,499	7,592
Sinhŭng 3, Sŏnhwa	1.5	0.23	9,937	8,539	9,143
Puksŏng, Sŏllin	1.0	1.07	9,974	9,472	10,782
Songwŏl	0.5	0.22	11,661	12,181	12,579
Hwasu 2, Songhyŏn 4	1.3	0.28	11,561	11,763	12,330
Songhyŏn 2	1.3	0.08	16,616	16,030	16,812
Songnim 1	1.5	0.21	10,701	11,016	12,319
Songrim 3, Sŏbu	2.0	0.21	9,945	11,479	11,557
Songhyŏn 3	1.7	0.67	14,584	14,055	14,584
Tohwa 2, Sŏbu	4.0	0.92	4,690	9,164	7,147
Chuan, Sŏbu	6.0	1.83	4,287	9,487	11,389
Mansu	10.0	6.19	2,414	4,917	7,773
Yonghyŏn 1, Sŏbu	4.0	1.02	10,957	15,211	17,272
Hagik 2	5.0	1.93	5,405	8,976	9,681
Sungŭi 2	3.5	0.47	10,625	13,319	14,107
Sungŭi 4	4.0	0.51	12,070	14,247	16,025
Pup'yŏng 3, Sipchŏng 2	8.5	1.27	9,777	12,978	12,754
Ch'ŏngch'ŏn	8.0	3.15	5,073	5,571	6,382
Chakchŏn	10.5	2.90	1,942	2,505	5,914
Pugae, Ilsin, Kusan	10.0	6.76	7,869	10,134	11,047
Kangch'on, Yŏnhŭi, Simgok	9.0	8.75	1,846	2,308	2,582
Kajwa	5.0	4.41	2,161	3,444	4,042

Source: Inch'ŏn, Inch'ŏn-si t'ongye yŏnbo, 1967, 1971, 1973.

TABLE A-6-12 Samch'ŏnp'o

Tong (Precinct)	Distance (km)	Area (km²) 1960–70	Area (km²) 1973	Population 1960	Population 1966	Population 1970	Population 1973
Tongsŏ	2.2	1.42	1.37	8,662	8,373	9,463	9,880
Sŏn'gu	1.3	0.63	0.60	8,322	8,854	8,852	9,041
Tongsŏgŭm	1.0	0.88	0.84	5,492	6,773	7,963	8,936
Tongjiwa	2.6	2.79	2.66	2,303	2,234	2,211	2,157
Pŏllyong	4.1	11.14	10.63	3,175	3,293	3,916	4,479
Pongni	2.8	3.70	3.53	2,394	2,453	2,243	2,231
Igungsa	5.0	5.40	5.15	2,434	2,614	2,266	2,184
Hyangch'on	2.1	3.09	2.95	2,827	3,018	2,951	3,149
Taebang	3.6	1.63	1.56	1,066	1,683	1,957	2,133
Silma	5.6	4.66	4.45	2,298	2,705	2,245	2,232
Nŭkto	2.4	0.86	0.82	1,326	1,421	1,335	1,333
Sinsu	2.4	0.98	0.94	1,247	1,316	1,400	1,385
Paeksin	7.0	9.33	8.91	1,300	1,377	1,263	1,212
Nodae	7.4	2.38	2.27	2,002	2,158	2,021	1,968
Songp'o	5.2	4.32	4.12	2,409	2,570	2,670	2,812
Chungnim	5.2	7.49	7.15	2,177	2,264	2,160	2,076

Source: Samch'ŏnp'o, *Samch'ŏnp'o-si t'onggye yŏnbo, 1961, 1967, 1971, 1974.*

TABLE A-6-13 Seoul

Tong (Precinct)	Distance (km)	Area (km²)	Population 1965	1970	1973
Sejongno, Ch'ŏngjin, Ch'ebu	1	1.46	25,943	20,283	18,708
Chongno 4, 5, 6	2	0.74	21,710	21,599	18,971
Namdaemun 3, 4, 5	1.5	0.41	12,935	12,588	10,560
Yegwan, Ŭlchiro 4, 5, Ch'ungmuro 4	2.0	0.78	30,805	24,446	20,967
Samsŏn 1, 2, 3, Tongsŏmun, Sŏngbuk 1	3.5	1.53	56,959	66,791	64,933
Chŏngnŭng 1, 2, Mia 1	5.0	2.88	53,427	99,952	92,455
Changwi 1, 2, Sŏkkwan	8.5	3.01	16,319	71,091	96,777
Mia 7, 8, 9, 10	7.0	2.38	40,322	86,992	101,148
Ch'ang, Ssangmun, Tobong	12.0	28.70	20,314	84,276	116,977
Sinsŏl, Pomun 1, 2, Anam 1	4.0	1.21	53,768	45,826	59,489
Yongdu 1, 2	5.0	1.26	63,635	67,275	38,837
Chŏngnŭng 1, 2, 3	7.0	1.93	64,647	83,837	85,313
Hwigyŏng, Imun 1, 2, 3	8.0	3.35	41,548	93,727	104,649
Chunghwa, Sinnae, Kongnŭng, Pyŏlloe	12.0	20.32	19,940	54,780	89,230
Kwanghoe, Sindang 1, 5, 6, 7, 8	3.5	1.74	66,467	80,841	75,897
Ch'ŏngnyang 1, 2, 3, Ŭngbong	5.5	1.71	48,497	82,227	84,781
Sŏngsu 1, 2, Chayang 1, 2	8.0	13.58	32,451	58,902	93,783
Ch'ŏnho, Sŏngnae, Kil, Amsa	15.0	21.90	37,568	86,307	90,439
Sindang 2, 3, 4, Kŭmho 1, 2	4.0	3.22	118,895	118,707	120,856
Hannam 1, 2, It'aewŏn, Pogwang	4.5	4.06	60,898	66,059	64,455
Togok, Naegok, Sŏch'o, Yangjae	13.0	46.18	15,434	19,474	26,835
Kŏyŏ, Ilwŏn, Segok	15.0	17.99	8,126	34,149	43,184
Namsan, Hoehyŏn, To, Tongja, Huam	2.0	1.61	60,266	53,736	90,975

(*continued*)

TABLE A-6-13 (continued)

Tong (Precinct)	Distance (km)	Area (km²)	Population		
			1965	1970	1973
Sŏbinggo, Hangangno 2, 3, Ich'on 1,2	5.0	7.51	68,688	60,745	72,887
Hŭksŏk 1,2,3	8.0	1.78	48,363	62,050	60,796
Sadang 1, 2	11.0	11.99	4,085	55,659	67,405
Karibong, Sihŭng 1, 2	14.0	15.78	20,239	74,771	102,446
Ahyŏn 1,3, Kongdŏk 1	2.5	0.98	81,456	83,494	60,593
Kongdŏk 2, Singongdŏk, Tohwa 1, 2, Yonggang	4.0	2.45	92,394	99,893	101,699
Sin'gil 1, 2, 4, Taebang 1, 2	8.5	4.85	48,384	61,332	109,416
Yŏngdŭngp'o 1, 2, 3	8.0	2.18	51,231	49,173	49,192
Yangp'yŏng 1, 2, Tangsan 2	8.0	5.13	40,156	59,944	64,615
Haptong, Ch'ungjŏng, Pugahyŏn 1, 2	1.5	1.18	55,371	58,377	61,129
Sŏgyo, Hapchŏng, Ch'angjŏn, Sangsu	6.0	4.96	35,776	76,159	90,793
Susaek, Sŏngsan, Sangam	8.0	13.46	23,918	54,652	62,275
Yŏngch'ŏn, Hyŏnjŏ, 1,2	2.0	1.02	47,166	62,629	60,637
Hongŭn 2,3, Hongje 3	4.0	4.02	40,717	79,342	77,902
Ŭngam 1, 2, Nokpŏn, Yŏkch'on	6.0	7.73	41,416	94,822	123,906
Ch'ŏngun, Hyoja, Nusang, Ogin	1.5	3.05	36,586	36,514	34,864
Sŏngbuk 2, Chŏngnŭng 3, 4	5.0	9.72	31,111	64,694	69,583

Source: Sŏul [Seoul] T'ŭkpyŏlsi, Sŏul [Seoul] t'onggye yŏnbo, 1966, 1971, 1974.

Note: Seoul has been divided into 88 districts for the purpose of traffic flow study. Each district consists of several tong (precincts).

TABLE A-6-14 Suwŏn

Tong (Precinct)	Distance (km)	Area (km²)	Population			
			1966	1970	1973	
P'alch'ang	0.3	0.36	4,457	4,294	4,436	
Yŏngch'ŏn	0.5	0.18	3,440	4,114	3,495	
Namhyang	1.0	0.34	7,074	8,841	9,099	
Sinan	0.8	0.48	9,863	11,275	11,421	
Maegyo	1.3	0.77	8,829	10,572	11,848	
Seryu 1	2.0	0.82	6,443	9,726	10,505	
Seryu 2	2.5	3.01	5,614	9,750	11,185	
P'yŏng	4.5	9.99	6,701	8,259	9,293	
Sŏdun	3.0	8.79	7,575	9,125	10,615	
Maesan	1.0	0.84	10,690	11,050	11,153	
Kohwa	1.5	3.65	10,416	14,097	16,026	
P'ajang	4.0	16.28	4,938	8,275	9,159	
Yŏnghwa	1.3	6.3	8,541	12,223	14,351	
Yŏnmu	3.5	7.68	7,530	10,541	11,495	
Chiman	1.8	3.33	11,380	15,919	17,455	
Ingye	1.5	3.37	9,009	12,019	13,318	
Maewŏn	3.2	7.94	2,474	3,814	4,529	
Koksŏn	4.0	9.54	2,689	3,307	3,488	

Source: Suwŏn, *Suwŏn-si t'onggye yŏnbo, 1967, 1971, 1974.*

Appendix to Chapter 7
Statistical Data on Land Values

TABLE A-7-1 Status of Land Use in Korea, 1972

Use	Area (million p'yŏng)	Share
Dry field	2,859.1	9.6
Paddy field	3,807.2	12.8
Residential	499.8	1.7
Salt field	39.0	0.1
Lake and pond	148.1	0.5
Miscellaneous	117.4	0.4
Temple	2.4	0.01
Parks	0.6	0.0
Railroad use	30.6	0.1
Forest	20,140.5	67.6
Piped water	3.3	0.01
Cemetery	83.2	0.3
Road	514.8	1.7
River	1,111.0	3.7
Ditch	413.6	1.4
Banks	20.2	0.1
Other	0.6	0.0
Total	29,791.4	100.0

Source: Computed from land use data in Naemubu, *Chijŏk t'onggye, 1974.*

Note: 1 p'yŏng = 3.3058 m² or 1/1224 acre.

TABLE A-7-2 Pattern of Land Use by Region, 1973

(million p'yŏng)

	Dry field		Paddy field		Forest		Residential		Others		Total	
P'yŏng	2,863		3,808		19,637		513		3,053		29,874	
Total Km²(1,000s)	9.5		12.6		65.0		1.7		10.1		98.9	
Share (%)	9.6		12.7		65.7		1.7		10.2		100.0	
	P'yŏng	*%*	*P'yŏng*	*%*	*P'yŏng*	*%*	*P'yŏng*	*%*	*P'yŏng*	*%*	*P'yŏng*	*%*
Seoul	20.3	10.8	23.8	12.7	58.1	32.9	41.1	21.7	41.6	21.9	189.9	100.0
Pusan	4.3	3.8	10.4	9.1	66.9	59.0	16.4	14.5	15.4	13.6	113.5	100.0
Kyŏnggi province	383.1	11.6	543.8	16.4	1,934.5	58.4	63.0	1.9	391.7	11.7	3,348.3	100.0
Kangwŏn province	388.2	7.6	184.7	3.6	3,524.5	69.4	29.2	0.6	954.5	18.8	5,077.3	100.0
N. Ch'ungch'ŏng province	247.3	11.0	223.6	10.2	1,585.2	70.5	30.7	1.4	157.5	7.0	2,249.6	100.0
S. Ch'ungch'ŏng province	302.7	11.4	524.8	19.8	1,528.3	57.7	59.8	2.3	233.0	8.8	2,647.6	100.0
N. Chŏlla province	214.6	8.8	491.5	20.2	1,457.6	59.8	45.0	1.8	229.1	9.4	2,437.4	100.0
S. Chŏlla province	411.4	11.3	637.7	17.5	2,290.7	62.7	73.3	2.0	241.1	6.6	3,652.7	100.0
N. Kyŏngsang province	484.7	8.1	631.3	10.5	4,349.0	72.6	84.8	1.4	443.3	7.4	5,990.1	100.0
S. Kyŏngsang province	256.4	7.1	528.6	14.6	2,489.2	68.8	59.7	1.7	282.1	7.8	3,617.2	100.0
Cheju Island	150.1	27.3	3.0	0.5	353.4	64.2	9.6	1.7	34.7	6.3	550.5	100.0

Source: Naemubu, *Chijŏk t'onggye, 1973.*

TABLE A-7-3 Pattern of Land Use in the Seoul Metropolitan Region, 1973
(%)

	Arable land	Residential site	Forest	Road	Others	Total
Seoul Metropolitan Region	27.5	2.9	56.4	2.3	10.7	100.0
Seoul	23.5	21.7	32.9	4.0	18.0	100.0
CBD	–	58.2	22.6	12.4	6.8	100.0
Kyŏnggi province	27.7	1.9	57.8	2.3	10.3	100.0
Total cities in Kyŏnggi	33.1	7.8	43.5	2.5	13.1	100.0
Total counties in Kyŏnggi	27.4	1.6	58.6	2.2	10.2	100.0

Source: Data are computed from Naemubu, Chijŏk t'onggye, 1973.

TABLE A-7-4 Average Land Value Index for Major Cities

(Base year = 1963)

City	1963	1964	1965	1967	1968	1969	1970	1971	1972	1973	1974
Seoul	100	168	225	495	755	1,390	1,445	1,860	1,966	1,997	2,610
Pusan	100	143	191	404	603	1,082	1,208	1,582	1,649	1,759	2,321
Taegu	100	151	188	476	676	1,381	1,458	2,002	2,070	2,230	2,668
Kwangju	100	151	206	436	637	933	1,059	1,474	1,473	1,414	1,605
Taejŏn	100	130	162	342	557	1,014	1,191	1,726	1,824	2,152	2,291
Inch'ŏn	100	161	198	431	671	–	1,327	1,857	1,885	1,955	2,235
Ch'unch'ŏn	100	148	199	304	510	–	941	1,068	1,080	1,094	1,100
Chŏnju	100	129	158	358	445	–	–	3,287	2,948	3,053	3,554
Suwŏn	100	176	184	299	510	–	–	2,570	2,689	2,723	3,020
Ch'ŏngju	100	130	191	310	528	–	–	2,082	3,602	3,924	4,303
Masan	100	113	213	531	787	–	–	1,718	1,748	1,866	2,967
Cheju	100	212	321	556	665	–	–	1,736	1,731	1,944	2,315
Average	100	151	203	412	612	1,160	1,233	1,912	2,056	2,176	2,582

Source: Han'guk Kamjŏngwŏn, *12 chuyo tosi chiga chisu*, June 1975.

TABLE A-7-5 Land Value Index for Major Cities
(Commercial and Residential Land)

	1956		1960[a]		1970		1975	
	Commercial	*Residential*	*Commercial*	*Residential*	*Commercial*	*Residential*	*Commercial*	*Residential*
Seoul	100	100	650	347	10,833	6,501	15,167	7,854
Pusan	100	100	406	406	12,187	6,093	18,687	10,154
Taegu	100	100	163	200	812	6,000	13,812	8,500
Masan	100	100	120	122			33,702	12,185
Inch'ŏn	100	100	325	325	17,334	4,551	21,668	6,502
Ch'unch'ŏn	100	100	217	216	21,668	10,823	43,337	15,152
Wŏnju	100	100	390	498			19,506	10,823
Kangnŭng	100	100	325	368			23,213	17,316
Taejŏn	100	100	325	130	15,168	3,901	28,169	6,502
Chŏnju	100	100	193	279			15,648	9,285
Kunsan	100	100	163	130			29,259	15,152
I-ri	100	100	162	216			36,556	17,316
Kwangju	100	100	394	473	15,757	7,092	21,666	9,456
Mokp'o	100	100	208	186			11,700	9,285
Yŏsu	100	100	338	279			20,801	9,285
Cheju	100	100	418	541			64,995	21,645
Average	100	100	300	295	13,334	6,423	26,118	11,634
Wholesale price index	100		123.5		398.4		948.2	

Source: Han'guk Kamjŏngwŏn, *T'oji siga chosa, 1956–1973, 1975.*

Note: [a]Data for Seoul are from the 1960 Land Price Survey, and for other cities are from the Land Price Survey in 1959.

TABLE A-7-6 Land Values – Seoul

(1,000 wŏn per p'yŏng)

Tong (Precinct)	Distance (km)	Residential Land Value			Commercial Land Value		
		1975	1973	1970	1975	1973	1970
Chongno 5	2.25	300	200	200	1,400	1,200	1,200
Kongp'yŏng	0.75	300	200	200	1,600	1,200	1,000
Chunghak	0.25	250	200	200	500	400	300
Waryong	1.25	200	150	100	500	350	300
Naeja	1.25	200	150	200	450	350	400
Myŏngnyun 1	2.75	200	150	200	250	350	300
Wŏnnam	1.75	200	150	150	350	300	250
Ŭlchi 3	1.25	300	250	200	1,400	700	800
Namdaemun 5	1.25	350	300	300	1,400	1,000	800
P'il 2	1.75	250	200	180	700	400	350
Chuja	1.25	250	200	200	500	350	500
Ch'ungmu	1.75	250	200	150	500	300	300
Sallim	1.25	250	200	200	1,000	700	600
Ojang	1.75	250	200	200	600	400	350
Sindang	3.25	200	150	200	800	350	500
Sŏngsu 1	6.5	80	40	30	150	80	60
Nonhyŏn	7.0	100	20	20	150	50	40
Nŭng	7.0	100	30	20	150	50	60
Kŏyŏ	15.0	30	20	10	70	20	15
Tongsomun 1	3.5	150	100	100	400	300	250
Samsŏn 5	3.5	150	100	80	250	200	150
Tonam	4.5	100	70	80	150	100	150
Panghak	13.0	50	20	10	70	30	50
Yŏmni	3.25	120	70	60	250	150	120
Tonggyo	4.5	150	90	70	250	200	120

TABLE A-7-6 (continued)

Tong (Precinct)	Distance (km)	Residential Land Value			Commercial Land Value		
		1975	1973	1970	1975	1973	1970
Pomun 2	3.75	150	100	70	300	200	150
Imun	8.0	100	50	40	250	150	150
Okchŏn	1.75	150	70	70	500	250	100
Migŭn	1.25	100	70	70	450	200	200
Hongje	3.5	100	50	50	350	200	120
Nokpŏn	6.0	100	50	40	200	100	80
P'yŏngch'ang	5.0	70	40	30	100	100	150
Malli 1	2.0	120	70	60	400	250	120
It'aewŏn	3.25	150	100	100	250	150	150
Yongsan 2	3.25	100	70	60	150	100	150
Sŏbinggo	5.0	80	40	40	100	120	100
Yŏngdŭngp'o 7	8.0	120	70	60	250	150	120
Mullae 1	9.5	80	50	40	200	100	80
Sin'gil	9.0	100	70	60	300	200	200
Hwagok	13.0	50	30	20	200	100	80
Sindaebang	10.0	80	40	40	200	100	100
Sillim	11.0	80	35	20	250	120	50

Source: Han'guk Kamjŏngwŏn, T'oji siga chosa, 1970, 1973, 1975.

TABLE A-7-7 Land Values – Pusan

(1,000 wŏn per p'yŏng)

Tong (Precinct)	Distance (km)	Residential Land Value			Commercial Land Value		
		1975	1973	1970	1975	1973	1970
Chungang 1	0.5	250	120	100	1,000	500	350
Tonggwang 4	1.0	200	120	70	500	300	220
Posu 2	1.3	220	120	100	400	250	200
Kwangbok 2	0.5	250	150	150	1,700	1,000	700
Ch'angsŏn 2	0.5	250	150	100	2,300	1,600	1,500
Namp'o 1	0.5	250	120	100	1,000	400	350
Yŏngju	1.5	180	100	80	400	300	220
Tongdaesin 1	1.8	200	100	90	400	200	150
Pumin	1.8	200	100	80	400	250	120
Ami 2	2.3	180	90	70	300	170	100
Ch'ungmu 5	1.2	120	80	70	250	150	100
Pŏmil	5.0	180	100	80	1,200	800	450
Namhang 1	1.2	150	70	60	400	200	150
Pongnae	0.7	100	50	40	200	100	70
Ch'ŏnghak	2.3	80	40	30	200	120	60
Ch'oŭp	9.3	80	40	25	200	120	50
Uam	5.0	60	30	30	250	130	100
Churye	6.3	60	30	25	120	50	30
Mora	11.0	35	20	10	120	50	25
Sumin	13.3	120	60	40	700	350	160
Pugok	15.0	80	35	25	300	120	70
Ch'ŏngnyong	20.0	25	15	10	100	50	30
Suyŏng	11.0	70	30	15	250	80	40

Source: Han'guk Kamjŏngwŏn, *T'oji siga chosa, 1970, 1973, 1975.*

TABLE A-7-8 Land Values – Taegu

(1,000 wŏn per p'yŏng)

Tong (Precinct)	Distance (km)	Residential Land Value					Commercial Land Value			
		1975	1973	1970	1965	1960	1975	1973	1970	1965
Tongin 1	1.25	100	70	60	10	3	300	170	170	25
Samdŏk 1	1.0	100	80	60	12	3.5	300	150	100	20
Kyo	0.25	150	100	100	18	4	1,200	800	600	150
Yongdŏk	0.25	120	120	50	10	3.5	800	600	500	60
Tongsŏng 2	0.25	170	150	100	20	3.5	1,700	1,100	550	90
Kongp'yŏng	0.75	120	80	60	10	3	500	250	150	25
Namsŏng	0.75	100	70	70	9	3	400	300	250	38
Changgwan	0.5	100	70	70	10	3	300	150	180	25
Chŏn	0.25	120	90	80	10	3.5	300	500	350	40
Puksŏng 2	0.5	120	70	180	10	4	800	250	200	45
Sŏmun 1	0.5	120	70	70	12	3	400	200	180	35
Ingyo	0.5	100	70	70	10	2.5	400	250	200	30
Talsŏng	1.25	100	60	40	7	1.5	400	300	250	20
Hyangch'on	0.25	150	100	100	15	4	1,200	800	600	120
Ch'ilsŏng 2	1.0	60	40	40	4	1	180	150	100	15
Ch'imsan	2.25	50	40	40	4	1	180	150	80	6
Pongdŏk	2.5	70	50	30	4	1	450	350	150	10
Pisan	3.0	100	60	30	4	0.8	700	450	150	20
Wŏndae	2.75	50	30	25	4	1.2	100	80	70	10
Sang	4.5	45	25	15	15	4	80	30	25	3
Bullo	6.0	15	10	3	15	0.4	25	15	10	6

Source: Han'guk Kamjŏngwŏn, *T'oji siga chosa, 1970, 1973, 1975.*

TABLE A-7.9 Land Values – Suwŏn

(1,000 wŏn per p'yŏng)

Tong (Precinct)	Distance (km)	Residential Land Value				Commercial Land Value	
		1975	1973	1968	1965	1975	1973
Kyo	0.5	50	50	15	4	170	120
Paltal 1-ga	0.2	70	60	20	8	200	150
Paltal 3-ga	0	70	60	30	10	700	500
Chung	0.4	60	50	12	6	350	400
Yŏng	0	70	50	30	8	700	600
Namsu	0.7	40	30	8	3	150	100
Puksu	0.75	50	30	8	2	150	120
Changan	0.75	40	30	6	2	100	80
Namch'ang	0	60	40	20	8	90	70
Maegyo	1.25	50	30	6	2	170	120
P'yŏng	2.5	15	7	1	0.5	30	25
Sŏdun	2.0	15	10	1.5	0.5	25	25
Maesan 2-ga	1.0	50	30	6	3	120	100
Maesan 3-ga	1.5	50	30	8	3	120	100
Hwasŏ	1.0	30	15	2.5	0.5	40	30
Yonghwa	1.25	40	30	5	1	100	60
Chi	0.5	40	40	10	5	120	120
In'gye	1.5	30	30	3	2	100	100
Omokch'ŏn	5.5	5	3	0.5	0.4	7	5
Chowŏn	1.75	30	15	1.2	0.3	50	30
P'ajang	3.5	20	10	1.0	0.3	30	10
Chŏngja	1.75	30	15	1.5	0.5	50	40

Source: Han'guk Kamjŏngwŏn, *T'oji siga chosa, 1970, 1973, 1975.*

Appendix to Chapter 8
Statistical Data on Housing

TABLE A-8-1 Major Economic Indicators Concerning Korean Housing

	GNP (in billion 1970 wŏn)			National Income (billion wŏn, current price)			Capital Formation (in billion 1970 wŏn)		
	Total	Housing[a]	%	Total	Rent	%	Total	Housing	%
1975	4,107.71	87.11	2.1	7,348.15	290.09	4.0	1,082.90	192.05	11.7
1974	3,825.50	79.92	2.1	5,141.62	220.54	3.9	1,101.62	171.20	15.5
1973	3,522.72	73.89	2.1	4,069.48	175.82	4.3	921.67	120.51	13.1
1972	3,023.63	69.10	2.3	3,241.87	140.31	4.3	667.93	89.46	13.4
1971	2,826.82	66.05	2.3	2,662.94	121.28	4.6	748.81	96.07	12.8
1970	2,589.26	62.87	2.4	2,177.73	102.85	4.7	704.66	87.93	12.5
1969	2,400.49	59.74	2.5	1,756.31	89.00	5.1	714.07	71.46	10.0
1968	2,087.12	56.84	2.7	1,349.07	72.44	5.4	509.05	66.97	13.2
1967	1,853.01	54.24	2.9	1,095.50	62.43	5.7	368.32	42.06	11.4
1966	1,719.18	52.15	3.0	901.66	46.78	5.2	317.49	35.57	11.2
1965	1,529.70	50.97	3.3	712.35	39.53	5.5	197.26	26.54	13.5
1964	1,441.99	49.67	3.4	630.16	33.26	5.3	188.18	23.83	12.7
1963	1,328.31	48.09	3.6	432.14	26.59	6.1	225.09	21.00	9.3
1962	1,220.98	47.01	3.8	303.58	20.91	6.9	119.88	18.05	15.1
1961	1,184.48	45.92	3.9	264.91	18.10	6.8	121.35	18.45	15.2
1960	1,129.72	44.76	4.0	215.59	16.78	7.8	96.59	23.28	24.1
1959	1,108.33	43.77	4.0	193.36	15.62	8.1	91.77	15.84	17.2
1958	1,067.15	43.39	4.1	184.86	14.51	7.8	117.73	12.39	10.5
1957	1,014.44	42.57	4.2	179.65	12.31	6.8	135.26	13.04	9.6
1956	942.21	41.65	4.4	139.76	10.14	7.2	75.72	14.09	18.6
1955	938.24	40.42	4.3	106.12	8.76	8.2	94.02	13.32	14.2
1954	890.18	39.37	4.4	60.12	7.12	11.8	91.55	19.25	21.0
1953	843.52	38.13	4.5	44.25	5.47	12.4	115.42	11.88	10.3

TABLE A-8-1 (continued)

	Consumption Expenditure (in billion 1970 wŏn)						Building Permits (No. of buildings)			Building Permits (floor area, m²)		
	Total	Food (%)	Rent & Water Charges (%)	Fuel & Light (%)	Furniture & Equipment (%)	Household Operation (%)	Total	Housing	%	Total	Housing	%
1975	2,682.77	44.8	3.9	4.5	3.9	1.1	120,950	101,887	84.2	18,420	11,623	63.1
1974	2,547.34	45.1	3.7	4.4	3.8	1.1	128,228	109,347	85.3	16,884	10,300	61.0
1973	2,415.82	45.4	3.7	4.4	3.4	1.1	117,359	96,551	82.3	16,572	7,924	47.8
1972	2,226.03	47.0	3.7	4.3	3.0	1.1	74,153	60,832	82.0	8,701	4,524	52.0
1971	2,080.12	47.0	3.7	4.5	2.9	1.0	89,112	67,834	76.1	9,619	5,594	18.2
1970	1,884.25	48.9	3.9	4.7	2.7	1.0	92,909	80,585	86.7	10,787	5,885	54.6
1969	1,705.63	50.3	4.0	4.6	2.7	1.0	75,183	63,239	84.1	9,572	4,706	49.9
1968	1,545.55	51.5	4.2	4.6	2.7	1.1	67,978	57,192	84.1	7,717	3,811	49.4
1967	1,396.87	52.9	4.4	4.8	2.6	1.1	57,357	48,077	83.8	5,888	3,213	54.6
1966	1,282.37	55.1	4.6	5.4	2.2	1.0	36,858	28,812	78.2	4,507	1,977	43.9
1965	1,124.20	.2	4.7	5.0	1.8	1.1	30,146	23,353	77.5	3,893	1,731	44.5
1964	1,123.20	56.9	4.9	5.3	1.9	1.2	20,067	15,020	74.9	3,140	1,279	40.7
1963	1,055.51	53.9	5.1	5.6	2.0	1.2	23,184	16,975	73.2	2,583	1,052	40.7
1962	1,017.73	55.9	5.1	4.7	1.9	1.3	15,917	9,924	62.9	2,180	813	37.3
1961	950.65	58.0	5.4	4.5	1.5	1.1						
1960	942.62	57.2	5.3	4.4	1.5	1.3						
1959	924.72	59.5	5.3	3.9	1.4	1.2						
1958	882.43	60.3	5.5	3.8	1.5	1.2						
1957	840.36	57.8	5.7	3.8	1.5	1.1						
1956	809.52	58.8	5.8	3.6	1.5	1.0						
1955	775.09	58.8	5.8	3.3	1.5	1.0						
1954	710.10	61.0	6.2	3.5	1.2	1.1						
1953	658.15	63.8	6.5	3.5	1.3	1.0						

Sources: Sŏul [Seoul] T'ŭkpyŏlsi, *Sŏul [Seoul] t'onggye yŏnbo, 1967, 1972, 1974, 1975;* Pusan, *Pusan-si t'onggye yŏnbo, 1972, 1973, 1974;* BOK, *Economic Statistics Yearbook, 1971, 1976, 1977.*

Note: ªGNP originated from the housing sector (due to ownership of dwellings).

TABLE A-8-2 Data for the Housing Model

(in 1970 prices)

	Urban Population (1,000s)	Number of Urban Households (1,000s)	Number of Urban Houses	Urban Housing Price (A)	Urban Housing Price Index (B)	Construction Material Index (real)	Wage Index	Housing Construction Cost Index	Urban per Capita Income (in wŏn)	GNP Deflator
1975	17,656	3,382	1,833,725	1,428	185.6	94.0	217.0	95.3	137,555	220.4
1974	16,660	3,192	1,739,129	1,607	166.4	97.1	171.7	97.1	128,639	177.2
1973	15,644	2,978	1,637,608	2,135	149.2	88.7	142.1	92.6	118,926	139.9
1972	15,021	2,797	1,547,967	2,002	144.4	86.3	136.1	92.4	102,653	127.7
1971	14,240	2,637	1,491,488	1,907	123.0	90.7	119.1	95.5	101,268	115.5
1970	13,549	2,472	1,428,508	2,918	100.0	100.0	100.0	100.0	97,135	100.0
1969	12,136	2,195	1,249,710	1,419	83.3	100.5	85.6	99.9	100,814	86.7
1968	11,288	2,038	1,109,400	2,148	71.5	109.0	70.2	103.8	90,158	76.6
1967	10,576	1,906	982,507	1,074	70.7	111.7	59.9	104.4	83,892	68.5
1966	9,970	1,793	931,514	1,225	50.0	125.0	41.9	108.4	84,945	60.1
1965	9,608	1,728	900,958	827	25.8	126.8	30.4	106.1	71,057	52.6
1964	9,259	1,665	876,194	1,047	20.7	115.8	26.3	97.3	68,235	48.6
1963	8,783	1,580	860,268	1,120	19.7	114.7	22.5	98.6	54,753	36.8
1962	8,105	1,458	842,265	1,451	18.7	138.5	18.7	116.5	51,423	28.6
1961	7,228		831,739							25.1
1960	7,068		822,793							21.8

Sources: BOK, *Economic Statistics Yearbook, 1976.* EPB, *Annual Report on the Family Income and Expenditure Survey, 1975.* Kŏnsŏlbu, *Kŏnsŏl t'onggye p'yŏllam, 1975.*

Note: Urban housing price (A) is computed from Taehan Chut'aek Kongsa, *Chut'aek chosa t'onggye, 1974.* Housing price is deflated by housing size. Urban housing price index (B) is computed from EPB/Bureau of Statistics, Population and Housing Census, 1975. Wage index is also computed from the household survey data. Housing construction cost index is computed from construction material price index (weight of 0.7) and wage index (weight of 0.3). Urban per capita income is computed from both household survey and national income data. Income, wage, housing price, and cost of housing are all deflated by the GNP deflator.

TABLE A-8-3 Population, Households, and Housing by Region, 1970 and 1975

(1,000s)

	1970				1975			
	Population	Households	Housing	Shortage ratio (%)	Population	Households	Housing	Shortage ratio (%)
Seoul	5,536.4	1,097.4	596.8	45.6	6,389.5	1,410.7	746.9	47.1
Kyŏnggi province	3,358.1	641.3	482.6	24.8	4,039.9	817.4	557.9	31.8
Pusan	1,880.7	371.9	212.6	42.8	2,454.1	504.0	257.1	49.0
S. Kyŏngsang province	3,119.4	574.2	497.8	13.3	3,280.1	628.8	513.3	18.4
Kangwŏn province	1,866.9	352.5	287.5	18.4	1,862.1	362.2	283.9	21.6
N. Ch'ungch'ŏng province	1,481.6	262.2	228.3	12.9	1,522.2	280.9	232.3	17.3
S. Ch'ungch'ŏng province	2,860.7	500.3	432.7	13.5	2,948.6	535.3	442.0	17.4
N. Chŏlla province	2,434.5	427.3	365.5	14.5	2,456.5	444.8	368.6	17.1
S. Chŏlla province	4,005.7	703.9	599.8	14.8	3,984.8	733.4	606.8	17.3
N. Kyŏngsang province	4,559.6	850.3	668.2	21.4	4,858.8	954.1	707.6	25.8
Cheju Island	365.5	83.0	71.4	14.0	412.0	92.2	72.5	21.4
Whole Country	31,469.1	5,864.3	4,443.0	24.2	34,708.5	6,763.8	4,788.9	29.2

Source: BOK, *Economic Statistics Yearbook, 1972, 1976;* EPB, *Report on Population and Housing Census, 1970, 1975.*

TABLE A-8-4 Housing Tenure and Shortage by Region, 1970

(1,000s)

	Housing Units	*Household*	*Shortage Ratio (percent)*	Tenure			
				Owner-Occupied		*Rented*	
				Household	*Ratio*	*Household*	*Ratio*
Seoul	583.6	1,067.2	45.3	512.8	48.1	554.4	51.9
Pusan	206.7	360.0	42.6	169.9	47.2	190.1	52.8
Kyŏnggi province	473.3	633.5	25.3	440.8	69.6	192.7	30.4
Kangwŏn province	280.9	350.1	19.8	251.4	71.8	98.7	28.2
N. Ch'ungch'ŏng province	223.3	260.9	14.4	209.3	80.2	51.6	19.8
S. Ch'ungch'ŏng province	425.4	497.7	14.5	397.9	79.9	99.8	20.1
N. Chŏlla province	359.9	425.7	15.5	336.6	79.1	89.1	20.9
S. Chŏlla province	592.9	700.5	15.4	557.8	79.6	142.7	20.4
N. Kyŏngsang province	654.0	843.7	22.5	598.2	70.9	245.5	29.1
S. Kyŏngsang province	490.0	571.3	14.2	462.1	80.9	109.2	19.1
Cheju Island	69.9	82.4	15.2	59.4	72.1	23.0	27.9
Urban	1,397.8	2,475.1	43.5	1,198.1	48.4	1,277.0	51.6
Semi-urban	394.8	527.9	25.2	354.0	67.2	173.9	32.8
Rural	2,567.2	2,790.0	8.0	2,444.1	87.6	345.9	12.4
Whole country	4,359.9	5,793.0	24.7	3,996.2	69.0	1,796.8	31.0

Source: EPB, *Report on Population and Housing Census, 1970*, Vol. 12–1.

TABLE A-8-5 Dwelling Sizes, 1970
(m²)

	Per Housing Unit		Per Occupant	
	Floor Area	Occupants	Floor Area	Room Area
Whole Country	45.7	7.0	6.6	2.9
Urban	48.1	8.8	5.5	2.7
Rural	44.4	6.0	7.5	3.1
Seoul	53.2	9.0	5.9	3.0
Pusan	42.1	8.6	4.9	2.6

Source: EPB, *Report on Population and Housing Census, 1970.*

TABLE A-8-6 Proportion of Urban and Rural Housing by Age, 1970
(%)

	Region		
Period	Urban	Rural	Whole Country
Before 1944	21.3	48.6	39.2
1945–1950	15.0	18.3	17.2
1951–1960	22.6	24.8	21.1
1961–1965	14.2	6.8	9.3
1966–1970	24.6	5.2	11.8
Total	100.0	100.0	100.0

Source: EPB, *Report on Population and Housing Census, 1970* Vol. 2 (10% Sample Survey, 4-4, Housing).

TABLE A-8-7 Proportion of Housing by Age in Seoul
(%)

Year	Age (years)					Total	Total Dwelling Units
	Less than 1	1–10	10–15	15–24	Over 24		
1960	9.4	42.3	12.8	35.4		100.0	
1965	4.2	35.7	21.8	17.5	20.7	100.0	345,657
1970	8.1	43.6	19.7	17.6	11.1	100.0	600,367
1972	2.9	47.7	21.9	13.8	13.7	100.0	665,182
1973	4.9	35.5	24.4	15.2	19.9	100.0	700,754
1974	6.0	46.0	20.4	15.3	12.3	100.0	736,656

Sources: Sŏul [Seoul] T'ŭkpyŏlsi, *Sŏul [Seoul] t'onggye yŏnbo, 1975*; EPB, *Report on Population and Housing Census, 1970.*

TABLE A-8-8 Construction of Public Sector Housing by Size and Constructors, 1973

Size (p'yŏng)	Total	%	Ministry of Construction	%	KHC	%	KHB	%
Total	45,502	100.0	26,047	100.0	2,629	100.0	13,826	100.0
Less than 9	500	1.2	500	1.9	–		–	
9–13	12,382	29.1	12,251	47.0	48	1.8	83	0.6
13.1–15	4,400	10.4	4,160	16.0	46	1.7	194	1.4
15.1–18	8,421	19.8	5,039	19.4	64	2.4	3,318	24.0
18.1–22	13,463	31.6	3,553	13.6	1,490	56.7	8,420	60.9
22.1–25	2,359	5.5	544	2.1	4	0.2	1,811	13.1
25.1–32	144	0.3	–		144	5.5	–	
32.1–40	490	1.2	–		490	18.6	–	
Over 40	343	0.8	–		343	13.0	–	

Source: Kŏnsŏlbu, Chut'aek pumun kyehoek charyo, 1977–1981, 1974.

TABLE A-8-9 Status of Illegal Housing
(for the 20 largest cities)

Cities	As of 1972	Existing Illegal Housing Improvement in 1973 On-the-Spot Improvement	Moved to Apt.	Resettlement	Other	Total
Seoul	163,543	3,874	–	1,486	2,817	8,177
Pusan	37,098	1,695	–	2,646	110	4,451
Taegu	10,744	1,301	29	92	1,565	2,987
Inch'ŏn	10,260	141	–	323	2,397	2,861
Kwangju	596	39	–	36	334	409
Taejŏn	3,501	3,048	–	–	371	3,419
Chŏnju	1,690	–	–	–	30	30
Masan	3,001	–	–	–	284	284
Mokp'o	294	25	–	–	58	83
Suwŏn	2,060	1,596	–	–	64	1,660
Ulsan	2,683	–	–	–	149	2,534
Ch'ŏngju	18	–	–	–	18	18
Ch'unch'ŏn	245	–	–	245	–	245
Chinju	232	–	–	–	76	76
Yŏsu	–	–	–	–	–	–
Kunsan	789	–	–	–	–	–
Wŏnju	38	–	–	38	–	38
Cheju	1,922	118	–	185	–	303
Kyŏngju	99	3	–	–	8	11
Sŏngnam	9,876	3,989	–	–	1,936	5,925
Total	248,689	15,829	29	5,051	10,217	31,126

(continued)

TABLE A-8-9 (continued)

Cities	As of 1973 (A)	In 1972	New Illegal Housing Improvement in 1973 Constructed	Removed	Difference	In 1973 (B)	As of 1973 (A+B)
Seoul	155,366	–	1,160	1,160	–	–	155,366
Pusan	32,647	–	1,759	1,759	–	–	32,647
Taegu	7,757	–	868	868	–	–	7,757
Inch'ŏn	7,399	–	369	369	–	–	7,399
Kwangju	187	–	227	227	–	–	187
Taejŏn	82	–	252	252	–	–	82
Chŏnju	1,660	–	99	99	–	–	1,660
Masan	2,717	–	231	231	–	–	2,717
Mokp'o	211	–	87	87	–	–	211
Suwŏn	400	–	156	156	–	–	400
Ulsan	2,534	–	206	206	–	–	2,534
Ch'ŏngju	–	–	88	88	–	–	–
Ch'unch'ŏn	–	–	37	37	–	–	–
Chinju	156	–	102	100	2	2	158
Yŏsu	–	–	56	56	–	–	–
Kunsan	789	96	144	30	114	210	999
Wŏnju	–	–	13	13	–	–	–
Cheju	1,619	12	45	27	18	30	1,649
Kyŏngju	88	–	21	21	–	–	88
Sŏngnam	3,951	–	–	–	–	–	3,951
Total	217,563	108	5,920	5,786	134	242	217,805

Source: Kŏnsŏlbu, *Chut'aek pumun kyehoek charyo, 1977–1981,* 1974.

TABLE A-8-10 Housing Finance by Sources

(in 1974 million wŏn)

	1970	1971	1972	1973	1974	1975
Total	155,900 (100.0)	160,800 (100.0)	145,200 (100.0)	199,900 (100.0)	299,300 (100.0)	326,000 (100.0)
1. Public	24,500 (15.7)	34,000 (21.1)	17,800 (12.3)	50,300 (25.2)	41,000 (13.7)	74,000 (22.7)
a. Government finance	1,418 (0.9)	1,749 (1.1)	1,942 (1.3)	5,558 (2.8)	904 (0.3)	16,201 (5.0)
b. National housing fund				7,406 (3.7)	17,379 (5.8)	20,840 (6.4)
c. Housing lotteries	411 (0.3)	789 (0.5)	1,028 (0.7)	1,690 (0.9)	1,937 (0.7)	1,667 (0.5)
d. Private housing fund	8,645 (5.5)	15,901 (9.9)	13,860 (9.6)	16,968 (8.5)	8,412 (2.8)	13,383 (4.1)
e. Foreign loan				4,000 (2.0)	8,000 (2.7)	12,000 (3.7)
f. Others	14,026 (9.0)	15,561 (9.7)	970 (0.7)	14,678 (7.3)	4,368 (1.5)	9,959 (3.1)
2. Private	131,400 (84.3)	126,800 (78.9)	127,400 (87.7)	149,600 (74.8)	258,300 (86.3)	252,000 (77.3)

Source: EPB, *Housing and Urban Planning for Korea's Fourth Five-Year Plan,* 1976.

Appendix to Chapter 9
Statistical Data on Urban Transportation

TABLE A-9-1 Major Indicators Concerning Transportation in Korea

	Share of GNP[a]	Share of Investment[b]	Share of Consumption Expenditure	Number of Vehicles								
				Total	Total Passenger Cars	Gov't	Private	Commercial	Trucks	Bus	Small Cars	Special Cars
1975	4.4	24.2	5.0	200,175	84,212	5,023	50,093	29,096	82,262	21,209	6,594	5,035
1974	4.7	22.1	5.5	183,544	76,462	4,837	44,618	27,007	76,833	19,583	6,516	4,150
1973	5.1	23.2	5.7	170,714	75,334	5,046	43,400	29,888	67,584	18,871	5,407	3,517
1972	4.8	29.1	5.8	150,035	70,244	4,507	36,412	29,325	55,116	17,550	4,398	2,728
1971	4.8	24.0	5.5	144,337	67,582	3,961	33,994	29,627	53,405	17,411	4,068	1,871
1970	4.8	23.8	5.7	129,371	60,677	3,547	28,687	28,443	48,901	15,831	2,865	1,097
1969	5.0	26.7	6.1	108,669	50,299	3,128	23,696	23,475	40,134	14,237	2,531	1,468
1968	5.2	24.9	6.0	80,951	33,112	2,787	14,397	15,928	31,582	12,786	2,188	1,283
1967	4.7	27.8	5.5	60,697	23,234	2,247	9,871	11,117	22,955	11,499	1,722	1,286
1966	3.9	23.2	5.5	50,160	17,502	1,845	7,481	8,176	19,432	10,888	1,322	1,016
1965	3.4	19.7	4.2	41,511	16,280	1,649	5,580	9,051	16,015	6,037	2,385	794
1964	2.9	16.6	3.7	37,815	14,586	1,527	4,487	8,572	14,951	5,440	2,160	678
1963	3.5	18.0	4.2	34,228	12,679	1,491	3,322	7,866	13,929	5,022	2,029	569
1962	4.2	25.2	4.5	30,814	11,074	1,374	2,571	7,129	13,093	4,406	1,846	395
1961	4.1	21.0	4.5	29,234	9,809	1,095	1,925	6,789	12,808	4,266	1,863	488
1960	3.9	18.9	4.3	31,339	12,776	1,950	4,224	6,602	13,426	4,195	588	354
1959	4.0	25.1	4.3	30,392	12,133	2,128	3,899	6,106	13,196	4,140	569	354
1958	3.3	18.3	3.7	28,993	10,766	1,686	4,426	4,654	13,366	3,954	521	326
1957	3.0	19.5	2.9	28,086	9,743	1,501	4,300	3,942	13,679	3,847	571	246
1956	2.5	19.2	2.1	25,328	8,428	1,423	3,984	3,021	12,740	3,312	589	259
1955	2.4	13.6	2.2	18,356	6,556	1,511	2,684	2,361	8,103	2,953	622	122
1954	2.1	13.9	2.0	15,950	5,017	1,214	1,814	1,989	7,466	2,542	650	275
1953	1.6	7.5	2.0	13,507	3,661	1,031	1,581	1,049	6,830	2,170	684	162

Source: BOK, *Economic Statistics Yearbook, 1971, 1976.*
Notes: [a]GNP originated in the transportation sector (including storage).
[b]Share of domestic capital formation in the transportation and communication sectors.

TABLE A-9-2 Number of Motor Vehicles by Region and Mode, July 1976

	Total	Automobiles	Bus	Truck	Special Vehicle
National Total	211,648	89,967	22,887	86,435	12,359
Seoul	90,537	51,532	6,941	29,371	2,693
Pusan	24,799	9,783	2,380	10,251	2,385
Kyŏnggi province	20,804	5,273	3,372	9,726	2,433
Kangwŏn province	6,935	1,771	911	3,831	422
N. Ch'ungch'ŏng province	4,617	1,064	692	2,526	335
S. Ch'ungch'ŏng province	10,405	3,285	1,179	5,159	782
N. Chŏlla province	7,010	2,244	922	3,311	533
S. Chŏlla province	10,435	3,290	1,751	4,950	444
N. Kyŏngsang province	21,693	7,489	2,340	10,340	1,524
S. Kyŏngsang province	12,156	3,399	2,089	6,001	667
Cheju Island	2,257	837	310	969	141

Source: Gyotong Shinbo-Sa, *The Monthly of Korean Transportations and Communications Review* 8.9 (September 1976), p. 125.

TABLE A-9-3 Status of Roads by Region

(km)

	Total	Paved		Unpaved	Under Construction
			%		
National Total	44,905	10,000	22.3	31,295	1,610
Seoul	5,785	3,057	52.8	2,728	–
Pusan	1,200	539	44.9	630	31
Kyŏnggi province	4,283	951	22.2	3,060	272
Kangwŏn province	4,515	693	15.4	3,282	541
N. Ch'ungch'ŏng province	2,664	522	19.6	1,825	317
S. Ch'ungch'ŏng province	3,838	711	18.6	2,737	389
N. Chŏlla province	3,321	486	14.6	2,548	287
S. Chŏlla province	5,629	753	13.4	4,182	695
N. Kyŏngsang province	6,735	1,221	18.1	4,767	747
S. Kyŏngsang province	5,057	748	14.8	3,977	382
Cheju Island	1,878	319	17.0	1,559	–

Source: Gyotong Shinbo-Sa, *The Monthly of Korean Transportations and Communications Review* 8.7 (July 1976), p. 23.

TABLE A-9-4 Modal Share of Passenger Transportation in Seoul, 1974 and 1975
(1,000s)

	1974				1975			
	Whole Day		Rush Hour		Whole Day		Rush Hour	
Total	7,175	100.0	2,393	100.0	8,100	100.0	2,754	100.0
Bus	6,071	78.5	2,097	87.6	6,224	76.8	2,318	84.2
Taxi	800	10.4	100	4.3	966	11.9	140	5.1
Subway	235	3.0	38	1.6	260	3.2	38	1.4
Others	69	8.1	158	6.6	650	8.0	258	9.4

Source: Gyotong Shinbo-Sa, *The Monthly of Korean Transportations and Communications Review* 7.4 (April 1975), p. 18.

TABLE A-9-5 De Jure versus Daytime Population in Seoul, 1966–1975
(1,000s)

	De Jure Population (A)	Daytime Population (B)	B/A
1966	3,805	3,575	0.94
1967	3,969	3,731	0.94
1968	4,385	4,135	0.94
1969	4,777	5,260	1.10
1970	5,536	6,170	1.11
1971	5,850	6,726	1.15
1972	6,076	7,048	1.16
1973	6,258	7,385	1.18
1974	6,438	7,725	1.20
1975	6,640	8,100	1.22

Source: Gyotong Shinbo-Sa, *The Monthly of Korean Transportations and Communications Review* 7.4 (April 1975), p. 18.

TABLE A-9-6 Road Conditions in Seoul, 1970–1974

		Paved	Graveled	Total Roads	Roads as % of Total Area
1970	Length	1,540	3,752	5,292	
	Area	10.3	24.8	35.1	5.7
1971	Length	1,933	3,528	5,471	
	Area	13.5	24.7	38.2	6.2
1972	Length	2,267	3,301	5,568	
	Area	14.5	24.9	39.4	6.4
1973	Length	2,397	3,198	5,595	
	Area	15.5	24.3	39.8	6.4
1974	Length	2,635	3,023	5,659	
	Area	17.3	23.3	40.6	6.5

Source: Sŏul [Seoul] T'ŭkpyŏlsi, *Sŏul [Seoul] t'onggye yŏnbo, 1975.*
Note: Unit: Length – km, Area – km^2

Appendix to Chapter 10
Statistical Data on Environmental Quality

TABLE A-10-1 Sources of Air Pollution in Korea, 1965, 1971
(1,000 ton/year)

Source	1965 Amount	1965 Percent	1971 Amount	1971 Percent	Percentage Increase 1965–1971
Vehicle	105.5	20.4	351.2	24.5	232.9
Factory	58.0	11.2	415.0	29.0	615.5
Thermal Power Plant	105.0	20.3	152.0	10.6	44.8
Heating	247.7	48.0	512.9	35.8	107.1
Total	516.2	100.0	1,431.1	100.0	177.2

Source: Suk-p'yo Kwŏn, "Hwan'gyŏng pojŏn ŭi tangmyŏn kwaje wa chŏnmang," 1974, p. 121.

TABLE A-10-2 Pollution Indicators in Seoul, 1970–1974

	1970	1971	1972	1973	1974
Water Supply					
Total (million m³)	159.8	198.8	207.9	226.3	244.2
No. of households with water service (thousands)	849.8	895.3	976.6	1,015.3	1,129.1
Supply ratio (%)	77.4	77.8	82.6	83.5	88.6
Consumption of Coal					
Total (thousand M/T)	5,014.2	5,170.1	5,044.2	6,112.5	6,433.6
Residential (thousand M/T)	4,720.0	5,037.5	4,980.3	5,967.6	6,202.5
Solid Waste					
Total (thousand M/T)	2,238.8	2,456.5	2,562.0	2,770.6	2,810.0
Pollution Industries					
No. of establishments				5,488	5,350
Exceeding permitted level				400	758

Source: Sŏul [Seoul] T'ŭkpyŏlsi, *Sŏul [Seoul] t'onggye yŏnbo, 1975.*

TABLE A-10-3 Status of Solid Waste Disposal
Under Municipal Service in Seoul, 1967–1974

Year	Population Served	Quantity Disposed (1,000 M/T)	Per Capita Refuse Disposed (M/T)
1967	3,619,895	1,454	0.40
1968	3,835,955	1,902	0.50
1969	3,851,899	2,001	0.52
1970	4,277,874	2,128	0.50
1971	4,921,731	2,384	0.48
1972	5,220,268	2,515	0.48
1973	5,491,520	2,516	0.46
1974	5,733,937	2,768	0.48

Source: Sŏul [Seoul] T'ŭkpyŏlsi, *Sŏul [Seoul] t'onggye yŏnbo, 1975.*

TABLE A-10-4 Urban Waste Disposal in Korea, 1963–1974

Year	Total Population (1,000)	Population Served (1,000)	Tonnage of Waste (1,000 M/T)	Per Capita Waste Collected (Kg)
1963	6,943.6	5,177.4	2,502.2	360.4
1964	8,506.6	6,633.3	2,852.6	335.3
1965	8,829.9	7,137.4	3,086.2	495.2
1966	8,012.3	6,198.3	3,443.9	429.8
1967	10,054.3	8,203.9	4,379.5	435.6
1968	10,882.6	8,166.3	3,815.5	350.6
1969	11,686.2	8,790.8	4,218.8	361.0
1970	12,182.4	10,940.1	4,605.2	378.0
1971	13,923.6	11,542.6	5,457.5	392.0
1972	15,081.0	12,455.7	6,196.0	410.8
1973	15,664	13,695.5	6,359.0	406.0
1974	16,660	14,013.0	7,162.4	429.9

		Disposition of Garbage (in 1,000 M/T)			
Year	Total Disposed	Buried	Burned	Compost	Other
1963	1,436.7 (100.0)	1,399.0 (97.4)	3.2 (0.2)	28.6 (2.0)	5.8 (0.4)
1964	1,675.3 (100.0)	1,554.6 (92.8)	9.9 (0.6)	51.1 (3.0)	59.8 (3.6)
1965	2,153.4 (100.0)	1,961.0 (91.1)	13.0 (0.6)	66.6 (3.1)	113.0 (5.2)
1966	2,570.7 (100.0)	2,341.5 (91.1)	15.6 (0.6)	86.5 (3.4)	127.1 (4.9)
1967	3,032.1 (100.0)	2,905.4 (95.8)	10.6 (0.4)	77.2 (2.5)	38.9 (1.3)
1968	2,677.8 (100.0)	2,581.0 (96.4)	5.8 (0.2)	51.1 (1.9)	39.0 (1.5)
1969	4,021.7 (100.0)	3,927.6 (97.7)	5.9 (0.1)	48.0 (1.2)	40.1 (1.0)
1970	4,533.4 (100.0)	4,425.0 (97.6)	11.6 (0.3)	28.8 (0.6)	68.0 (1.5)
1971	5,263.5 (100.0)	5,167.8 (98.2)	20.6 (0.4)	32.5 (0.6)	42.6 (0.8)
1972	5,356.8 (100.0)	5,255.1 (98.0)	35.6 (0.7)	35.9 (0.7)	30.2 (0.6)
1973	5,922.8 (100.0)	5,848.0 (98.7)	26.3 (0.4)	12.2 (0.2)	36.3 (0.6)
1974	6,903.1 (100.0)	6,761.0 (97.9)	60.2 (0.9)	30.0 (0.4)	51.9 (0.8)

Source: Ministry of Health and Social Affairs, *Yearbook of Public Health and Social Statistics, 1972, 1975.*

Note: Figures in parentheses indicate ratios.

Appendix to Chapter 10

TABLE A-10-5 Estimated Future Air Pollution Emissions, 1975–1981
(1,000 ton/year)

Source	1975	1977	1979	1981
		Year		
Transportation	304.5(15.8)	351.5(15.6)	396.3(14.3)	437.7(13.9)
Plant	828.5(43.1)	1,009.3(44.8)	1,300.9(47.0)	1,528.5(48.6)
Power Station	224.2(11.7)	246.9(10.9)	349.9(12.6)	377.6(12.0)
Housing	564.5(29.4)	645.6(28.7)	721.9(26.1)	801.9(25.5)
Total	1,921.7(100.0)	2,253.3(100.0)	2,769.0(100.0)	3,145.7(100.0)

Source: Ch'ŏr-hwan Ch'a, "Tosi kaebal kwa hwan'gyŏng munje," in papers submitted to the seminar on National Development and Human Environment in Korea, 1975, p. 12.

Note: Estimated through unit coefficient of pollution emission by fuel.

TABLE A-10-6 Coverage of Solid Waste Disposal in Seoul, 1972–1981
(1,000s)

	1972	1974	1976	1981
Total Number of Households	1,151	1,310	1,400	1,490
Total Population	5,851	6,550	7,000	7,450
Number of Households Served	1,022	1,239	1,400	1,490
Population Served	5,220	6,195	7,000	7,450
Number of Households Not Served	129	71	–	–
Percent of the Number of Households Served of the Total Number of Households	88.9%	94.6%	100%	100%
Annual Amount of Refuse Disposal (M/T)	2,515	2,905	3,215	3,339

Source: Sŏul [Seoul] T'ŭkpyŏlsi, Sijŏng Kaeyo, December 1973, p. 260.

TABLE A-10-7 Particulate Concentration in Seoul by Land-Use Zone and Year[a]
(ton/km[2]/month)

Land Use	Year					
	1969	*1970*	*1971*	*1972*	*1973*	*1974*
Industrial and Semi-Industrial	25.1	31.1	32.90	38.58	31.1	18.6
Commercial	29.0	39.6	34.38	31.22	33.3	17.7
Residential	20.7	18.4	20.58	18.29	22.2	11.2
Green[b]	11.8	14.3	17.09	12.79	18.5	10.7
From the core of CBD:						
5 km	–	–	22.29	–	–	–
5–10 km	–	–	27.17	–	–	–
10–15 km	–	–	35.72	–	–	–

Source: Sŏul [Seoul]-si Pogŏn yŏn'guso, *Yŏn'gu pogoso*, Seoul, 1974.

Notes: [a]Averages observed bimonthly from April to December of each year.
[b]Includes green-belts and parks, etc.

TABLE A-10-8 Average Amounts of BOD in the Han River
(p.p.m.)

	Near the Kooiri Reservoir	*Near the Bokwang Reservoir*	*Near the Noryangjin Reservoir*
1967	14.2	26.3	23.2
1968	18.0	44.3	26.9
1969	20.3	34.9	30.7
1970	6.2 – 18.6	18.8 – 50.6	15.6 – 39.5
1971	4.0 – 13.5	40.2	30.1
1971 (DO)	9.1	6.4	7.4

Source: Suk-p'yo Kwŏn, "Hwan'gyŏng pojŏn ŭi tangmyŏn kwaje wa chŏnmang," 1974.

Note: BOD is biochemical oxygen demand, a measure of oxygen demand made on streams by organic discharges.

Notes

ONE   *Introduction*

1. The purposes of this volume do not require a precise definition of LDCs. The term refers to the relatively poor countries of the world.

2. Kingsley Davis, *World Urbanization, 1950–1970,* Population Monograph Series No. 4 (Berkeley, 1970).

TWO   *A Survey of Urbanization in Korea*

1. For a decade following the end of World War II, Japan's urbanization exceeded any ever recorded in Korea, but this obviously reflected in large part the return of residents who had fled the wartime devastation of the cities. It is interesting to note that the Korean War appears to have had no effect on the 5-year data in Table 1. The statements in this paragraph are hardly affected by the partition of Korea in 1945, since North and South Korea were about equally urbanized at that time.

2. Including migration of about half a million refugees from North Korea during 1950–1955. The inclusion of these refugees hardly affects the total. See Chapter 5.

3. Agriculture here includes forestry and fisheries.

4. For Korean data, see Ministry of Home Affairs, *Municipal Yearbook of Korea, 1974*; for U.S. data see U.S. Government, *U.S. Population Census, 1970.*

THREE   *Causes and Comparisons of Urban Growth*

1. Allen C. Kelley, Jeffrey G. Williamson, and R. J. Cheetham, *Dualistic Economic Development: Theory and History* (Chicago, 1972).

2. Edward F. Denison, *Accounting for United States Economic Growth, 1929–1969* (Washington, D.C., 1974).

3. Hollis Chenery and Moises Syrquin, *Patterns of Development, 1950–1970* (Oxford, 1975).

FOUR   *Primacy and the City Size Distribution*

1. In *World Urbanization.*

FIVE   *Migration*

1. This chapter, contributed by John E. Sloboda, University of Michigan, draws heavily on the fuller treatment of population movements included in Tai Hwan Kwon, "Population Change and Its Components in Korea: 1925–1966," unpublished PhD dissertation, Australian National University, 1972, and the study of demographic changes and development prepared for this series.

2. Based on population figures given in Chosŏn Ch'ongdokpu, *Chosŏn in'gu ŭi hyŏnsang* (Seoul, 1927), pp. 265–289.

3. Ehn-Hyun Choe, *Population Distribution and Internal Migration in Korea* (Seoul, 1966), p. 11.

4. Sŭng-je Ko, *Han'guk iminsa yŏn'gu* (Seoul, 1973), p. 269.

5. Yunshik Chang, "Population in Early Modernization in Korea," unpublished PhD dissertation, Princeton University, 1966.

6. John J. Stephen, "The Korean Minority in the Soviet Union," *Mizan,* XIII.3 (December 1971), 140.

7. Sŭng-je Ko, pp. 205–214, 235.

8. In accordance with Japanese practices, the minimum population required for calssification as an urban place changed from 20,000 to 30,000 in the mid-1930s.

9. According to a 1938 survey of the permanent domiciles of Koreans registered in Japan, only 3.4% were from the northern provinces. See Sang-hyŏn Kim, *Chae-Il Han'guk Kŏjumin yoyak* (Seoul, 1969), p. 44.

10. The decline in the price of rice may have helped squeeze into tenancy small cultivators who lacked the capital necessary to reap a share of the major gains in productivity that occurred during this period.

11. Many may also have gone in small boats.

12. Manchuria was, in fact, a major center of activities for Korean nationalists, leftists, and anti-Japanese guerrilla activities.

13. Senji Tsuboe, Zai Nihon Chōsenjin no gaikyō (Tokyo, 1965), p. 14, and Sang-hyŏn Kim.

14. The domestic draft labor plan called for the mobilization of 850,000 men. See Tai Hwan Kwon, "Population Change," p. 232.

15. Ibid., p. 243.

16. I. B. Taeuber and G. W. Barclay, "Korea and the Koreans in the Northeast Asian Region," *Population Index* 16.4 (1950).

17. In making his estimates Tai Hwan Kwon employed the following procedures and assumptions:

1. The estimation of the population in South Korea at the time of Liberation from the 1944 census using estimated life-table survival ratios and the assumption that the 1940–1944 immigration patterns persisted through Liberation, September, 1945.

2. Japan was assumed to be the only destination of emigrants after 1940.

3. The estimation of net migration into South Korea during 1945–1949 from the estimated population at the time of Liberation and the 1949 census using the forward projection census survival ratio method.

4. Estimation of the net migration from Japan to South Korea during this period based on the assumption that 90% of the Koreans repatriated from Japan went to South Korea.

5. The rough estimation that 40% of the Koreans in Manchuria and elsewhere in East Asia were repatriated during this period with one-half of these coming to South Korea.

6. Calculation of north-south movement as the difference between estimated net migration into South Korea and the estimated number of overseas repatriates entering the south.

Tai Hwan Kwon, "Population Change" pp. 241–246.

18. Tai Hwan Kwon, "Population Change," pp. 235, 268.

19. See Ehn-Hyun Choe, p. 28; and G. T. Trewartha and W. Zelinsky, "Population Distribution and Change in Korea, 1925–49," *Geographical Review* 45.1:1–26 (January 1955).

20. Tai Hwan Kwon, "Population Change," (p. 277) suggests that more than half may have settled in urban areas.

21. Tai Hwan Kwon's task was complicated by evidence of substantial age misreporting and under-enumeration in the 1955 census and later post-war censuses among young adult males.

22. Tai Hwan Kwon, p. 290. Based on adding one-third of the reported missing and P.O.W. to the known number of those taken north. He notes that many of these may have died en route during the two North Korean withdrawals.

23. Ibid., p. 292.

24. Ibid., p. 294.

25. Tai Hwan Kwon estimates net rural-urban migration during this

period at 722,000 persons, using the assumption that the number of North Korean refugees in each area in 1955 is equivalent to the *net* gain from the north in the area.

26. Han'guk Nongŏp Hyŏptong Chohap, *Han'guk nongŏp ŭi che munje*, (Seoul 1969), pp. 332–336.

27. The quality of the 1955, 1960, and 1966 censuses has been examined in detail by Tai Hwan Kwon, "Population Change," pp. 9–25. A revised version of his assessment of the 1960 and 1966 censuses appears in *A Study of the Korean Population 1966,* The Population and Development Studies Center, Seoul National University, 1974, by H. Y. Lee, T. H. Kwon, Y. S. Chang, and E. Y. Yu.

28. Tai Hwan Kwon, "Population Change."

29. Tai Hwan Kwon, "Estimates of Net Internal Migration for Korea, 1955–1970," *Bulletin of the Population and Development Studies Center*, Vol. IV (1975) pp. 54–103. Kwon includes a detailed description of the adjustment made.

30. Under the traditional age reckoning system, an individual's age is equal to the number of lunar new years passed since birth, plus one. Correspondence to the Western notion of completed (solar) years is further complicated by the difference in the length of lunar and solar years and the additional month in lunar leap years which causes noticeable heaping among cohorts born in these years.

31. Estimated post-migration births to migrant women are also reckoned as part of national increase, although this increase is also ultimately due to migration.

32. In 1957, Ch'ungju and Samch'ŏnp'o ŭp (towns) were upgraded to si (city) status. In 1955 these had a combined population of 103,600. Annexations to Kwangju, Taegu, and Chŏnju added areas with a 1955 population of 69,751 to these cities.

33. Tai Hwan Kwon, "Population Change," p. 303.

34. Suwŏn, Kangnŭng,* Ch'ungju, Kunsan,* Sunch'ŏn, P'ohang,* Kyŏngju, Kimch'ŏn, Masan,* Ch'ungmu,* Chinhae,* Samch'ŏnp'o* (asterisks indicate port cities).

SIX   *Structure of Cities*

1. See Edwin S. Mills "Urban Density Functions," *Urban Studies,* February 1970; and Mills, *Studies in the Structure of the Urban Economy* (Baltimore, 1972).

2. See Mills and Ohta.

3. D_0 is a somewhat artificial notion since, in fact, relatively little land is devoted to residences in central business districts of most large cities.

SEVEN   *Land Values*

1. BOK, *Economic Statistics Yearbook, 1976,* pp. 3, 261.
2. Edwin S. Mills, *Urban Economics* (Glenview, Ill., 1972).
3. It is likely that the quality of the appraisals on which Table 27 is based has improved gradually. If so, it may mean that the more recent appraisals have kept up with market values better than earlier appraisals, imparting an upward bias to estimates of land price increases.
4. The theoretical ideas in this section refer to land rents, not to land values. As indicated earlier, the distinction is important. Available data are for land values, not rents. Land value functions estimated below have the same exponents as land rent functions, provided land values are the same multiple of land rents everywhere in an urban area. This might not be the case if, for example, future capital gains were expected to be more rapid near the fringes of the urban area than near the center.
5. See Mills and Ohta, p. 699.

EIGHT   *Housing*

1. *U.N. Statistical Yearbook, 1974.*
2. Byung-Nak Song and Raymond J. Struyk, "Korean Housing: Economic Appraisal and Policy Alternatives" KDI Working Paper No. 76-03 (Seoul, 1976).
3. Kŏnsŏlbu, *Chut'aek pumun kyehoek charyo, 1977–1981,* 1974.
4. Song and Struyk, "Korean Housing."
5. William A. Doebele, "Land Policy in Seoul and Gwangju [Kwangju], with Special Reference to Land Readjustments" (Washington, 1976).

NINE   *Urban Transportation*

1. EPB, *Preliminary Outline of the Fourth Five-Year Development Plan* (April 1976), p. 193, and "A Summary Draft of the Fourth Five-Year Development Plan, 1977–1981" (July 1976).
2. Motor vehicles include buses, trucks, cars, and motorcycles.

TEN   *Environmental Quality*

1. EPB, *The Third Five-Year Economic Development Plan, 1972–1976* (1971), and "A Summary Draft of the Fourth Five-Year Development Plan."

Bibliography

Statistical

Andong. *Andong-si t'onggye yŏnbo* (Andong statistical yearbook), *1963, 1967, 1971, 1973, 1974.*

Bank of Korea (Han'guk Ŭnhaeng). *Economic Statistics Yearbook, 1949,* 1955, 1971, 1976, 1977.

——. *National Income in Korea, 1973, 1975.*

Chŏlla-namdo (South Chŏlla province). *Chŏlla-namdo t'onggye yŏnbo* (South Chŏlla province statistical yearbook), *1974.*

Ch'ŏnan. *Ch'ŏnan-si t'onggye yŏnbo* (Ch'ŏnan statistical yearbook), *1967, 1971, 1974.*

Ch'ŏngju. *Ch'ŏngju-si t'onggye yŏnbo* (Ch'ŏngju statistical yearbook), *1966, 1971, 1974.*

Chōsen Sōtokufu (Japanese Government General in Korea). Chōsen Sōtokufu *tōkei nenpō* (Statistics Yearbook), *1910, 1915, 1920, 1923, 1925, 1926, 1930, 1932, 1935, 1936, 1940, 1941.*

Economic Planning Board. *Korea Statistical Yearbook, 1952, 1965, 1970, 1971, 1975.*

——. *Report on Population and Housing Census, 1955, 1960, 1966, 1970, 1975.*

——. *Annual Report on the Economically Active Population, 1974.*

——. *Special Labor Force Survey Report, 1974.*

——. *Yearbook of Migration Statistics, 1974.*

——. *Housing and Urban Planning for Korea's Fourth Five-Year Plan.* 1976.

——. *Preliminary Outline of the Fourth Five-Year Development Plan.* 1976.

——. *Annual Report on the Family Income and Expenditure Survey, 1963-1974.* 1975.

Gyotong Shinbo-Sa (Kyot'ong Sinbosa). *The Monthly of Korean Transportations and Communications Review.* 1975, 1976.

Han'guk Chut'aek Ŭnhaeng (Korea Housing Bank). *Han'guk chut'aek kŏnsŏl ch'ongnam* (General status of Korean housing construction), 1975.

Han'guk Kamjŏngwŏn (Korea Appraisal Board). *12 chuyo tosi chiga chisu* (Land value index of 12 major cities in Korea). June, 1975.

———. *T'oji siga chosa* (Land value survey), *1956–1973, 1975.*

Han'guk Ŭnhaeng (Bank of Korea). *Chiyŏk kyŏngje t'onggye* (Regional economic statistics). June, 1975.

Inch'ŏn. *Inch'ŏn-si t'onggye yŏnbo* (Inch'ŏn statistical yearbook), *1967, 1971, 1973.*

Kangnŭng. *Kangnŭng-si t'onggye yŏnbo* (Kangnŭng statistical yearbook), *1967, 1971, 1974.*

Kŏnsŏlbu (Ministry of Construction). *Chut'aek pumun kyehoek charyo* (Data for the housing sector plan for the Fourth Five-Year Economic Development Plan), *1977–1981.* 1974.

———. *Kŏnsŏl t'onggye p'yŏllam* (Survey of construction statistics). 1975.

———. *Kukt'o mit sanŏp ipchi pumun kyehoek* (National land use and industrial location plans for the Fourth Five-Year Economic Development Plan), *1977–1981.* 1976.

Korean Institute for Family Planning. *A Study on National Family Planning and Fertility.* 1974.

Kwanju. *Kwangju-si t'onggye yŏnbo* (Kwangju statistical yearbook), *1967, 1971, 1974.*

Kyŏngsang-namdo (South Kyŏngsang province). *Kyŏngnam t'onggye yŏnbo* (South Kyŏngsang province statistical yearbook), *1974.*

Ministry of Agriculture and Fisheries. *Report on the Results of Farm Household Economy Survey, 1975.*

Ministry of Health and Social Affairs. *Yearbook of Public Health and Social Statistics, 1972, 1975.*

Naemubu (Ministry of Home Affairs). *Chijŏk t'onggye* (Land registration statistics). 1973.

Ministry of Home Affairs (Naemubu). *Municipal Yearbook of Korea, 1969, 1972, 1974.*

Ministry of Transportation. *Korea Port-Phase Two Development Study*, Vols. I–X. February 1976.

———. *Korea Transportation Survey Draft Report.* June 1966.

———. *Statistics Yearbook of Transportation, 1963, 1968, 1974, 1975.*

Pusan. *Pusan-si t'onggye yŏnbo* (Pusan statistical yearbook), *1967, 1971, 1974.*

Republic of China, Economic Planning Council. *Taiwan Statistical Data Book, 1974.*

Samch'ŏnp'o. *Samch'ŏnp'o-si t'onggye yŏnbo* (Samch'ŏnp'o statistical yearbook), *1961, 1967, 1971, 1974.*

Sŏul (Seoul) T'ŭkpyŏlsi (Seoul Metropolitan Government). *Sŏul (Seoul) t'onggye yŏnbo* (Seoul statistical yearbook), *1967, 1971, 1972, 1974, 1975.*

Suwŏn. *Suwŏn-si t'onggye yŏnbo* (Suwŏn statistical yearbook), *1967, 1971, 1974.*

Taegu. *Taegu-si t'onggye yŏnbo* (Taegu statistical yearbook), *1967, 1971, 1973.*

Taehan Chut'aek Kongsa (Korea Housing Corporation). *Chut'aek chosa t'onggye* (Housing statistics). December 1974.

Taejŏn. *Taejŏn-si t'onggye yŏnbo* (Taejŏn statistical yearbook), *1967, 1971, 1974.*

United Nations. *U. N. Demographic Yearbook, 1970.*

———. *U. N. Statistical Yearbook, 1974.*

United States Government, Bureau of the Census. *Statistical Abstract of the United States.* Washington, D.C., Government Printing Office, annual.

———. *U. S. Population Census, 1970.* Washington, D.C., Government Printing Office, 1970.

Yŏnse (Yonsei) Taehakkyo Konghae Munje Yŏn'guso (The Yonsei University Pollution Research Institute). *Che 4-ch'a kyŏngje kaebal 5-gae nyŏn kyehoek, chut'aek mit tosi kyehoek pumun kyehoek* (Housing and urban sector planning for Korea's Fourth Five-Year Economic Development Plan, 1977–1981). 1976.

General

Ban, Sung Hwan (Pan, Sŏng-hwan). "The New Community Movement in Korea." Korea Development Institute, Interim Report No. 7502.

Beier, G., et al. "The Task Ahead for the Cities of the Developing Countries." World Bank, Staff Working Paper No. 209. July 1975.

Ch'a, Ch'ŏr-hwan. "Chawŏn kaebal kwa hwan'gyŏng oyŏm taech'aek" (Resource development and measures to control environmental pollution). Paper presented at the First Population Policy Seminar held at the Korea Development Institute, March 30–31, 1976.

———. "Tosi kaebal kwa hwan'gyŏng munje" (Urban development and environmental problems). Proceedings of the National Conference on Human Environment—National Development and Human Environment in Korea. Sponsored by the Korea Atomic Energy Research Institute and Graduate School of Environmental Studies, Seoul National University. December 1975.

Chang, Yunshik (Chang, Yun-sik). "Population in Early Modernization: Korea." Unpublished PhD dissertation, Princeton University, 1966.

Chenery, Hollis and Moises Syrquin. *Patterns of Development 1950–1970.* Oxford, Oxford University Press, 1975.

Cho, Lee Jay (Cho, I-jae). *Estimates of Current Fertility for the Republic of Korea and Its Geographical Subdivisions: 1959–1970.* Yonsei University Press, 1974.

Choe, Ehn-Hyun (Ch'oe, Ŭn-hyŏn). *Population Distribution and Internal Migration in Korea.* Seoul, Economic Planning Board, Bureau of Statistics, 1966.

Chosŏn Ch'ongdokpu (Japanese Government General in Korea). *Chosŏn in'gu ŭi hyŏnsang* (The population situation in Korea). Seoul, 1927.

Clark, Colin. *Population Growth and Land Use.* London, St. Martin's Press, 1967.

Davis, Kingsley. *World Urbanization, 1950–1970.* Population Monograph Series No. 4. Berkeley, University of California Press, 1970.

Denison, Edward F. "The Sources of Economic Growth in the United States and the Alternatives Before Us." Committee for Economic Development, Supplementary Paper No. 13. 1962.

——. *Accounting for United States Economic Growth, 1929–1969.* Washington, D.C., The Brookings Institution, 1974.

Doebele, William A. "Land Policy in Seoul and Gwangju [Kwangju], Korea, with Special Reference to Land Readjustment." Washington, D.C., World Bank draft, January 1976.

Economic Planning Board. *The Third Five-Year Economic Development Plan,* 1972–1976. Seoul, 1971.

——. *A Summary Draft of the Fourth Five-Year Economic Development Plan, 1977–1981,* Seoul, 1976.

Han'guk Chut'aek Ŭnhaeng (Korea Housing Bank). *Yungja chut'aek silt'ae chosa* (Survey report on the Korea Housing Bank loan housing). 1974.

Han'guk Kwahak Kisul Yŏn'guso (Korea Institute of Science and Technology). *Chihach'ŏl sunhwansŏn kŏnsŏl ŭl ŭihan kisul mit kyŏngjesŏn chosa* (Feasibility study on the proposed construction of the circular metropolitan subway system), May, 1975.

——. *Hwan'gyŏng pojŏn ŭl ŭihan tosi mit chiyŏk kyehoek e kwanhan yŏn'gu* (A study on urban and regional planning for environmental preservation). April 1975.

——. "Pusan-si kyot'ong kibon kyehoek" (Basic transportation plan for the city of Pusan). February 1974.

——. *Sŏul [Seoul] T'ŭkpyŏlsi t'onghaeng silt'ae chosa* (Traffic survey in Seoul). February 1974.

Han'guk Nongŏp Hyŏptong Chohap (Korea National Agricultural Cooperative Federation). *Han'guk nongŏp ŭi che munje* (Various problems of Korean agriculture). Seoul, 1969.

Han'guk Sanŏp Ŭnhaeng (Korea Development Bank). *Han'guk kyŏngje 10-nyŏnsa* (Ten-year economic history of Korea). 1971.

Hoover, Edgar M. *An Introduction to Regional Economics.* New York, Alfred A. Knopf, 1971.

Hwang, Myung-Chan (Hwang, Myŏng-ch'an). "Self-Help Site Development in Korea: An Overall Evaluation." Paper Presented to the Habitat Forum, the U.N. Conference on Human Settlements, Vancouver, Canada, May-June 1976.

Inch'ŏn-si (the City of Inch'ŏn). *Han-gang sujil oyŏm chosa pogosŏ* (Research report on the water quality of the Han River). December 1973.

Kelley, Allen C. and Jeffrey G. Williamson. *Lessons from Japanese Development.* Chicago, University of Chicago Press, 1972.

——— and R. J. Cheetham. *Dualistic Economic Development: Theory and History.* Chicago, University of Chicago Press, 1972.

Kim, Ch'a-bong. "Sujil oyŏm ŭi yŏnghyang kwa taech'aek e kwanhan yŏn'gu" (A study on the effects of water pollution and control measures). Unpublished thesis, Yonsei University, 1973.

Kim, Chol. *Kankoku no jinko to keizai* (The Population and Economy of Korea). Tokyo, Iwanami Shoten, 1965.

Kim, Kwang Suk (Kim, Kwang-sŏk). "Household Savings Behaviour," Planning Model and Macro-Economic Policy Series. Ed. Chuk-Kyo Kim (Chŏk-kyo Kim). Seoul, Korea Development Institute, 1977.

Kim, Sang-hyŏn (Kim, Sang-Hyon). *Chae-Il Han'guk kŏjumin yoyak* (Abstract of Korean residents in Japan). In'gu Munje Yŏn'guso (The Institute of Population Problems). Seoul, 1969.

Kim, Tae-yŏng. "Sŏul [Seoul] sinae saengsan mit sodŭk ch'ugye" (Estimate of production and consumption in Seoul). Korea Development Institute, Research Report No. 75-03, January 1975.

Kim, Tae-yŏng and Hyo-gu Yi. *Uri nara in'gu idong ŭi t'ŭkching 1965–1970* (Characteristics of migration in Korea 1965–1970). Korea Development Institute, Working Paper No. 76-01, May 1976.

Ko, Sŭng-je. *Han'guk iminsa yŏn'gu* (A study of Korean emigration). Seoul, Changun'gak, 1973.

Kongŏp Tanji Kwallich'ŏng (The Agency for Industrial Estates Management). *Kongŏp tanji ŭi hyŏnhang* (Present status of industrial estates). I, II (March 1976).

Kŏnsŏlbu (Ministry of Construction). *Chut'aek chŏngch'aek kwa changgi kŏnsŏl kyehoek* (Housing policy and long-run housing construction plan). May 1975.

Korea Housing Bank (Han'guk Chut'aek Ŭnhaeng). *Eighth Annual Report.* 1974.

——. *Housing Finance Quarterly Review.* Vol. 6 (1973), Vol. 7 (1974), Vol. 8 (1975).

Korea Industrial Development Research Institute. *Study on Housing Policy Formulation.* December 1974.

Korea National Agricultural Cooperative Federation (Han'guk Nongŏp Hyŏptong Chohap). *National Land Values Survey, 1974.*

Kwŏn, Suk-p'yo. "Sŏul [Seoul] T'ŭkpyŏlsi taegi oyŏm paech'ullyang" (Air pollutant emission in Seoul), *Bulletin of the Korea Pollution Control Association*, 1972.

——. "Hwan'gyŏng pojŏn ŭi tangmyŏn kwaje wa chŏnmang" (Present problems and future prospects of environmental preservation in Korea). Research Report of Yonsei University Pollution Research Institute, 1974.

Kwon, Tai Hwan (Kwŏn, T'ae-hwan). "Population Change and Its Components in Korea: 1925-1966." Unpublished PhD dissertation, Australian National University, 1972.

——. "Estimates of Net Internal Migration for Korea, 1955-1970." *Bulletin of the Population and Development Studies Center,* Vol. IV (November 1975), 54-103.

Kwon, Tai-Joon. "An Evaluation of the Capacity of a Legal System to Facilitate an Urban Development Program: The Case of Gwangju (Kwangju) Squatters Relocation," *Korean Journal of Public Administration* 10.2 (1972).

Lee, H. Y. (Yi, Hae-yŏng), T. H. Kwon (T'ae-hwan Kwŏn), Y. S. Chang (Yun-sik Chang) and E. Y. Yu (Ŭi-yŏng Yu). *A Study of the Korean Population 1966.* The Population and Development Studies Center, Seoul National University, 1974.

Li, Wen Lang. "An Analysis of Internal Migration in Korea." Research Report of the American Public Health Association in Agreement with the U.S. Agency for International Development. October 1974.

Mills, Edwin S. "Urban Density Functions," *Urban Studies.* February 1970.

——. "City Sizes in Developing Economies," in Raanan Weits, ed., *Rehovoth Conference on Urbanization and the Developing Countries.*

Rehovot, Israel, Continuation Committee for the International Conference on Science in the Advancement of New States, 1971.

———. *Studies in the Structure of the Urban Economy.* Baltimore, The Johns Hopkins University Press, 1972.

———. *Urban Economics.* Glenview, Illinois, Scott, Foresman and Co., 1972.

——— and Katsutoshi Ohta. "Urbanization and Urban Problems," in Hugh Patrick and H. Rosovsky, eds., *Asia's New Giant—How the Japanese Economy Works.* Washington, D.C., The Brookings Institution, 1976.

Muth, Richard F. *Cities and Housing: The Spatial Pattern of Urban Residential Land Use.* Chicago, University of Chicago Press, 1969.

National Commission on Urban Problems. *Three Land Research Studies.* U.S. Government Printing Office, 1968.

Nelson, Joan M. "Migration, Integration of Migrants, and the Problems of Squatter Settlement in Seoul," Korea: Report on a Field Survey for the Smithsonian Institution, Harvard Center for International Affairs the Woodrow Wilson Center, Smithsonian Institution. May 1972.

Nippon Fudōsan Bank Research Institute, Ltd. Nippon no chikahyoka to fudōsan torihiki sōgaku (Estimates of total land value and total amount of real estate transactions). Tokyo, 1973.

Orishima, Isao. "Land Use and Land Price," *Real Estate Appraisal.* May 1973.

Patrick, Hugh and Henry Rosovsky, eds. *Asia's New Giant—How the Japanese Economy Works.* Washington, D.C., The Brookings Institution, 1976.

Renaud, Bertrand. "The Evolution of the Urban System in Korea 1910–1970," *Bulletin of the Population and Development Studies Center,* Seoul National University, Vol. III, September 1974.

———. "Industrial Location and Regional Policy in Korea," in *Asian Survey.* Berkeley, University of California Press, 1974.

———. "Economic Growth and Income Inequality in Korea." World Bank Staff Working Paper No. 209. February 1976.

Rho, Chae-Shik. "Environmental Problems in Korea." Paper presented at the Workshop on Systems Development, July 12–15, 1977, Ministry of Science and Technology, Seoul.

Robert R. Nathan Associates, Inc. *Seoul Metropolitan Region.* First Cycle Report. Technical Report prepared for the United Nations, January 1975.

Sloboda, J. E. "Housing, Land, and Socio-Economic Integration—Viewed through the Housing Problem in Seoul, Korea." Cambridge, Harvard University, unpublished paper. 1972.

Song, Byung-Nak (Song, Pyŏng-nak). "The Distribution and Movement of

Jobs and Industry—the Seoul Metropolitan Region." Korea Development Institute, Working Paper No. 74-11. November 1974.

—— and Raymond J. Struyk. "Korean Housing: Economic Appraisal and Policy Alternatives." Korea Development Institute, Working Paper No. 76-03, Seoul, 1976.

Song, Pyŏng-nak (Song, Byung-Nak). "Han'guk sudokwŏn ŭi konggan kyŏngje punsŏk" (A study on the Seoul region). Korea Development Institute, Research Report No. 75-16, December 1975.

Sŏul [Seoul] Sanŏp Taehak, Tosi Konghak Yŏn'gubu (Seoul Industrial College Urban Engineering Research Unit). "Sudokwŏn chihach'ŏl chŏnch'ŏl unhaeng ŭi p'yŏngka mit sahoe kyŏngjejŏk hyokwa punsŏk" (Socio-economic appraisals of the Seoul metropolitan subway system). Seoul, July, 1975.

Sŏul [Seoul]-si Pogŏn Yŏn'guso (Seoul Metropolitan Government Board of Health). *Yŏn'gu pogoso* (Research report). 1974.

Sŏul [Seoul] T'ŭkpyŏlsi (Seoul Metropolitan Government). *Chongno chihach'ŏl mit sudokwŏn chŏnch'ŏl kaet'ong ŭi hyokwa* (Impact of the opening of the Chongno subway line and electrification of the railroads in the Seoul region). Proceedings of the Seminar on the Impacts of the Opening of the Chongno Subway Line, August 1974.

——. *Sijŏng kaeyo* (Survey of municipal affairs), 1973, 1974, 1975.

Sovani, N. V. "The Analysis of Over-Urbanization," *Economic Development and Cultural Change,* Vol. 12, 1964.

Stephen, John J. "The Korean Minority in the Soviet Union," *Mizan* XIII.3 (December 1971).

Taehan Chut'aek Kongsa (Korea Housing Corporation) and Kŏnsŏlbu (Ministry of Construction). "Chut'aek konggŭp ch'okchinch'aek mit chŏryŏmhwa pangan" (Policies for promotion of housing supply and measures for reducing housing production costs). Proceedings of the Seminar on Promotion of Housing Supply, Seoul, 1975.

Taehan Min'guk Kongbosil (Republic of Korea, Office of Public Information). *Han'guk ŭi 1949-nyŏn in'gu sensŏsŭ sokpo* (Preliminary report of the 1949 census of Korea). 1950.

Taeuber, I. B. and G. W. Barclay. "Korea and the Koreans in the Northeast Asian Region," *Population Index* 16.4 (1950).

Trewartha, G. T. and W. Zelinsky. "Population Distribution and Change in Korea, 1925–49," *Geographical Review* 45.1:1–26 (January 1955).

Tsuboe, Senji. *Zai Nihon Chōsenjin no gaikyō* (The general condition of Koreans in Japan). Tokyo, Gannando, 1965.

United Nations. *Urban Land Policies and Land-Use Control Measures.* Vol. II, *Asia and the Far East*; Vol. VII, *Global Review.*

The World Bank. *Housing.* Sector Policy Paper. May 1975.

——. "The Task Ahead for the Cities of Developing Countries." Staff Working Paper No. 209. July 1975.

Yoon, Jong Ju (Yun, Chong-ju). *A Study of the Population of Seoul.* Seoul, Seoul Women's College Press, 1975.

Index

Agriculture: workers in, 7, 17, 185, 190–196, 203, 225–226; workers leaving, 15, 175; growth in, 29; input demand for, 32; under Japanese, 62, 64; wartime damage to, 76; land productivity in, 99, 175; effects of on environment, 156–157

Air: quality of, 156, 161; discharges into, 157, 158–165, 283, 285; concentrations in, 162–165, 286

Algeria: housing in, 120

Allocation: of resources, 29, 171, 204–211; of labor, 40, 41, 171; of land, 33–35, 99, 101, 109, 110–114; of investment funds, 118

Andong, 50, 86, 95, 236, 237

Anyang Stream, 167

Armistice of 1953, 75

Automobiles. *See* Motor vehicles

Bangladesh: population density in, 11

Banking: employment in, 16, 190–196

Beverages: expenditures for, 31

Binghamton, N.Y., 89–90

Birth rates: 4; rural vs. urban, 8, 232

Buildings: substituted for land, 33, 35–36, 104; and urban density, 92; taxes on, 115; conversion of, 126

Buses, 143, 144; Korean reliance on, 145–150, 155; in Seoul and Pusan, 146–148, 150, 151; imported vs. domestic, 150; advantages of, 152; future prospects for, 152–154. *See also* Motor vehicles

Capital: accumulation, 29, 32, 38; substituted for land, 108; formation, 122, 212–215

Capital gains, 116, 133

Carbon monoxide, 158, 162, 168

Census, 5, 56, 71, 73, 77

Central Business District (CBD), 108–110

Cheetham, 28

Cheju city, 81, 256, 257, 271–272

Cheju Island, 72, 79, 80, 193, 196, 267, 278

Chemical industries, 53

Chenery, Hollis B., 37, 41, 42

Chientao district, 57

China: population density in, 11; Koreans in, 57, 59, 63, 66; Korean relations with, 57

Chinese Communists, 75

Chinhae, 50, 53

Chŏlla province, North and South, 67, 71, 72, 75, 192–193, 196, 267, 278

Ch'ŏnan, 50, 87, 95, 236, 239

Ch'ŏnggye Stream, 167

Ch'ŏngju, 49, 86, 95, 236, 240, 256, 271–272

Ch'ŏngnyang-ni, 147

Chŏnse, 133, 134, 135

Ch'ungch'ŏng province: North, 67, 72, 75, 76, 192, 195, 267, 278; South, 67, 72, 75, 79, 192, 195, 267, 278

Cities: definition of, 6–7; characteristic of, 10; Seoul, Tokyo, NY, 12; declining densities in, 15; sizes of, 44–54, 173–174; structure of, 82–91, 92–93; decentralization in, 82–91, 92; transportation in, 145

Cities, Korean: population densities of, 11–12, 85–87, 95, 96; employment patterns in, 16–17; populations of, 47–54; out-migrations from, 80; land values in, 104–106; illegal housing in,

303

Harvard East Asian Monographs

46. W. P. J. Hall, *A Bibliographical Guide to Japanese Research on the Chinese Economy, 1958–1970*

47. Jack J. Gerson, *Horatio Nelson Lay and Sino-British Relations, 1854–1864*

48. Paul Richard Bohr, *Famine and the Missionary: Timothy Richard as Relief Administrator and Advocate of National Reform*

49. Endymion Wilkinson, *The History of Imperial China: A Research Guide*

50. Britten Dean, *China and Great Britain: The Diplomacy of Commerical Relations, 1860–1864*

51. Ellsworth C. Carlson, *The Foochow Missionaries, 1847–1880*

52. Yeh-chien Wang, *An Estimate of the Land-Tax Collection in China, 1753 and 1908*

53. Richard M. Pfeffer, *Understanding Business Contracts in China, 1949–1963*

54. Han-sheng Chuan and Richard Kraus, *Mid-Ch'ing Rice Markets and Trade, An Essay in Price History*

55. Ranbir Vohra, *Lao She and the Chinese Revolution*

56. Liang-lin Hsiao, *China's Foreign Trade Statistics, 1864–1949*

57. Lee-hsia Hsu Ting, *Government Control of the Press in Modern China, 1900–1949*

58. Edward W. Wagner, *The Literati Purges: Political Conflict in Early Yi Korea*

59. Joungwon A. Kim, *Divided Korea: The Politics of Development, 1945–1972*

60. Noriko Kamachi, John K. Fairbank, and Chūzō Ichiko, *Japanese Studies of Modern China Since 1953: A Bibliographical Guide to Historical and Social-Science Research on the Nineteenth and Twentieth Centuries, Supplementary Volume for 1953–1969*

61. Donald A. Gibbs and Yun-chen Li, *A Bibliography of Studies and Translations of Modern Chinese Literature, 1918–1942*

62. Robert H. Silin, *Leadership and Values: The Organization of Large-Scale Taiwanese Enterprises*

63. David Pong, *A Critical Guide to the Kwangtung Provincial Archives Deposited at the Public Record Office of London*

64. Fred W. Drake, *China Charts the World: Hsu Chi-yü and His Geography of 1848*

65. William A. Brown and Urgunge Onon, translators and annotators, *History of the Mongolian People's Republic*

66. Edward L. Farmer, *Early Ming Government: The Evolution of Dual Capitals*

67. Ralph C. Croizier, *Koxinga and Chinese Nationalism: History, Myth, and the Hero*

68. William J. Tyler, tr., *The Psychological World of Natsumi Sōseki*, by Doi Takeo

91. Leroy P. Jones and Il SaKong, *Government, Business, and Entrepreneurship in Economic Development: The Korean Case*
92. Edward S. Mason, Dwight H. Perkins, Kwang Suk Kim, David C. Cole, Mahn Je Kim, et al., *The Economic and Social Modernization of the Republic of Korea*